Dead Silence

It took twenty years to solve the case of who shot Danny Paquette in his own backyard. Not twenty years of complete mystery—for the police seemed to be perpetually close to cracking the case open—but twenty years of silence. Though some regarded his killing as a senseless murder, many more weren't the least bit sorry that Danny Paquette was dead.

Only one person's finger pulled the trigger, but dozens of others pressed their fingers to pursed lips in silence. That perfectly aimed bullet ruined many other lives in addition to the one it ended that day. But as the years passed and the silence grew, many people judged the crime righteous and justified. Many knew. No one spoke. Their reasons varied, but the act of frontier justice was all made easier to bear because of one thing:

Danny Paquette had it coming.

OUR LITTLE SECRET

The True Story of a
Teenage Killer and the Silence of
a Small New England Town

Kevin Flynn and Rebecca Lavoie

BERKLEY BOOKS, NEW YORK

THE BERKLEY PUBLISHING GROUP
Published by the Penguin Group
Penguin Group (USA) Inc.
375 Hudson Street, New York, New York 10014, USA
Penguin Group (Canada), 90 Eglinton Avenue East, Suite 700, Toronto, Ontario M4P 2Y3, Canada
(a division of Pearson Penguin Canada Inc.)
Penguin Books Ltd., 80 Strand, London WC2R 0RL, England
Penguin Group Ireland, 25 St. Stephen's Green, Dublin 2, Ireland (a division of Penguin Books Ltd.)
Penguin Group (Australia), 250 Camberwell Road, Camberwell, Victoria 3124, Australia
(a division of Pearson Australia Group Pty. Ltd.)
Penguin Books India Pvt. Ltd., 11 Community Centre, Panchsheel Park, New Delhi—110 017, India
Penguin Group (NZ), 67 Apollo Drive, Rosedale, North Shore 0632, New Zealand
(a division of Pearson New Zealand Ltd.)
Penguin Books (South Africa) (Pty.) Ltd., 24 Sturdee Avenue, Rosebank, Johannesburg 2196,
South Africa

Penguin Books Ltd., Registered Offices: 80 Strand, London WC2R 0RL, England

The publisher does not have any control over and does not assume any responsibility for authors' or third-party websites or their content.

OUR LITTLE SECRET

A Berkley Book / published by arrangement with the authors

PRINTING HISTORY
Berkley mass-market edition / May 2010

Copyright © 2010 by Kevin Flynn and Rebecca Lavoie.
Cover photography by Age Fotostock.
Cover design by Lesley Worrell.

All rights reserved.
No part of this book may be reproduced, scanned, or distributed in any printed or electronic form without permission. Please do not participate in or encourage piracy of copyrighted materials in violation of the authors' rights. Purchase only authorized editions.
For information, address: The Berkley Publishing Group,
a division of Penguin Group (USA) Inc.,
375 Hudson Street, New York, New York 10014.

ISBN: 978-0-425-23465-5

BERKLEY®
Berkley Books are published by The Berkley Publishing Group,
a division of Penguin Group (USA) Inc.,
375 Hudson Street, New York, New York 10014.
BERKLEY® is a registered trademark of Penguin Group (USA) Inc.
The "B" design is a trademark of Penguin Group (USA) Inc.

PRINTED IN THE UNITED STATES OF AMERICA

10 9 8 7 6 5 4 3 2 1

If you purchased this book without a cover, you should be aware that this book is stolen property. It was reported as "unsold and destroyed" to the publisher, and neither the authors nor the publisher has received any payment for this "stripped book."

Most Berkley Books are available at special quantity discounts for bulk purchases for sales, promotions, premiums, fund-raising, or educational use. Special books, or book excerpts, can also be created to fit specific needs.

For details, write: Special Markets, The Berkley Publishing Group, 375 Hudson Street, New York, New York 10014.

To my parents, without whom much would be impossible.
—KF

To my children, for whom I would do anything.
And to Victor Paquette, who said the families of victims
should never give up,
even when they think they have no other choice.
—RL

Acknowledgments

The authors would like to thank the many people who assisted in this project and without whom this story could not have been told. We are deeply grateful for your support.

First, thanks to the many people in law enforcement who worked on different parts of this case for twenty years. Their fastidious notes were instrumental in preserving the facts and statements of their contemporaries, even those who later chose not to participate in this project. The authors would like to recognize the cooperation of Jeffery Strelzin and Joan Bissonnette from the New Hampshire Attorney General's Office; Mark Armaganian and Roland Lamy (ret.) of the New Hampshire State Police; William Simpson of the Hopkinton Police Department; and Stephen Agrafiotis and Bill Shackford of the Hooksett Police Department.

Thanks to the many people who shared their recollections of those in this book. They include Victor Paquette, Richard Baron, Joan Fossum, Heather Bouchard, Lisa Brown, Paul McDonough, Ronnie Wise, Steve Chamberlain, Peter Heed, Rick Patenaude, Dick Campbell, Court Burton, George Naum, Michael Manzo, and Lisa Windhurst Terry. In particular, the authors would like to thank Eric Windhurst for his candid and frequent discussions.

The authors would like to acknowledge the assistance of two people within the circle of silence surrounding this crime.

Their names are not listed for their protection, but they know the contribution they made to this book.

This project would not have come to the page were it not for Jamie Malanowski and Chris Napolitano at *Playboy*. Thank you to Sharlene Martin and Martin Literary Management. Also, much grateful praise for the work of Gary Mailman, Eloise Kinney, and our creative mentor, Shannon Jamieson Vazquez, at The Berkley Publishing Group.

Contents

Prologue ... 1

Part One: The Murder of Danny Paquette

1. On a November Morning in New Hampshire . . . 5
2. The Gypsy 13
3. A Troubled Life 22
4. A Magic Bullet 30
5. Roads Diverged in a Wood 42
6. It Runs in the Family 53
7. Bad Blood 61
8. You Can't Go Home Again 74
9. It Will All Work Out 84

Part Two: The White Knight

10. The New Girl 93
11. The Captain 101
12. Bury the Truth 110

13. Everyone Comes Home . . . Eventually	120
14. The Letters	128
15. Persons of Interest	135
16. Guilty Feelings	146

Part Three: The Hail Mary

17. The Chief	157
18. The Investigator	167
19. Tell Me the Truth	176
20. Best Friends	187
21. Live Free or Die	194
22. Everybody Dies for a Reason	202
23. Rumor and Innuendo	213

Part Four: Nothing Is As It Seems

24. The Gang of Five	223
25. The Prosecutor	234
26. A Model Life	243
27. The State Versus . . .	254
28. Surprise Ending	264
29. Many Rivers to Cross	275
Epilogue	286

Prologue

DANNY Paquette's killer walked into the visitors' room at the New Hampshire State Prison for Men. He was cheerful—even pleased—to see a new face, someone who hadn't known him before he was arrested.

The killer claimed to be a popular man. To get someone new in to see him, the killer had to drop someone else from his visitors list. It was his old dentist, he said, and prison rules said she couldn't be added back to the list for at least one year. "I'm the only one in here with a waiting list of people wanting to get in to see me," he said.

At first he did not want to talk about the details of that day, instead hoping to drop the story altogether. "Please don't reopen old wounds," he said. But on the other hand, he did understand why so many people were still interested in the story. There were many questions still left unanswered. Who else was involved? What convinced him to do it? How did he go twenty years without being caught? The only question that didn't need to be asked was, "Why?"

"I've had plenty of people—very prominent people—say to me they would have done the same thing," he said. The killer claimed that he still got letters every day that called him a hero.

That's because everyone knew he killed a child molester.

* * *

IT took twenty years to solve the case of who shot Danny Paquette in his own backyard. Not twenty years of complete mystery—for the police seemed to be perpetually close to cracking the case open—but twenty years of silence. Though some regarded his killing as a senseless murder, many more weren't the least bit sorry that Danny Paquette was dead.

Only one person's finger pulled the trigger, but dozens of others pressed their fingers to pursed lips in silence. That perfectly aimed bullet ruined many other lives in addition to the one it ended that day. But as the years passed and the silence grew, many people judged the crime righteous and justified. Many knew. No one spoke. Their reasons varied, but the act of frontier justice was all made easier to bear because of one thing:

Danny Paquette had it coming.

Part One

THE MURDER OF DANNY PAQUETTE

There are four kinds of homicide: felonious,
excusable, justifiable, and praiseworthy.

—Ambrose Bierce, *The Devil's Dictionary*

— 1 —
On a November Morning in New Hampshire . . .

ON November 9, 1985, the morning that Danny Paquette was murdered, he had planned a full day's worth of work. It was a Saturday, but nonetheless, Danny liked to stay busy. He had a strong work ethic, something he probably learned from his father. The old man had run the Paquette family dairy farm in the 1960s, getting up early in the morning to milk the cows before heading off to put in eight to ten hours as a construction foreman.

Danny's latest girlfriend, Ruth Szeleste, was new to New Hampshire, having come to the Granite State from Western Pennsylvania with her ex-husband and three teenage sons six months earlier. Like a lot of women in town, she'd found Danny Paquette extremely attractive. She'd liked his rugged looks and his bad-boy demeanor, though her boys hadn't shared her admiration. In fact, the boys and their mother's new man had recently had a falling out, which had been brewing for weeks over inane stuff such as the fact that Danny wanted the kids to get their rusty car off his property, and they resented the way he said it. At the heart of matter, Ruth's boys were sure that Danny was just using their mother. In turn, Danny had no patience with the boys, whom he considered lazy.

Danny Paquette was thirty-six years old when he died. Ruth

had warmed his bed the night before; her sons had spent the night back at her place. Danny had a voracious sexual appetite, so she made sure to please him. Even though she hadn't known him long, she'd already learned that the only side you'd ever want to be on was Danny Paquette's good side.

* * *

RICHARD Duarte got up around seven o'clock on the morning of November 9 and ate breakfast. He wanted to get an early start that Saturday. His plans were to get over to Danny Paquette's place and work on the car he was keeping in Danny's garage. He'd bought the 1954 Ford from Danny, who was also letting him use his tools to work on it. The men were friends who'd bonded over cars, and Duarte had already spent the previous evening at Danny's, monkeying with the Ford until 10:30 p.m. After getting dressed, Duarte drove to the local parts dealer before driving back to Danny's place, on Whitehall Road in Hooksett, New Hampshire, a small town on the north side of Manchester, the state's largest city.

Danny's property had lots of land, a house, a nice barn, and a decent-sized garage. It was perfect for Danny's real job; he was a welder by trade, and a damn good one. Auto repair was just a hobby. As Duarte pulled up Danny's driveway at 9:00 a.m., he passed the welded metal sculptures that his friend had fabricated out of leftover parts from his steady stream of jobs. Unlike other men in the welding trade, Danny wasn't afraid to also consider himself an artist.

Duarte found Danny Paquette with Ruth Szeleste in the garage. They were laughing about something.

"You're awful," Ruth scolded Danny, who slapped her on the ass as she made her way out. "I'll leave you to do your work."

Danny got one last long look at Ruth walking away before speaking to Duarte. Finally, he took a deep breath and said, "I've been waiting for that kid who helps me out to give me a call." He rubbed his hands on a rag. "OK, let's get to work." There was no doubt Danny was in a good mood.

Danny told his friend about some people he expected to come over that morning. "You have *got* to meet these two Canadian guys," Danny said to Duarte, who had his head under the hood. "They chew cigars and speak broken English. It's a friggin' riot."

"When are they coming?"

"This morning. I made a fuel tank for them."

As if on cue, Duarte heard a truck pull up and a pair of doors swing open and close. He saw the Canadians come up and shake hands with Danny, but Duarte kept his attention on his troublesome Ford.

The Canadians, Gaby Caron and Eugene Blouin, had met Danny only a week earlier. Blouin's brother-in-law, Gil Daigle, had been one of Danny Paquette's neighbors for seven years, and it was Daigle who'd recommended Danny's services to Blouin and Caron.

Just as Danny described, the men spoke with the thick French Canadian accents common to Quebec, and not unfamiliar to New Hampshirites. Canadians had been traveling south to work in Manchester's textile mills for the past hundred and twenty-five years.

"Danny," Caron asked (pronouncing the name "Dan-NEE"), "can you do dat t'ing to da tank?" The men had earlier talked about getting a toolbox welded on top of a fuel tank that they'd bought from Danny.

Danny laughed and led the men out of the garage and around the corner. He had his welding equipment set up next to a bulldozer.

Blouin noted the bulldozer (which he called a "bill-do-ZUR") and asked if it belonged to Gil Daigle, his brother-in-law.

"Yep. I'm going to do some more work on it this morning," Danny said.

Danny fired up the torch, welded a two-inch piece of pipe onto the tank, installed a leather pipe, and then welded a strap over the pump. Danny's speed impressed the Canadians. It took him only about six or seven minutes to complete the task.

The guys joked around some more. Blouin showed Danny how to balance ten nails on the head of one, a trick that really impressed the welder.

"Hey, is there a party going on here I wasn't invited to?" Gil Daigle ribbed, as he walked up Danny's driveway and saluted the other men. He had come over to borrow a caulking gun for a home project.

Caron looked at his wristwatch and realized that he and Blouin had to leave for an 11:00 a.m. appointment they had at the Chevrolet dealership. Duarte yelled for a missing part, and Danny told him to look in the trunk of one of the other cars nearby.

"Can I give you a hand with that?" Daigle helped Blouin lift the fuel tank onto the back of his 1977 Chevy pickup before following Danny around the corner to look at his bulldozer.

"What do you think, Danny?"

"I should have it ready for you today," he said. "I'm still waiting on this kid from work to show up to help me paint some of the tanks."

Just then, seventeen-year-old Court Burton walked up the driveway, waving nervously. The kid stood around as Danny accepted a check for $244 from the Canadians, then went scrounging for the caulking gun Daigle needed.

Daigle walked home to put it to use while he waited for Danny to finish working on the bulldozer. The Canadians pulled out of the driveway and aimed their truck toward Manchester for their appointment. Driving down Whitehall Road, they passed a series of hunters who had just pulled to the side of the road and disappeared into the woods, toting rifles on their backs.

* * *

COURT Burton had met Danny Paquette while working construction. Danny had a steady job welding for a utility company, but he also made plenty of money on the side as a freelance, or "gypsy," welder working by the hour at construction sites. Danny took an interest in Burton, and even though he was more than twice the kid's age, he quickly befriended the teen laborer.

"I like your work ethic," he'd told Burton. "You work hard. You take pride in what you do. You'll go far." Danny would then bitch to Burton about his girlfriend's teenage boys, and how they didn't live up to his particular standards of manliness.

Burton had agreed to come by Danny's place in Hooksett on Saturday, even though he didn't have a way to get there. Danny had been expecting him to call for a pickup. Instead, the kid had hitchhiked, which had taken longer than he'd expected. Although he was late, Danny didn't seem upset.

"Help me weld a plate on this bulldozer; then I'm going to have you mix some paint so you can paint my fuel tanks."

Burton was eager to help. He followed Danny back across the garage and around the corner. As he walked past the garage door, he saw another guy inside tinkering with a vintage Ford. Danny told him that Duarte was working on the old car's brakes.

"Danny, do you mind heating the star gears again?" Duarte asked. Danny paused to help his friend while Burton watched.

Danny then led the kid over to Daigle's bulldozer and handed him a metal plate. "Hold it right here while I weld it in place." Danny was wearing his leather gloves and overalls and dropped the face guard on his welding helmet. "Don't look," he teased Burton, just as plumes of yellow and orange sparks blossomed from his electric torch.

The bulldozer sat by itself, but it was far from the only vehicle on the Paquette property. There were several cars, including the one abandoned by Ruth's sons, and some Danny planned to use for parts or a future restoration project. Some had less potential than others and were mostly used for target practice; they were filled with bullet holes, the product of thrill shooting and boredom among Danny and his friends. Compared to the well-kept ranch-style and gambrel-roofed homes that abutted Danny's property, the Paquette place was a bit of an eyesore.

The bulldozer was parked alongside an outbuilding. Through the opening in the driver's cab, it was possible to see the woods along the far end of the land, about three hundred yards back. It was early November and well past the peak of the foliage season, though not all of the trees had given up the last of their brown, dying leaves. The day was cloudy, a little cool. It was the first day of hunting season in New Hampshire, but the woods were still quiet.

Danny switched off the arc and lifted his mask. The plate securely in place, he led Burton back into the garage. "Here's how I want you to mix this paint," he told the kid, then left him with Duarte in the garage as he went out to finish his work on Gil Daigle's bulldozer.

* * *

DUARTE was getting frustrated with the breaks and the star gears. He had someplace to be at 11:00 a.m. and he'd thought he'd be further along with the Ford by now.

Duarte didn't mind the kid who was hanging out in the

garage. It was the kind of thing he expected from Danny. It seemed Danny was always helping out kids in the neighborhood, fixing their tricycles or bikes. He had heard Danny talk about some of the young girls who lived in his neighborhood, too, saying there was one who he'd been dating on the side. Duarte wasn't sure how old the girl was—maybe fifteen? He also knew that Danny had shown an interest in Duarte's own teenage daughter. He'd talked to her about it, but it wasn't just the inappropriateness of such a relationship that bothered Duarte. He worried that somehow his daughter might come between him and Danny. He worked almost seventy hours a week and had few friends. There weren't many people he trusted, and he didn't want to lose a friend.

Duarte cleaned up the shop, intent on coming back and figuring out some more about the 1954 Ford he'd gotten himself into. It was close to eleven o'clock, so Duarte started to walk outside to clean his hands before he left.

Crack!

The noise was sudden, and loud enough that he heard it clearly over the noise of Danny's welding generator. Duarte had been a U.S. Marine in Vietnam, and the noise reminded him of an M2 Carbine rifle shot or of a helmet falling on a rock. Though his mind drifted to the jungle, his senses involuntarily pulling him back into combat, he shook it off and headed toward the garage door.

When Duarte made it to the door, he saw Court Burton standing in the opening. The kid had been coming to look for him. There was panic in his eyes.

"There's something wrong with Dan," he said.

* * *

RICHARD Duarte looked toward the bulldozer. The first thing he saw was Danny Paquette's empty welding helmet rolling on the ground. He looked for his friend, but didn't see him standing next to the dozer as he should have been. Instead, Danny was lying flat on his back, his arms outstretched, the electric torch still humming on the ground.

Jesus Christ, he's arced himself, Duarte thought.

Duarte ran and kneeled next to the man, thinking Danny

had been accidentally electrocuted. He grabbed Danny's legs and picked them up.

"Go call the fire rescue!" he ordered the kid. In 1985, the emergency number 911 had not yet been instituted in the more rural parts of New Hampshire. Burton turned and ran around the corner, out of sight.

Duarte felt helpless, unsure of what to do. He dropped Danny's legs and started pumping on his chest. He didn't know if it was doing any good. He put his hand up to Danny's mouth and nose and couldn't feel any breath coming out.

"Wake up, Danny! Wake up!"

Duarte stood up to look for the kid, but he was nowhere in sight. He got back down on his knees and started pumping on Danny's chest again.

Duarte's hands were pumping steadily, rhythmically, but his head was whipping around like mad. He was looking everywhere for help. Then he saw a neighbor outside a house across the street.

* * *

KEVIN Cote was walking to the end of his driveway with a handful of envelopes he was about to stick in the mailbox when he noticed someone waving frantically at him from the Paquette place.

"Call the Rescue!" the man shouted across the street. "I think Danny's been electrocuted!"

Cote shouted to his wife to call the fire department, then dashed across Whitehall Road and followed the man to check on his fallen neighbor.

When they got to the bulldozer, Cote saw the torch was still running, and though Danny Paquette still had on both of his leather gloves, he was sprawled flat on his back, spread-eagled and not moving. Cote was afraid to touch the body, wondering if it was still electrified. He followed the running torch to the extension cord back to the welding machine. The two men choked off the generator and ripped the cables out. Cote thought it was now safe to touch the unconscious man.

Cote kneeled at Danny's head and started mouth-to-mouth respirations. Duarte started pumping on Danny's chest again.

This time, as he pressed down on the breastbone beneath the leather overalls, Duarte felt something wet. He looked at the palms of his hands. Cote could hear something bubbling inside Danny's mouth.

"He's bleeding." The two men looked at each other, unsure of what to do next. Had he *not* been electrocuted after all?

Duarte jumped up from Danny's limp form and ran into the garage. He was trying to find something to stop the bleeding. He grabbed some plaster of Paris and brought it back outside. Cote had continued CPR while Duarte was gone.

"Put this on him!" Duarte called out. Cote wasn't sure what the plaster was supposed to accomplish, but he relinquished his efforts at chest compressions to allow the man to smear the white paste across Danny's torso.

Cote looked up to see another person, a teenage boy, standing over the scene. "Where you been?" Duarte snapped.

"The Rescue's on the way." In the distance, they could hear the sirens coming.

Richard Duarte, Kevin Cote, and Court Burton waited for the sirens to reach them and rescue their friend. They'd done all they could; now all they could do was wait.

In those fleeting moments, they still believed Danny had been injured while working on the bulldozer. They'd all been so busy just before Danny collapsed, and then so preoccupied with running to help try to save his life when they saw his fallen form, none of them had thought twice about the sound they'd heard, not even for a moment.

But that moment had passed anyway; even before Danny Paquette had hit the ground, the muzzle of a hunting rifle had already retracted silently into the trees across the barren field, leaving a puff of blue smoke in its wake.

— 2 —

The Gypsy

VICTOR Paquette wanted to sleep in on Saturday morning, but his dog started barking at 7:00 a.m. He was wiped out, having worked a long day on Friday. Victor was a welder, just like his younger brother Danny. Unlike Danny, though, Victor worked off the back of his truck, going wherever the work was. It was a different kind of life, and even though the work was sometimes hard to find, it suited him.

"Goddamned dog," he muttered. "Always gets me up early."

Victor dragged himself into the bathroom. His teenage daughter was thinking about moving into his apartment with him. He liked that idea, so he spent the morning cleaning the sink and shower to make the place more presentable. Victor didn't give a damn about his bathroom being clean, but he knew it was the kind of thing girls cared about.

Victor was tall and beefy, with a round face and a bald head. His beard was mostly thick and black, but it had started to gray at the chin. His eyes were deep-set. In the past, his gaze had been stern enough to prevent punches being thrown, to give pause to anyone thinking about starting trouble with him. Victor was a biker and had been a bouncer at some of the nastiest establishments in the state. No one wanted to cross him, but Victor got into a lot of fights anyway.

At 9:00 a.m., the phone rang. It was Laverne Gauthier*.

"I worked five to nine this morning," she told Victor. "I'm done so I'm going shopping. Can I stop by?"

Shopping was code for what she would tell her husband she was doing while she was actually rolling in the sheets with Victor. As long as she didn't actually come home with bags of expensive purchases, Laverne's husband seemed OK with her alibi.

An hour later, the woman slipped into Victor's house in Hooksett and nuzzled up to him. The two had met a year ago at a coffee truck while on break from their respective jobs. Victor had been doing some work in Manchester's turn-of-the-century brick mill yard, and Laverne was making sweaters at one of the few textile mills to have survived the Great Depression. After weeks of coffee breaks designed to coincide with hers, Victor called the woman and invited her to stop by his house. She did, and they'd been seeing each other ever since. The ground rules were simple: they met at Laverne's convenience and at Laverne's discretion.

"I don't want any problems," he told her. The last time he'd dated a married woman it had ended badly. At Christmastime the year before, a private investigator had followed Victor and his date back to his home in Hooksett. Victor had grabbed the guy by the jacket lapels and threatened him, told him to get lost.

This time was different. Victor really liked Laverne. Loved her, he told people. She wasn't anything like his two ex-wives. His first marriage had lasted nine years and resulted in a son and daughter. His first wife had since remarried, and Victor thought her new husband was a hell of a guy. His second marriage lasted just a year and a half; Victor hadn't seen his second wife since 1977.

"What the fuck are you doing still married?" he'd ask Laverne.

"I want to give the marriage more time," she said. Victor just smiled. He knew that she just liked him in bed, nothing more. He liked the sex, but he also liked talking to her. As far

---

* Denotes pseudonym

as making a commitment to her, he did the best be could. He'd decided not to see anyone else because he didn't want to give Laverne the clap or herpes.

Victor thought they got along well. In all the time they were together, they'd only had one fight, when Victor tried to pull her shorts off and Laverne slapped him in the face.

"Nobody slaps me," he said. The heat vanished from the room as Victor went still, leveling his bouncer's gaze on Laverne. "You better get out." Laverne apologized, then left. Since then, things had been good, so Victor was happy to be Laverne's "shopping" destination for yet another long morning.

The phone rang again at 10:15 a.m., after Laverne had arrived. It was Victor's son, Doug. He wanted to come over later with a buddy and do some shooting on the hill behind the house. He came over about once a month to target shoot. Doug had a 12-gauge shotgun and Victor often lent the young men his .22 rifle.

Victor hung up and said the boys were coming over at noon, so he tossed Laverne onto the bed and decided to make the most of the time they had left.

* * *

AMONG the Hooksett police officers dispatched to Whitehall Road was twenty-six-year-old Stephen Agrafiotis. It was his day off, so he was surprised when his sergeant called him in. The kid was a rookie, fresh out of the criminal justice program at St. Anselm College, and was now working for his hometown police department. He heard the call was for an electrocution or a cardiac arrest. It wasn't immediately clear to first responders what had happened.

The members of the Hooksett Fire Rescue had found Kevin Cote and Richard Duarte hunched over Danny Paquette's lifeless body, furiously doing chest compressions and attempting mouth-to-mouth. They were puzzled by the makeshift bandage of plaster covering the victim's chest. When they moved Danny, they uncovered a puddle of blood beneath the body.

Officer Agrafiotis pulled up to the house in his black-and-white cruiser, put on his uniform cap, and approached the other men assembled on the scene. The Hooksett Police Department had only about a half-dozen officers, so nearly the entire force was gathered on the property. Police Chief John Oliver was conferring with two of the department's more experienced detectives, while the other uniformed officers were carefully walking the property looking for something.

"The witnesses say they heard one crack, which could have been a gunshot." The cops were comparing notes.

"One shot? It could have been a hunter," someone offered. "Hunting season started today."

Chief Oliver motioned to one of his sergeants. "You're coming with me to the hospital. Let's hear what the doctor says." He then pointed to the detectives. "State police will be here any minute. Fish and Game, too. We'll need to collect all witness statements; then we'll have to go up and down Whitehall Road and some of the back roads and get every license plate on every car pulled over. There must be fifty hunters parked in this area."

"What about me, Chief?" Agrafiotis asked.

The town's top cop took a long look at Agrafiotis, who stood there looking like a puppy eagerly awaiting a scrap from the table. The chief sized up the rookie's readiness for a homicide.

"Get your camera," he told him. "Take pictures."

* * *

VICTOR Paquette and Laverne Gauthier were engaging in a sex act even Victor thought was filthy when the phone rang again. It was close to noon, and he didn't want to ignore the call in case it was his son.

"Yeah?" he yelled into the phone, half out of breath. It wasn't his son Doug, as he expected; it was Bobby Dube, a friend who lived near his brother Danny.

"Danny's been hurt bad. He's bleeding a lot," Dube said. Dube had been out hunting that morning when he heard about the incident. He went first to Danny's house and then ran home to call Victor. "They're taking him to Elliot Hospital."

By the tone of his friend's voice, Victor knew it was serious. He threw on some jeans and left for the emergency room. Twenty years later, when he thought about that day in 1985, Victor could still remember checking out Laverne's ass on his way out the door and thinking, *I'll finish that job another day.*

* * *

CORPORAL John Barthelmes of the New Hampshire State Police had caught the Danny Paquette case, which became known in the records as I-85-147. Barthelmes was tall and thin and clean-cut. He was destined for bigger things within the state police force.

Barthelmes surveyed Danny Paquette's property. The plot of land was large. On the left side of the uphill driveway was a good-sized house with a small garage set next to it. On the right side, there were more outbuildings: a larger garage, a workshop and office, and a white metal shed. Cordwood was piled near the porch. The land was littered with scatterings of abandoned cars, orphaned tires, and stray lengths of metal. If it weren't for Danny's profession, this collection would have held the title of local junkyard.

Barthelmes passed beneath an object hanging from a tree. It looked like a pie plate with something cut out of the bottom. There was another one hanging decoratively from the workshop. From the road, one could make out the inverted heart-shaped symbol welded through the metal. It was the ace of spades—the "Death Card."

"Just heard from the hospital a short time ago," a Hooksett officer told Barthelmes. "The victim's dead."

The policemen on the scene were moving gingerly around the bulldozer, looking in the bark of trees and examining the wood siding on all the outbuildings. They were searching for the bullet. The doctor who'd examined the body hadn't found it lodged in Paquette's chest. Officers were also searching the interior of Tri-town Ambulance number 500 for it, in case it had fallen from his body on the ride to Elliott.

The Hooksett detectives began sharing their notes with the state police corporal. If this became a homicide investigation, the case would no longer be handled at the local level. There were strict protocols in the state of New Hampshire. The State Police Major Crime Unit would handle the legwork, and the elite prosecutors of the attorney general's Homicide Unit would bring the case to court. But it wasn't considered a homicide, not yet.

"A friend of the victim's came to the scene before he was

transported," the local cop explained. "Guy's name is Bobby Dube. He said the victim had some problems with his girlfriend's sons."

Barthelmes listened carefully. The cop said he remembered responding to a call back in August about an intoxicated female at Paquette's. When he arrived, he found Danny Paquette outside nursing a bloody nose.

"I just got into a fistfight with this guy because he thinks I'm using his mother," Paquette explained. "She's inside, drunk, and I want her out of my house."

* * *

RUTH Szeleste decided to move into Danny Paquette's house in June 1985, four months before he was shot, but she kept her own place in nearby Candia. She wanted her three boys to move to Danny's with her, but they were reluctant and chose to split their time between both houses. Danny was never asked his opinion about opening up his home. No one had lived with him there since before his second divorce, years earlier.

The dislike between Ruth's children and Danny was mutual. Danny especially didn't care for her oldest son, Vincent, who was laid-back and into music, not particularly driven by any aspiration. He didn't fit Danny's image of what a man was, and he had no problem telling Vincent that. Mark, the middle boy, liked many of the same things that Danny did. He had a penchant for cars and liked to fix them up. But he was messy and didn't put tools back, which pissed Danny off to no end.

Mark had spent that summer working on his mother's 1977 Chevy Nova, which Ruth had wrecked. The remains of the yellow Nova were parked at Danny's. Her son wanted to put a new front end on it, and one Sunday evening, Mark traveled to Whitehall Road to do some work on the car.

"Where's your brother?" Danny asked when he caught Mark rummaging through the workshop.

"Hal? I left him at home."

Hal was Danny's favorite. He was the youngest of the boys, and he generally did whatever Danny told him to do. The boy would paint or cut wood or do whatever needed to be done around the house. Mark, on the other hand, could barely hide his contempt for Danny from behind his thick eyeglasses. He thought his mother could do much better than this guy.

"Get out," Danny told him. Mark was nonplussed. They argued and called each other names until Danny ran him off his land.

Two weeks later, Vincent called Mark and asked him to go to Danny's house to pick up their little brother, Hal. Their mother was there, but she was drunk. Mark pulled into the driveway quickly and honked for Hal, hoping to get in and out without encountering Paquette.

"Hey, asshole," Danny called to Mark. "Before you leave, put the goddamned lug nuts on your mother's car." He waved a fist at the kid. He had likely been drinking himself, along with Ruth.

"Kiss my ass," Mark told him.

"Mark . . . Mark . . ." His mother came out of the house and staggered to the car. "Will you go to the store and get me some more Daniel Boone?"

"What?" He didn't want to go on a booze run, and he certainly didn't want to come back to the Paquette place once he left. But he also didn't want to make things any worse. "OK, Mom. I'll do it."

Suddenly, Danny put his foot on the driver side door and punched Mark through the open window. The young man struggled with the door but couldn't open it. Danny hit him four times in the face, knocking his glasses off.

Ruth yelled at the two of them, trying to get Danny away from the car. When he finally backed off, Mark was able to open the door. He got out of the car and moved right to Danny, then socked him once in the nose, hard. Beneath his fist, Mark felt the small bones in Danny's nose break and a torrent of blood start to flow.

Danny grabbed Mark's car keys and threw them into the tall grass. "I'm going to teach your kid a lesson," he told Ruth. Hal, Ruth, and Mark all scrounged in the brush for the keys. Danny put a ladder up against the side of the house and climbed up to the roof for a better view of the search. As soon as he was at the top, Mark ran for the ladder and pulled it away, stranding him on the roof. The young man had trouble controlling the cumbersome ladder, and it smashed a window on its way down.

As Danny shimmied down the side of the house, Mark and Hal found their keys, got into their car, and started to pull away. Danny picked up a steel bolt that he found on the ground and threw it at the retreating car, shattering the back windshield.

The fight left Danny Paquette with a broken nose and two black eyes. He called the police, not to file a report against Mark, but to throw a drunken Ruth out of his house.

About five weeks later, Ruth and Danny set their differences aside and started dating again. None of Ruth's boys approved.

* * *

WHEN Victor Paquette got to Elliot Hospital, no one would talk to him about his brother's condition. The nurses were stalling him. It didn't take him long to figure out that Danny was dead.

"Cut the fucking bullshit," he said to one of the nurses. The biker used his imposing figure to intimidate her. "I'm a grown boy. I've seen all kinds of fucking death. Where's my brother?"

Victor was escorted to an examination room in the morgue. There were four men in the room: two police officers, a pathologist, and an assistant. There was also a woman, a prosecutor from the attorney general's Homicide Unit. Danny's naked body was lying on the examination table.

Victor was speechless at first. Local police knew the Paquette brothers were very different from each other, ran with different crowds. But Victor and Danny were extremely close. Devastated by the sight of his beloved brother lying on a steel table, Victor struggled with the feelings roiling inside of him.

There is no way, no way *I'm not going to know what happened to my brother,* Victor thought to himself. *I ain't putting my head down. I ain't walking out the door and not checking everything, including his asshole if I have to. Not this time!*

"Show me," he ordered the cops. With the help of the pathologist, they pointed to a tiny bullet hole in Danny's chest. The single shot was in the center of the torso, slightly above an imaginary line between the nipples.

"Show me the back," Victor said. They propped Danny's

body up and pointed out the exit wound. It was higher on his back than the hole in his chest had been. It was also to the right of the spinal column. There was only one hole.

"Who's this?" Victor asked, motioning to the woman standing in the corner of the room.

"I'm with the attorney general's office," she said. "We prosecute homicides in this state."

Victor chuckled to himself. This process was not new to him or his family. "The attorney general doesn't prosecute homicides," he said. "You bury them."

Satisfied that he had seen everything he needed to see on his brother's corpse, Victor turned to leave the morgue. He stopped and asked the prosecutor one more thing.

"You must know Kathy McGuire."

The woman nodded. "Yes. Assistant Attorney General McGuire is assigned to the homicide unit."

Victor pointed to the dead man on the table, who had once been married to a woman named Denise Messier, whose brother Philip was McGuire's husband.

"Well, that," he said, "is her ex-brother-in-law."

* * *

ASSISTANT Attorney General Kathleen McGuire wouldn't hear about Danny Paquette's death until Sunday morning after a series of phone calls among her husband's family. The news was shocking and upsetting, not only because of what it meant for her sister-in-law and nieces, but also because any crime that could be tied to her in any way could potentially compromise her professional life. McGuire was an ambitious homicide prosecutor, her career thus far above reproach.

But the worry Assistant Attorney General McGuire must have felt at hearing the news that Danny Paquette was gone forever was probably tempered by another emotion: relief. Whether she would have admitted it or not, Danny dying solved a big problem for her, one that had been foremost in her mind for months.

— 3 —

A Troubled Life

No one could have predicted during Danny Paquette's childhood that the investigation of his killing would render such a lengthy list of suspects. He was born on January 4, 1949, in Manchester, New Hampshire, the youngest of six children in a family of modest means. Besides Victor, Danny had another older brother, Arthur, and three older sisters, Joanne, Marion, and Nadine. His parents, Arthur Sr. and Rena, ran a dairy farm on Brown Avenue in a city where farming was becoming less and less common. A generation before Danny's birth, the neighborhood had been pastoral, teeming with working farms. But during his childhood, airplanes flew over the Paquette farm every day. The land was near the city's airport, Grenier Field. Alan Shepard, the first American in space, had learned to fly there. And a generation later, the streets had all been paved, grand shopping malls sprouted from the fields, and a bustling regional airport that competed with the likes of Boston's Logan operated at the end of Brown Avenue.

When Victor and Danny came home each day, they'd take off their school clothes and put on their work clothes. There was much for them to do. There were a hundred cows milking all the time. Arthur had also thought he'd try adding some hogs to the mix, though the smell of pig waste was so strong that no one in the family could stand it, and Arthur moved the passel to the back end of the property. The only actual crop the Paquettes grew was silage corn as feed for the animals. When it was time to harvest the crop, neighbors would come and help. The Paquettes would return the favor each season.

But farming was never enough to pay the bills at the Paquette home. Arthur would milk the herd in the morning and then head off to work in the city on a construction site. Rena would see the kids off to school. For the two youngest, this routine was all Victor and Danny knew; even when the others had grown and only they remained, their mother was the constant caretaking presence in their lives.

* * *

IN the winter of 1964, Danny's mother, Rena Paquette, died unexpectedly while she was alone in the house with Danny. The death raised all sorts of troubling questions for the family. It hit them all hard, and afterward, Victor often caught Danny sleepwalking through the cold farmhouse. He'd guide his little brother safely back to bed, then return to his own fitful rest, punching pillows and tossing blankets.

Within a matter of months after Rena's death, Arthur Paquette remarried. The man was not ready for the life of a widower, and he needed a companion. He met a woman named Marguerite and brought her into the home on the Brown Avenue dairy farm. Arthur's sudden nuptials stung all of the children, particularly Victor and Danny, who now had to share their mother's house with an unwanted stepmother. All of the children believed Marguerite was after Arthur's insurance money. Joanne stopped speaking to her father, resentful of the way he had treated her mother when she was alive. Danny's relationship with Marguerite was chilly; Victor's was downright toxic.

Victor soon left home, joined a trade union, and started down a road of rebellion. Danny stayed at home, but the seeds of rebellion were sown within him also.

* * *

NOT long after his mother's death, teenage Danny fell in love with a neighbor girl named Denise Messier. Denise also lived on Brown Avenue, just up the street from the Paquette farm. When they were little, all the neighborhood kids would play together. But as they grew into their teens, Danny couldn't help but notice Denise's strawberry blond hair and bright smile. She was his "girl next door."

When Danny was about sixteen or seventeen years old, he got a job working in the Elm Street Hotel in downtown Manchester. Denise, who was one year younger, also worked there, as a chambermaid. Their adolescent romance was facilitated by their unsupervised proximity at work, and by the dark halls and empty rooms at the hotel.

Denise's pregnancy was a family scandal. Her father was a Manchester police officer, her brother Phil headed for the military. Prospects for teenage mothers in the mid-1960s were few, and abortion was not an option in conservative New Hampshire. One day, friends were told that Denise was no longer staying at the family home on Brown Avenue. The rumor was that she'd been "sent away" to an unwed mother's farm and gave birth to a son, but when she came back, there was no baby. She was also forbidden from ever seeing Danny Paquette again.

* * *

AS the supply of troops for the Vietnam War failed to meet the demand, hundreds of young men from the Granite State were drafted to go to war. Danny Paquette got his draft papers in 1968 and shipped off to Army Basic Training. He was an infantryman who handled rockets, and there was no doubt he'd be going to Vietnam. His brother Victor was already in the New Hampshire National Guard, a unit that never seemed to get called up, and the older brother worried about his young brother getting shot in the jungles of Southeast Asia. There was a lot of anxiety in Victor's home while Danny was in Basic. Victor would sometimes snap at his new wife, Corrine, unable to express his concern for his brother. But when Danny came home on leave after Basic, he learned his unit's orders had been changed. Instead of Vietnam, they were going to Germany.

During this time, Danny dated a girl from Manchester named Stephanie. She was a knockout, and everyone could see why Danny was attracted to her. Stephanie was unlike many of the girls in the city; she was into "flower power" and dressed like a hippie, with daisies and sunflowers tucked behind her ears or braided in her hair. She was different from anyone Danny had ever known.

The army infantryman soon found out that his new girlfriend was pregnant. Still smarting from the loss of his first true love and the son he never knew, Danny decided to do things differently this time. He asked Stephanie to marry him. She agreed.

The couple got married in 1969. Stephanie stayed in New Hampshire to have the baby, while Danny began his fifteen-month hitch in Germany. She gave birth to a baby girl and named her Jennifer, but while she nested in the United States, her thoughts were overseas with her husband. She wrote to Danny, asking if they could come to Germany and live there with him. The infantryman agreed and arranged for housing.

Unfortunately, living together in a West German city was isolating for the family. Danny realized how little he actually had in common with his wife. He wasn't exactly open to new things, and here was his freethinking new wife. Stephanie was also a peacenik. Danny was no hawk on the war, but he was in the U.S. Army and had a sense of duty about it. West Germany seemed a lonely place for them, even when they were together.

Stephanie was also realizing Danny was not the man she'd thought he was when she married him. There were annoyances that became arguments that became fights. There was something about his personality that scared her. Danny was easy to anger and increasingly suspicious of her.

"You're not to leave this apartment without me," he told her. She could go nowhere outside of his company. She told friends his behavior was "impossibly bizarre." She and the baby soon returned to the United States, living on the money Danny sent home and awaiting the end of his tour of duty.

Sergeant Daniel Paquette was honorably discharged from the U.S. Army in 1971. He came back to New Hampshire and tried to readjust to life on the home front. But like so many veterans of that time, Danny found it hard to shed his demons.

One night Stephanie drew herself a bath to soak away the stresses of young motherhood and a strained marriage. Danny walked into the bathroom. According to the paperwork she'd later file, a mundane discussion became heated and then exploded.

"You leave me alone," she pushed back. "Or I'll take our daughter, and you'll never see us again."

"You fucking bitch," he spat at her. "I'll fucking kill you!" He picked Stephanie up and threw her into the tub fully clothed. She sat there, sloshing uncomfortably in the hot water, her legs hanging over the side, and stared at the father of her child.

Stephanie Paquette was granted a divorce in 1971.

* * *

DANNY and Victor began spending a lot of time together. Danny had a little place in Hooksett and Victor liked to get away from his own house every once in a while. Danny had a neighbor named Ray Foot who knew welding, and he taught the brothers everything he knew about the trade. Danny already had some experience with gas welding, having worked on hot rods with his buddies. Victor had worked odd jobs in construction, so he knew welding was a valuable skill. Both men had aptitude; Danny also had artistry.

One afternoon in 1973, Victor walked into Danny's place to find a young woman lounging on the sofa. She looked familiar, but Victor couldn't place her face immediately.

Then it hit him: it was Denise Messier, the girl who'd had Danny's baby when she was sixteen.

They all sat around, shooting the shit; then, as casual as can be, Danny said to Victor, "By the way, we're getting married."

The hulking man stared blankly at his brother. "Oh," he said.

"What do you say to your brother?" Victor would later recall. "'What are you, fucking nuts?' But I couldn't say that." He wouldn't say anything to his brother that might hurt Danny's feelings.

* * *

WHILE Danny was in the army, Denise had been working at a Dunkin' Donuts shop in Manchester. There she'd met a boy named Tom Benzel, whom she married in 1969. The couple had one child: a girl they named Melanie.

Two years into the marriage Denise announced she wanted out. She told her husband she was taking their one-year-old daughter and moving to Alaska. Benzel was also unhappy with the union, so he did not stand in her way, but he was surprised that she chose such a far-flung destination. He didn't think Denise knew anyone in Alaska.

Nevertheless, Denise moved to Anchorage and obtained a divorce from Benzel in 1971 while she was living there with Melanie. She told her ex-husband that he would not have to make child-support payments. She had a good job as a bookkeeper and could support them herself.

In 1973, Denise returned to New Hampshire with her toddler to visit her family. She bumped into Danny Paquette, the man whom she'd loved as a teenager. She was surprised to realize that there were still sparks between them. Their second courtship was of the whirlwind variety. Danny promised her that together they would find the son they put up for adoption and create the family they were always meant to have. Denise made one last trip to Alaska, to break up with the boyfriend she had there and to retrieve her belongings.

The childhood sweethearts were married on December 10, 1974. For the first time, Danny seemed truly happy. He and Denise had two more children, Caroline and Audrey. Danny went to court and adopted his stepdaughter because he didn't want Melanie to be the only one in the family with a different last name. They found a large stretch of land on Whitehall Road in Hooksett, complete with raggedy outbuildings that seemed perfect for operating a welding business.

In 1978, Danny and Denise incorporated "Paquette Welding Inc.," with Danny listed as president and secretary and Denise as vice-president and treasurer. The couple that had fallen in love more than a decade earlier finally had a second chance at a life together, but in 1980, the marriage started to fall apart. In March, Denise took the girls and left their country home for an apartment in the city. She wanted a divorce, and Danny couldn't accept it. He'd call her every day either begging or threatening. He'd show up at Denise's workplace and make a scene, crying uncontrollably.

On a Saturday in June, Danny stormed into Denise's Manchester home and began yelling that he wanted his children back. He grabbed Denise and threw her down on the couch. He put his hand over her mouth and nose. She couldn't breathe.

He was right on top of her, looking into her terrified eyes, yelling. The children, ages ten, two and a half, and ten months, were all in the room.

On Monday morning, Denise filed for a restraining order.

Danny was morose, always weeping about his children. He had lost his mother when he was so young, and he felt like he was losing his family all over again. He didn't recognize his own role in the pattern. It was, in part, his abusive behavior that led to this situation, just as it had in his first marriage.

A hearing on the divorce was slated for December 1980. The pressure was starting to get to Danny. On the second of November, Denise got a phone call from a friend of Danny's.

"Is Danny there?" he asked urgently.

"No, why?"

"He told me he's not ready for a divorce and he was going to take care of things his own way."

"What did he mean by that?" Denise asked nervously.

"He just bought a .45 pistol. He says he's going to go over there and kill you and then kill himself."

Denise called Danny and confronted him with this. "Did you get a gun?" she demanded.

"Yes," he told her. "And when I see you, I'm going to shoot you."

Denise hung up, called the police, and then fled to her mother's house. Her mother took great delight in reminding her daughter what she'd said about Danny Paquette back when he was sixteen: that he wasn't anywhere close to good enough for her daughter.

* * *

THE next day, while Denise was driving to work, a black-and-white 1951 Ford pickup truck pulled alongside her on Elm Street. She knew it immediately. It was Danny.

"You motherfucking bitch! I swear to God, I'll kill you!"

Not knowing whether Danny had the .45 in the truck with him, Denise hit the accelerator and took off. Elm Street was the city's busiest thruway, and Denise had to dodge cars sitting at lights or waiting to make left turns through oncoming traffic. In her rearview mirror she could see Danny's truck barreling down on her, his vanity plate of "FIXER" clinging to the metal bumper.

Denise was able to lose him at a red light. This time she drove straight to the police station and waited until the cops could find Danny and bring him in.

During his court appearance, Danny seemed agitated. The judge found that he had willfully violated the restraining order and ruled he should be held in the Hillsborough County House of Corrections. Danny leaped across the table, lunging for the judge. Bailiffs and attorneys all grabbed him by the shoulders, trying to restrain him.

Danny Paquette was later taken from the county jail to the state mental hospital and was committed for one year.

* * *

IN 1980, New Hampshire Hospital in Concord was a warehouse of the insane, the disabled, and the retarded. Lawsuits on behalf of the patients would modernize and improve treatment options there, but at the time of Danny's commitment, conditions were straight out of a Ken Kesey novel.

In August of 1981, the court granted the Paquettes their divorce on the grounds of irreconcilable differences. Danny was able to keep the home in Hooksett and therefore keep his livelihood. He paid seventy-five dollars per week in child support and had weekend visitation rights with all the girls. Because of his past relationship with Denise, all parties agreed that it was best if she was not around when Danny was with his daughters.

As far as Danny knew, this arrangement was working out, but several months after returning home from the state mental hospital, he went to his ex's apartment in Manchester to pick up his daughters only to find the place empty. Denise had told no one of her plan or her destination; she knew Danny would find a way to get it out of anyone who knew.

Danny never saw Denise, their two biological daughters, or his adopted daughter, Melanie, again.

— 4 —

A Magic Bullet

SUNDAY, November 10, 1985, was a gray day, just as Saturday had been. Victor Paquette stood with his sister Joanne behind a plastic roll of tape protecting the fifteen-thousand-pound bulldozer and watched the cops walk around in search of the bullet that had pierced Danny's heart. The older brother stared off into space, his usual sharp look lost. He rubbed his forehead under his checkered Trilby hat.

Officer Steve Agrafiotis was moving around the property with a video camera in his hand. He was recording as much of the scene as he could for posterity. The images would be important for investigators if they needed to revisit conditions from this day. It would also be a useful tool to show to a jury—if one would ever be called to hear this case.

Agrafiotis framed up his video shots carefully and lingered on whatever he was shooting. He was giving a sort of running commentary about what he was seeing, explaining for future viewers about what was in focus.

"This is the front of 898 Whitehall Road," he began, showing the house where Danny lived. He captured the driveway, filled with police cars. The officers who made cameos in the Agrafiotis film did so by walking through the shot while scanning the ground for clues or by getting caught standing tall and somber while the rookie panned left to right, right to left.

"This is the view of the yard where the incident took place.

I am facing north by . . ." The narrator paused to consult some unseen resource or perhaps just guess. ". . . by northeast."

Agrafiotis took some video of the Case 450 bulldozer. It was surrounded by yellow tape, tied off on the door of one of the outbuildings. He scanned around, pointing out Danny's tools. "This is the torch that the victim had been using at the time of the incident." He zoomed in and out of the weld on the left track, which Danny had been about to repair.

While Danny had been lying in the yard awaiting medical transport, one of his rescuers had lightly traced the outline of his body in the dirt. It wasn't exactly like the chalk outlines of detective fiction, but it could clearly be seen in the sleeping yellow grass.

"The dark spot in the middle of the screen is blood," Agrafiotis said, zooming in on the spot underneath the ghostly shoulders and head. "This is the only blood found on the scene."

The young patrolman climbed up on the dozer to get the property from the victim's point of view. A taller cop—and they *all* were taller than him—ribbed Agrafiotis to beware of low-flying birds while he was up there.

From where he was, Agrafiotis could see just how far back the tree line was from the bulldozer. Through the camera, it seemed the woods stood at an impossibly far distance from where Danny Paquette had been standing when he died. It was maybe three hundred yards. He pulled away from the eyepiece so he could really take in what he was seeing, a mental parallax error. Agrafiotis wasn't the only investigator on the scene who made note of how far away the edge of the woods was.

As he got down, he walked past Victor Paquette, who had been standing quietly with his sister Joanne. Victor held a coffee cup in his hand, but he was gesticulating so wildly, the cup had to be empty. Agrafiotis knew both Victor and Danny. Although their reputations around town were spotted, they never got into any serious trouble with the Hooksett police.

"Victor, I'm sorry about your brother," Agrafiotis said, extending his hand. Victor, who was more than a foot taller than the young cop, looked at his hand, then reached out to accept the gesture.

"I appreciate you saying that," Victor told him.

* * *

AGRAFIOTIS lugged the VHS camera through the empty field to the tree line. He wanted views from the left, the right, and straightaway to the bulldozer. Zoomed all the way back, the yellow dozer was far enough away not to appear visible on the screen. Away from the busy road, Agrafiotis could hear the wind rustling the bare branches and a flock of Canada geese squawking at one another. As he slowly pushed the telephoto lens closer to the crime scene, the depth of field changed and the bulldozer came into focus. At that moment, a Fish and Game officer stood where Danny had been before dying. The officer's red jacket perfectly contrasted the sharp yellow edges of the dozer cab. But with the zoom lens peering directly in, the video captured how little of the victim's body would've been exposed. The chest from the sternum up, the shoulders, and the head.

If this was an intentional shooting, Agrafiotis likely mused, *this is what the killer saw right as he squeezed the trigger.* It was an awfully small target for a shooter to hit from a great distance.

Agrafiotis noticed one other thing: something suspended over the head of the proxy victim. He moved the camera up to get a better view. It was something round and glimmering in the sun. It was hanging from either a tree or from the building. Then he realized what it was. A singular shape cut out of a metal circle, most likely by the dead man.

The ace of spades.

* * *

NEW Hampshire State Police detective sergeant Roland Lamy arrived at the scene to take over the investigation from Corporal Barthelmes. In his early forties, broad-shouldered, and bald, Lamy was gruff, profane, and brash. The other cops he worked with were fiercely loyal to him—the ones who could stand him, that was. He got along well with the press, who seemed to tolerate his blunt manner. In later years, some would draw comparisons between Lamy and Andy Sipowicz, Dennis Franz's character on *NYPD Blue*. Not only because both had Everyman features and a knack for rubbing people the wrong way, but because Roland Lamy was considered the best police detective on the force.

Roland Lamy had gotten into law enforcement in 1964 at age twenty-two. By 1971, he had been assigned to the NHSP Major Crime Unit. It seemed he always got his man. That was because Lamy was bold and aggressive as well as wickedly smart. He always knew where the line was and never crossed it. But he would wander right up to it and dance around it. Judge David Souter, who would someday sit on the U.S. Supreme Court, once famously declared of the detective's actions in a case, "Sergeant Lamy did not violate the Constitution." It was a weak endorsement, implying that Lamy did everything but.

Coming into this investigation, the detective knew there were some unsavory characters he'd have to find a way to control. Not the least of whom would be the victim's brother.

From the onset, Victor Paquette did not like Roland Lamy. Though they were equally physically imposing, he thought that Lamy had already sized him up, pegged him for a lowlife, and figured that Lamy would assume Danny's life wasn't worth the time and expense it would take to seek justice. But Victor Paquette would fight to make sure the cops followed through and did their jobs.

Lamy *had* sized up Victor, long before these tragic circumstances. He knew the guy was a biker and had been into drugs. He knew Victor got into a lot of fights. And he assumed the victim's brother would not be candid about whatever he knew, but he decided to question him anyway.

There was, for a brief moment, some weakness in Victor's eyes. He had been vacillating between denial and anger, looking over the Case 450 bulldozer where his brother was killed. Lamy's initial questions were perfunctory, asking where Victor had been at the time of the shooting, how he'd heard about it. Victor answered in the same absentminded way he had for Chief Oliver or Corporal Barthelmes, or any number of friends and relatives to whom he'd had to explain the day's events.

"Victor," Lamy asked next, softening the tone of his voice, "what do you think happened here?"

Victor swallowed hard. "I think that someone might have mistook my brother for me and killed the wrong guy."

Lamy gently prodded further. "Why do you say that?"

"Well, I'm currently screwing a married woman from Manchester. And if her husband found out, he could have learned that I am a welder," Victor said.

"Go on."

"If he found that out, he might have looked up Paquette Welding in the phone book. And if he did that, he would have come to my brother's place and shot the wrong guy."

* * *

TO begin with, investigators of case I-85-147 had few ideas about the identity of Danny Paquette's killer. But the most telling clue about the shooter's identity had to be the shot itself. It was, for lack of a better term, a dead-on bull's-eye. The bullet had pierced the man's heart from a distance of at least three hundred yards. The hospital pathologist determined that the shot, which went through the man's leather overalls, had killed Danny before he even hit the ground. Danny might have been dead before the report of the shot reached his own ears. There are very few people who could make a shot like that. The triggerman was either extremely skilled or extremely lucky.

The most crucial piece of evidence from the crime scene was still missing: the slug from the weapon. Investigators believed the bullet had come from a rifle, but someone surely could have made the shot with a handgun. Without the bullet, there would be no way to definitively identify the murder weapon. The bullet was the only physical evidence that could lead them back to the killer.

The autopsy suggested that when Danny was shot in the chest, the bullet exited out his left shoulder above the entry wound. Presuming their victim was standing up straight when he was shot, the bullet would have been traveling on an incline on its way out of the body. And the angle was steep—approximately thirty degrees—so the trajectory would have been like a football punt. A straighter path through Danny's chest would have bored the bullet into the Cotes' house across the street. Instead, the tack of the exit wound suggested that the slug had launched high over the neighborhood, shot over the town like a circus cannon.

The bullet, likely the size of a pencil-top eraser, could have come down anywhere in a town that was covered with woods, wetlands, and ground cover of old and newly fallen leaves. There were certainly other bullets to be found as well, especially as enthusiastic hunters began the season traipsing Hooksett's dense woods.

As detectives were still triaging the scene and searching hopelessly for the bullet, another call came in, which threw the investigation into confusion. Another pair of bodies had been discovered in the woods not far from where Danny Paquette was shot.

* * *

ALLENSTOWN'S shared border with Hooksett cuts through Bear Brook State Park, a ten-thousand-acre gem preserved for camping, hiking, fishing, and hunting. Less than two miles from Danny Paquette's home to the northeast, at the same time investigators were combing the property, a hunter made a gruesome discovery.

Two bodies, covered in canvas. The hunter had pulled back the material to take a closer look and uncovered the body of a woman, who looked to have been in her midtwenties, and that of a young girl, aged eight or nine.

The victims had been discovered nude, and state police investigators realized immediately that there had been some advanced decomposition. They knew the older woman had curly light brown hair, but they couldn't determine what color her eyes had been. The girl had a similar hairstyle. Both victims had suffered blows to the head. There was also some evidence of dismemberment. The investigators believed the victims were related—maybe mother and daughter, maybe sisters—because of similar dental characteristics.

Bodies weren't discovered in the woods of New Hampshire towns every day. This was a coincidence investigators couldn't ignore.

Unfortunately, it was a coincidence that would lead them even further away from the truth of what really happened to Danny Paquette.

* * *

NOVEMBER 9, 1985, was officially the first day of hunting season in New Hampshire, but target shooting was a popular sport year-round. On that morning, a group of sportsmen were shooting bottles in a sand pit at a quarry owned by Manchester Sand and Gravel in Hooksett. They had done this many weekends before, blasting glass back into dust with birdshot or small-caliber bullets.

The members of the Fish and Game Department had championed the theory—without much passion—that a stray bullet must've killed Daniel Paquette. It was not that they completely believed it, but their expertise was in investigating hunting accidents, not homicides.

"What do you think about the likelihood he was killed by a stray shot from the woods?" Barthelmes asked the lead conservation officer while he was examining the bulldozer.

"Stray bullets can travel a mile, two miles with fatal velocity. It's possible."

"But probable?"

The Fish and Game officer pointed out the steel panels surrounding the bulldozer's cab. "If your victim was standing here, then it's unlikely the shot could have come from the left-hand or right-hand sides."

"Explain why not."

"The opening he was standing in was only one foot, ten inches. If it had come on an angle, say five degrees to the right or left, the bullet would have been deflected by the bulldozer. Standing here, in the open well of the cab between the dashboard and seat, the only way he could have been struck in the chest was straight on. Meaning the shot came from due north."

The men looked due north, considering whether a bullet could have come from that direction and accidentally struck Danny Paquette in the heart.

They'd soon learn that the answer to that, surprisingly, was yes.

One mile due north from the bulldozer's cab, the sportsmen at the Manchester Sand and Gravel pit were still blasting bottles to smithereens.

* * *

ONE of the most surreal pieces of evidence came from a local man who had a bird's-eye view of the scene. At 11:00 a.m., the time Danny Paquette was shot, the man had been drifting silently over the house in a hot-air balloon, videotaping the ground view from above.

Investigators scoured each frame of the tape, hoping the camera had caught a glimpse of someone with a weapon, someone out of place, a car somewhere it wasn't supposed to be. Eventually, however, though intriguing, the hot-air balloon tape proved useless.

* * *

THE only clue to the firearm used in the shooting, beside the gunshot wound in Danny Paquette's corpse, was the noise heard by Danny's apprentice, Court Burton, and Danny's friend, Richard Duarte. Detective Roland Lamy asked Officer Steve Agrafiotis to drive to Nashua and bring the witness Burton back to the shooting scene for a test, as he'd been the one outside when the shot was fired.

Lamy fired up the welder and made Burton stand where he had been when Danny was shot. An officer walked seventy feet away and discharged several types of firearms into the air.

"How about that one?" he was asked. The officer had just fired a .308 rifle.

"No," Burton thought deeply about it. "No, that doesn't sound right."

The signal was given to fire the .22. "What about that?"

"No. It's much too loud."

The crew fired several more rifles and a shotgun. None of the shots sounded like the one burned in Burton's memory. Finally, the officer removed his service revolver from its holster and fired the .38 into the air.

"That was very close," Burton said when he heard the .38. "That could be it."

* * *

DISPROVING that the fatal shot came from an errant hunter was harder than first imagined. Philosophically speaking, it's always more difficult to eliminate improbable possibilities than to definitively prove facts. Such was the conundrum with the hunter theory.

Detectives had copied down license-plate numbers from

dozens of cars and pickups pulled over on area roads on the morning of November 9. Investigators divvied up the list and started contacting drivers to see if they had been hunting at the time of the shooting. They also put a call out through the media to ask those who had been hunting or target shooting at the sand pit to come forward. Experts would be able to match the weapons to the bullet . . . if one could ever be recovered.

There were a handful of Hooksett residents who volunteered their weapons. It was believed a great number more did not. New Hampshire's libertarian streak lives on in more ways than even the state's "Live Free or Die" motto would suggest, and such a request from the government would have been met with reluctance. But there was also the more practical matter that few citizens would want to face the legal consequences if it were determined that their rifle had been the one that fired the deadly shot.

* * *

MONDAY morning after the shooting, a man named Nicolas Johnson* walked into Riley's Gun and Ammo Shop on Route 3 in Hooksett. Riley's was one of the town's heritage businesses. It was among the largest such establishments in the state, and certainly the best gun shop within an hour's drive in any direction.

Johnson placed a Brno 30-06 rifle and a box of ammunition on the counter. "I want to return this gun," he said.

"What's wrong with it?" the clerk asked.

"Nothing's wrong. I've been thinking about getting rid of this gun since Danny Paquette died. It doesn't seem right to have it."

The comment seemed odd to the clerk, especially the part about Paquette. The man confessed he had been out shooting on the day of the incident. According to the sales slip, Johnson had purchased the weapon only two weeks earlier. The clerk checked the box of ammo; three rounds were missing.

The clerk notified Hooksett police, who looked into Johnson's background. He lived at a spiritual commune, tucked away

---

* Denotes pseudonym

in Hooksett's back woods. The residents believed in holistic health through sauna, massage, and acupuncture. Patrolman Agrafiotis accompanied the veteran detective who questioned Johnson.

"Why did you want to return that rifle?"

"It didn't seem right to have it. Not after Danny died."

"The death affected you?"

"Oh, yes," he said. "I've been very sad since then."

Johnson explained that he'd been a casual acquaintance of Danny Paquette's, that they'd had mutual friends. On Saturday, November 9, Johnson had spent the morning shopping with another man from the commune. In the afternoon, they took the Brno rifle into the woods behind their compound down the road from the Paquette house. Johnson said he had fired a couple of shots, but couldn't remember at what.

After reading about the discovery of Paquette's body in the Sunday paper, Johnson had undergone a Zen-like epiphany. He decided he didn't want the rifle anymore. He couldn't recall why he purchased it in the first place.

* * *

AUTHORITIES soon ruled that the discovery of the two female bodies, found just miles away the day after Danny Paquette's death, were not related to their Hooksett investigation. Judging by the level of decomposition, the bodies had been in the park anywhere from six months to three years. Hundreds of man-hours went into identifying the victims. They scoured missing-persons reports, school-attendance records, and campsite registrations. Investigators theorized everything from a serial killer to a Mob hit. The only thing they were ultimately certain of was that trying to link the two murder scenes had been a waste of time.

* * *

ANDY Myers's* first maintenance call of the day on Tuesday, November 12, was for a neighborhood in Hooksett. Myers was a lineman for New England Telephone. The trouble report said

---

* Denotes pseudonym

that service to some homes on Whitehall Road had been interrupted over the previous weekend. He took the slip and left the dispatch center in his bucket truck.

Myers worked by checking line voltages at the main terminal. The telephone lines were strung lowest on the utility poles, with high-power electric lines running along the top. The terminal checked out fine, so he moved eastward on Whitehall Road. Every ten poles Myers stopped and checked the line with a special probe. When he heard the steady drone of the dial tone coming through the wire, he packed up and moved down another ten poles.

When he got to the area of 898 Whitehall, Myers's probe no longer played a dial tone. He knew he had passed the trouble spot. The lineman did a visual inspection of the wire and saw something in front of the Paquette house. Maneuvering the truck under the line, he rode the bucket skyward to take a closer look. On the underside of the telephone wire, Myers could see a small hole in the plastic covering. Inside that hole was a bullet. Myers surveyed the damage, looked at his wristwatch, and decided it was a good time for a coffee break before he dislodged the bullet. There was a McDonald's near the main terminal. He went to the restaurant, where he met up with a coworker.

"You'll never believe what I just found on Whitehall Road," Myers told him. "A bullet lodged into the line."

The coworker was incredulous. "Don't you know someone was shot and killed in that neighborhood Saturday?" Myers hadn't heard the news, but when he learned who the victim was, he experienced a strange sense of déjà vu. The last time Myers had been to Hooksett, he had had Danny Paquette weld a trailer hitch onto his pickup truck.

Within an hour, the property at 898 Whitehall Road was once again swarming with police vehicles. At the investigators' request, Myers wrapped a white piece of tape around the black telephone line where the bullet had struck it. Agrafiotis took a new set of photographs, this time framing the tagged phone line up with the bulldozer. Even to the naked eye, the trajectory of the shot was as plain as day. It had come from the woods due north, straight into the cab, then up an inclined slope from Danny Paquette's shoulder to the wire above the road.

Once the cops diagramed the scene, they asked Myers to remove a five-foot section of cable and turn it over to them. He did so, then completed the line splice and restored service to the neighborhood.

Later, a state police ballistics expert would report in case file I-85-147 that the bullet recovered from the telephone wire was a .270 caliber. It had normal lans and grooves and could likely be matched with a weapon if one were produced. The bullet was covered in white and red material. It was determined the white material was bone fragment, consistent with the wound on Danny's scapula. The red material was blood, but in 1985 there was no test that could definitively link the blood to Danny Paquette.

Hot damn, Detective Lamy thought. Everyone knew it had been a one-in-a-million chance that the bullet had struck the phone line instead of continuing into the sky. *We finally have our first solid clue in this case.*

— 5 —

Roads Diverged in a Wood

THE men who comprised the task force investigating Danny Paquette's death, case file I-85-147, met in a reserved room at the Hooksett Police Department. It had been empty, but its walls were slowly being filled with notes and photographs, used coffee cups, and the remains of cold lunches.

New Hampshire State Police assumed the lead role in the task force, with Sergeant Roland Lamy heading up the investigation. There were four members of the New Hampshire State Police assigned to the investigation, including Lamy: Corporal John Barthelmes, Sergeant Tom Winn, and Trooper Colon Forbes. The attorney general's office also assigned three prosecutors to the case, although their role was strictly advisory, as there was no determination yet whether the Paquette shooting was accidental or homicidal. Fish and Game had two senior investigators on the task force as well, and the local Hooksett Police Department was represented by Chief James Oliver, Sergeant Frank Beliveau, and other senior officers.

Chief Oliver may have been top cop in tiny Hooksett, but he hadn't started out as a small-town policeman. Oliver had been a New York City detective before seeking a change of pace in New England, and while on the NYPD, Oliver had been with the Bureau of Special Service and Investigation (BOSSI). BOSSI members were intelligence operatives, charged with everything from providing security for VIPs to infiltrating extremist groups. Oliver knew his way around a sensitive investigation.

Patrolman Steve Agrafiotis was not officially assigned to the case, at least not as an investigator, but Agrafiotis's strong work ethic became well known during the investigation. It was a small department, and when the other members of the task force would come to the Hooksett Police Department, they would often find Agrafiotis typing up reports on the shooting or volunteering for the drudgery that the seasoned veterans didn't want to do.

Agrafiotis was the grandson of a World War I hero, and that work ethic ran in the young officer's blood; his grandfather, Christopher Agrafiotis, had been an American doughboy wounded in Cantigny in 1918, during what was the United States' first sustained offensive of the war. Shrapnel ripped open his gas mask during battle, and after taking in lungfuls of mustard gas released by the Germans, Private Agrafiotis was taken out of the trenches and written off as a dead. But the scrappy Greek American recovered and insisted he be returned to the First Division to continue to fight in France. After his unit ran into a machine gun nest, Agrafiotis and his lieutenant were the only survivors; yet the two still managed to capture ten German soldiers—and when Agrafiotis's superior was gunned down, the private single-handedly herded the enemy combatants to the Allied front. Agrafiotis marched the POWs into camp by himself and earned a Silver Star. The legacy of his grandfather loomed large both in Steve Agrafiotis's home and around the city of Manchester, where Agrafiotis would see his grandfather's name on local war monuments.

The young man might never have met his grandfather, but he knew this much about him: Agrafiotis brought his men in.

Whenever the task force would meet to discuss I-85-147, Patrolman Agrafiotis was always nearby. He offered to get guys coffee, to type up their notes, to do anything that would let him remain part of the investigation.

"Roland, come here." Chief James Oliver summoned the lead investigator, Roland Lamy, to a quiet corner of the room. "Give the kid something to do. Let him put together notes, follow up on license-plate numbers. He'll do a good job."

Sergeant Lamy agreed to give Agrafiotis some work. It was

no skin off his nose; Lamy wasn't sure they were even looking at a homicide. He thought the unlikely precision of the shot was too perfect to have been intentional. He leaned toward Danny Paquette's death being an accident.

Manchester Crimeline was offering a one-thousand-dollar reward for information leading to the arrest and conviction of any individual responsible for the death of Danny Paquette, which, as far as Lamy was concerned, meant that every nut job in the 603 area code would soon be calling in. And in fact, in the days following the shooting, several people did phone the anonymous tip line to offer the investigators different paths to follow.

One caller said a biker named "Jimma" Bolduc* was behind the shooting. Another called to say that one of Danny's ex-girlfriends had married a known drug user and burglar who bragged he had been contracted to kill someone. Still another reported that Danny had been dating a sixteen-year-old girl from Manchester who had a brother in the U.S. Marines, and the brother and sister had conspired to shoot him.

* * *

WHEN detectives searched Danny Paquette's home, looking for clues as to why someone might target him, among the items they discovered was Danny's little black book. There were at least sixty phone numbers listed in it. Some were family; some were business associates. Others belonged to married women in the area, women who pretended to not know who Danny Paquette was when investigators called to ask about the nature of their relationships with him.

They went door-to-door in the neighborhood, asking residents what they knew about Danny Paquette and who might've wanted to kill him. The men quizzed dozens of people, rang more than seventy-five phone numbers, and traced nearly one hundred license plates, all in the hunt for clues. Officer Agrafiotis had the unenviable job of taking the senior investigators' notes and creating a series of index cards filled with facts for later use in cross-referencing clues and alibis.

---

* Denotes pseudonym

Not *all* tales about Danny were ugly. One neighbor told Corporal John Barthelmes that Danny Paquette was an extremely nice guy who loved to work hard and was always in his workshop getting his hands dirty with cars or welding. He described Danny as someone who wasn't overly outgoing but who was golden to the people he knew and liked. The man described how Danny would make time to fix bikes for the boys on the street or would allow a neighbor's girl to ride her horse in his expansive back field.

But another neighbor described Danny as cold, someone who never gave her the time of day. The woman had been friendly with Danny's ex-wife Denise before she left him and took their three daughters with her. Perhaps it was this past association that caused the tension. The woman said there were rumors that Danny had molested one of the daughters, which is why Denise had taken off.

Hooksett Police Department sergeant Frank Beliveau was told that Danny had been dating a teenage girl at the same time he dated Ruth Szeleste. The informant didn't know the girl's name, only that she was someone from the neighborhood. The man had seen her at Danny's. She had blond hair and glasses, and she was even younger than the sixteen-year-old girl whose brother was in the U.S. Marines; this girl was only fifteen years old.

Even the local barber had a story. When Beliveau stopped for a high and tight cut at Roy's Barber Shop in North Manchester on his lunch break between interviews, the old barber mentioned to the trooper that he, too, had known Danny Paquette. Danny had told him that he was sleeping with a woman in the city who had a rich husband.

When Beliveau returned to the Whitehall Road section of Hooksett, yet another neighbor said that Danny had visited him recently, sporting two black eyes after the scuffle with Ruth's sons. Knowing his neighbor was a martial arts instructor, Danny had asked if he could teach him some techniques.

"You know that fight I had? Well, it ain't over," Danny reportedly told the instructor. "They're coming back."

One of the friends listed in the black book also pointed out that Danny had been in a motorcycle accident about three years earlier, and the woman who'd been riding on the back of his bike had been killed. The friend mentioned that the woman's brother-in-law held Danny responsible.

Danny's cleaning lady confessed to Sergeant Lamy that she wouldn't come to the house unless her sister or her mother came with her. She said Danny would proposition her while she cleaned up. The offers weren't threatening or overbearing, and they never came with any unwanted physical contact. There was something in his manner that disturbed the woman, but her brother-in-law was a friend of Danny's so she didn't want to drop him as a client.

She also reported that a biker named Jimma Bolduc had a grudge against Victor. That was the same name one of the Crimeline callers had given.

* * *

ANOTHER of Danny's neighbors, the Ouimettes,* told Sergeant Lamy they didn't know anything about any improprieties over at the Paquette place. Mr. and Mrs. Ouimette said they had never had any reservations about letting their two daughters play with Danny's children when the three little girls had lived there. Lamy asked if he could speak privately with the Ouimette girls. The younger daughter was Michelle, then almost thirteen years old. She remembered there being tension in the Paquette house when she visited, but that had been almost five years earlier. The older daughter was Jacqueline. She was nervous and cried when she talked to Lamy, but she denied that Danny Paquette had ever attempted any sort of physical contact with her. Still, the sergeant did not like the way the girl was answering his questions, and he wrote down in his notes that Jacqueline was evasive and seemed to be hiding something. He also noted that the girl had blond hair and glasses and was fifteen years old, the same description given for Danny's underage girlfriend.

* * *

ONE night after dinner, Sergeant Lamy got a call at home that a man had just walked into a neighboring town's police department and wanted to clear up a murder.

---

* Denotes pseudonym

Barry Gardener* stumbled into the Pembroke Police Department out of the rain at about eight thirty in the evening, asking for Lieutenant Lucien Bouffard. Gardener insisted that he had to speak to him. The corporal on duty escorted the man into Bouffard's office and closed the door.

"I'm scared and I want to get something off my chest," Gardener began, according to Bouffard. "I have information on a murder. I know who did it. I was there, man. But I want protection."

"I've got to know what you're talking about, Barry," the lieutenant told him. "Give me some details."

"No. No fucking way. Not unless I get protection."

"It doesn't work that way. What do you know? What case is this about?"

"I'm not saying. I don't fucking trust cops."

Bouffard told Gardener that he had a friend at the state police who might be able to help. By coincidence, the friend he was referring to was Roland Lamy; at that time Bouffard knew neither that Gardener was referring to Danny Paquette nor that Lamy was now lead detective in that case.

Lamy got there about an hour later. Right off, Lamy recalled, he sensed that Gardener had either been drinking or doing drugs, although the man didn't smell of alcohol or appear intoxicated.

"What do you know?" Lamy asked him.

"That Danny Paquette," Gardener began out of the blue, "was a real asshole. He abused kids, his girlfriend."

"What do you know about his death?"

"I was there when it happened. I didn't do it, but I was there. He was shot with a three-oh-eight caliber rifle, right through the heart."

"This rifle, did it have a scope on it?"

"You don't need a scope at the close range he was shot."

By this point, Lamy knew Gardender was lying about having been present when Danny was killed, but he wondered what other information he might have. He leaned forward in his chair. "So what's this all about, Barry? Why did Danny Paquette get shot?"

---

* Denotes pseudonym

Gardener also leaned forward, joining Lamy in the conspiratorial gesture. "Paquette owed me four thousand dollars in back payments on cocaine. He had a *bad* habit, a serious need for the stuff."

"Go on."

"But he didn't just owe me. There are seven other coke dealers he owes even more money to. He ran up a big fucking bill. So the eight of us all paid shares of six hundred dollars a person on a contract to kill Paquette."

"So you all did this?" Lamy quizzed. "You all chipped in six hundred dollars to pay to have Paquette whacked?"

"Yes."

"Eight times six hundred," Lamy pondered. "How much is that exactly?"

Gardener froze up, rolled his eyes inside his head. "Twenty-four hundred dollars?"

"That's forty-eight hundred dollars."

"Like I said, man," he came back, "I paid my share."

"Who did the shooting?"

"This guy named Kevin who lives in Massachusetts. He comes up to Pembroke to sell drugs. We paid him to do it." Gardener's face grew stony and serious. "I want guaranteed written immunity for what I've told you. I still have more information. I want protection!"

Lamy explained that the system didn't work that way, and that Gardener would have to offer some proof that he was truthful about this information.

"Offer of proof?" Gardener sputtered. "What do you mean, man? I was *there*. What more do you need?"

The witness became increasingly agitated, claiming he'd be killed if he didn't receive immunity and protection. Lamy looked him square in the eye and told Gardener he was free to leave.

* * *

VICTOR Paquette called Sergeant Roland Lamy often, asking about the status of the investigation into his brother's death. Lamy assured him that the investigation to find Danny's killer was aggressive and thorough. God knew they were compiling an ever-growing list of people who could have done the deed.

In Lamy's experience, the family members of murder victims were often consumed with an overwhelming feeling of helplessness, with no grasp on what had happened so far or what would happen next. Many of them clung to police officers and prosecutors, revering them as the justice-seeking champions of their loved one's memory. Their gratitude was deep and endless.

This was not the case, Lamy sensed, with Victor Paquette, who seemed contemptuous of the police. The detective was sure Victor had more to say, but was holding out. Lamy prodded Victor for information on Danny's possible drug connections.

"He never did the fucking the stuff," Victor told him. "He'd bitch at me whenever I smoked pot. He didn't put up with any of it."

"What about your own drug use, Victor?" Lamy pressed. "Did you ever do cocaine?"

"My last blast was a quarter gram only. I don't use it," he offered without reservation. "I bought an eight ball on New Year's. What a waste of money!"

"What do you about know Billy Couteau*?" Lamy asked him. Billy "the Knife" Couteau was suspected of being a major cocaine dealer in Manchester.

Victor hesitated. Lamy probed further.

Couteau was known to hang out at the Zoo, the seediest of bars imaginable, with his gang of thugs. Among them was his collector and enforcer, Jimma Bolduc, a character with a reputation for shaking down other dealers and slapping women around. There were about a million excuses the police could have used for shutting the Zoo down, but they never did. The bar served a purpose of limiting where crimes like drug dealing and prostitution took place in the city. It was like a one-stop shop for rounding up the usual suspects.

"Danny wasn't into that crowd," Victor finally stated. But although Danny may not have hung out at the Zoo, his brother did.

* * *

---

* Denotes pseudonym

DETECTIVE Roland Lamy felt he needed to know more about Victor's background, so he met secretly with Victor's married girlfriend, Laverne Gauthier.

"I don't know if he's into anything illegal," Laverne told him. "But there's another side to Victor that I don't know."

Lamy asked her what she meant, but she couldn't elaborate. She said that since Danny's shooting, Victor had slept with a handgun underneath his pillow.

"Do you know of any fights Victor might have had in the past six months?"

"He's had an ongoing feud with someone. I think the guy's name is Jimma Bolduc." It was the third time Bolduc's name had surfaced.

Laverne said she'd heard Victor talking to two friends about an incident that had happened at the Zoo the previous winter. Victor said he was in the men's room when Bolduc's little brother kicked in the door. Words were exchanged. Victor punched the younger Bolduc in the face, pulled his jacket over his head, and then punched him about ten times in the ribs.

There were six guys who witnessed the fight and asked Victor to stop. The two men Laverne overheard Victor talking to had been among those who'd seen the fight. One of them said that Jimma Bolduc had accosted him two weeks later wanting to know what role he'd played in beating up his brother.

Victor told his friends he would take care of Jimma Bolduc.

Before he ended the interview, Lamy asked Laverne where her husband had been at the time of Danny's shooting. Having been in bed with Victor, she couldn't say for certain, but she vouched that as far as she knew, her husband didn't own any guns and didn't even know how to shoot. Lamy asked her to check their bank accounts and see if any large amounts of cash had been withdrawn.

She contacted Lamy the next day after examining her husband's bankbook. She told the investigator that no large sums of money had been withdrawn over the past year. She said her husband had been working on his van from 10:00 a.m. to 3:00 p.m. the day of the shooting.

However, Laverne also remembered that her husband had said something later that day that upset her. She'd caught her husband gazing blankly out the window as the sun set. "There's a crow," he'd remarked absently, staring at the black bird. "That's a sign of death."

* * *

DETECTIVE Lamy approached Victor Paquette about the situation with Jimma Bolduc. Victor confirmed Laverne's story: Bolduc's kid brother got into a beef with him at the Zoo because Victor had been friendly with the brother's girlfriend. The girlfriend had told Victor that the relationship was not good and asked if she could move in with him, "just to have a roof over her head." Victor said he'd declined to extend an invitation.

After he heard that Bolduc had hassled his friend about the fight, Victor sought the man out. "I'm the only one who hit your brother," he reportedly told Bolduc. "Do you have a problem with that?"

The biker said no.

Victor said they considered the issue settled. He said he'd seen Jimma Bolduc at least twenty times since then and there hadn't been a problem.

* * *

SEVERAL days after he staggered into the Pembroke Police Department to confess the drug hit on Danny Paquette, Barry Gardener was asked to come in for questioning in Hooksett. Detective Roland Lamy and Corporal John Barthelmes conducted the interview. Sitting in were three homicide prosecutors from the attorney general's office.

Gardener repeated his story of the drug bounty on Paquette and his role in it. This time he said Danny Paquette was a dealer, not a user, and the coke debt was a rip-off of other dealers. When he was done, Lamy turned the tables on Gardener.

"Your story is bullshit."

"Hey, man, it's the truth."

"No, it isn't. None of this adds up."

Gardener sat silently for a moment. "All right," he admitted. "I made the whole story up."

Gardener explained that he had heard details about the shooting while working construction. Court Burton, the teen who'd been helping Danny that morning, likely told some coworkers who passed it along. Gardener admitted he usually did an eight-ball of cocaine a week. The night he'd confessed, Gardener said that he'd drunk six beers at the American Legion hall, six beers at a nearby pub, six more beers back at the Legion, then had gotten thrown out of the pub when they wouldn't let him drink more on credit. Mad, drunk, and frustrated, he'd walked into the police station and fabricated the Paquette story. Gardener gave no reason for the lie, other than that he'd been intoxicated.

After kicking Barry Gardener out of the station, Lamy slammed his pen and pad on the table. They had wasted valuable time chasing down this fictitious lead. Meanwhile, they still had a veritable rogues' gallery of suspects, a spinning wheel of motives, and were no closer to finding out why Danny Paquette had been killed.

— 6 —

It Runs in the Family

DANIEL Neal Paquette was buried on Wednesday, November 13, 1985. The family first gathered for a prayer service at 9:15 a.m. at the Goodwin Funeral Home in Manchester. Victor greeted the mourners at the funeral home; among those who came to pay respects were his aunts, his father's sisters.

Victor had always been a disappointment to his aunts, and he knew it. They disapproved of his divorce, of his heavy drinking, of his biker demeanor—yet it never seemed to bother them that Danny had also been divorced or that he also rode motorcycles.

Victor figured that the aunts probably blamed him for getting Danny into bikes in the first place, and for the trouble that he got into as a result. After Danny's divorce from Denise, Victor had taken his brother on a ride from New Hampshire to Daytona Beach. When they got back home, Danny bought a Harley Dresser. About a year later, while taking a Labor Day weekend drive to the White Mountains, a Subaru pulling into the Champney Falls scenic rest stop cut Danny off along the Kancamagus Highway. The impact was nearly head-on. Danny's female passenger, a girl named Diane Boothby, was thrown twenty-five feet and fractured her skull. She lay sprawled in the middle of the road, fifteen miles from the nearest town. A growing crowd watched helplessly while they waited for another motorist to drive through the mountain pass and call an ambulance. Danny had only sprained his wrist.

After five days in the hospital, Diane Boothby died.

The state police determined that the twenty-one-year-old driver of the Subaru was at fault, but the aunts believed that Victor was really to blame. After all, it was Victor who'd gotten Danny interested in motorcycles, wasn't it?

Still, although Victor politely shook his aunts' hands when they entered the funeral home, he felt that surely, in the back of their minds, they must be blaming him for this, too. Surely, somehow, Danny's death must be Victor's fault.

His aunts' disapproval always stung, but on this day it truly hurt.

* * *

TO understand the Paquette family, one had to look back to the winter of 1964, when citizens of New Hampshire's Queen City were outraged, despondent, and hysterical over the recent death of a young woman who had been brutally murdered. There were clues that her death was related to another murder, and there was a legitimate fear that a Jack the Ripper was living among the terrified residents of Manchester.

On January 13, 1964, a teenage girl named Pamela Jean Mason had been walking to a babysitting job. Pamela had a lovely face and black hair that she liked to spray up in a bouffant style. She was fourteen years old, sweet, and popular with the freshmen boys at West High School. Pamela had placed a flier in a Laundrorama advertising her services as a babysitter. She got a lot of jobs.

On this night, Pamela's mother had left for work in a blizzard that had enveloped the region. When her mother was gone, Pam received a telephone call looking for a babysitter. She made her younger brother dinner, then walked out into the snowstorm to take the job.

When Pamela did not return to her home that night, family and friends scoured the city. The police searched roads and alleys. Did she duck into a friend's apartment to escape the storm? Had she been struck by a plow? Where was she?

For a whole week, the city asked, *Where is Pam?* Curiosity grew into concern, then flowered into dread. Some of the girl's belongings, her gloves and books, were found scattered across the west side. Each morning and each afternoon, the papers splashed her beautiful photograph on the front page, imploring the public to help find her.

On the eighth day, Pamela Jean Mason was found. Her body was discovered in a snowbank along Interstate 93 in South Manchester. She had been bound, beaten, stabbed, and shot. She had been repeatedly sexually violated. She had been held against her will and tortured, perhaps for hours on end.

The city was heartbroken for the Mason family. *Why had this happened?* Newspaper editorials and letters to the editor all asked the same question over and over.

Manchester police detectives noticed some disturbing similarities between the Mason case and another unsolved homicide from four years earlier. In February of 1960, an eighteen-year-old girl named Sandra Valade had gone missing during the height of a snowstorm. She had been walking from a bus stop after swimming lessons at the YWCA. She had also been molested, stabbed, and shot by her abductor. Her body had also been found dumped in a snowbank, her belongings strewn across the city. It was as if the killer was taunting the police.

Media attention over the Pam Mason case was intense and furious. Each day, the chief of police and the state attorney general were peppered with impatient questions from reporters who demanded to know who had killed Pam and what they were doing to locate him. In the streets, in diners, in bowling alleys, in church meeting halls, and in the mills, all discussion was about only one topic. The dread people had felt about the missing girl turned into panic once she was found. It was the closest thing to mass hysteria in the city's history.

* * *

DURING school hours, Rena Paquette, Danny and Victor's mother, worked in the Laundrorama where Pamela Mason had hung her advertisement. Like everyone else in Manchester, she had become drawn to the case, following the stories in the papers and looking at the babysitting ad on the wall with a mixture of trepidation and sorrow.

"I think I know who did it," Rena told her husband, Arthur, at dinner one night when he'd finished his chores on their farm.

Her teenage sons had already left the table. Arthur didn't believe his wife until she added, "The killer's mother told me."

The fork clanged hard on the dinner stoneware. A moment of silence hung in the air. "What in God's name are you talking about, Rena?"

"I got a call from her today."

Arthur asked the woman's name. It was a name he knew, someone from her work, but not someone Rena was particularly close with.

"Why did she call you?"

"I'm not sure," Rena paused. "She knows her son did it. I don't think she can bring herself to turn him in. I think she wants someone else to do it for her."

"No," Arthur said. "I mean, why did she call *you*?"

Rena pursed her mouth, afraid to speak. "Because he killed one of the girls," she said, "in our pigsty."

"That's ridiculous!" Arthur said. "I don't want you getting involved." Rena knew the tone in his voice meant that was to be the end of the subject.

But it wasn't the end of the phone calls Rena received at home from the suspect's mother. Her pleas seemed very compelling. There was so much reverence for Pamela Mason at the Laundrorama, no one would take the babysitting ad off the wall. Each time people saw it their blood boiled anew. Each time Rena Paquette saw it, she thought of the telephone-caller's son.

Rena called the Manchester police and talked to an officer who had been fielding hundreds of calls about the Pamela Mason case. She explained what she knew and felt unburdened after passing the information on to the authorities.

That weekend, a pair of Manchester police detectives came to the Paquette farm on Brown Avenue and asked to speak to Rena. Arthur looked disapprovingly at this wife before leaving them to talk in the living room.

Rena told the detectives what she believed: that Pamela Mason's killer was a man named Edward Coolidge, a bakery delivery driver. A man of about twenty-five years old with a wife and baby daughter, he also had known violent tendencies and was unaccounted for at the time of Pamela's murder. Rena told them this information had come to her from Coolidge's mother, who was also the owner of the Laundrorama, and therefore Rena

Paquette's boss. Edward Coolidge had come in to the business to visit his mother. He'd seen Pamela's babysitting ad and copied down the contact information.

The detectives thanked Mrs. Paquette and left the farm.

* * *

THAT Monday morning, February 3, 1964, Arthur Paquette got up early to milk the herd before breakfast. He still had to get to work on the construction site. He came inside to the kitchen to the smell of eggs and bacon. Rena, dressed in a morning coat and slippers, was at the stove.

The cry of pre-dawn winds howled around the corners of the barn and the farmhouse. "Where are the boys?" he asked his wife.

"Victor's getting dressed for school. Danny has a dentist appointment this morning, so I told him I'd let him sleep late before taking him."

Arthur slid into his chair, and Rena brought a hot pan to the table and pushed the eggs onto Arthur's plate. "I'm going to talk to his mother," Rena declared.

"You are not. I want you to keep your nose out of this Pamela Mason stuff," Arthur said. Things had escalated since the police had visited over the weekend; they had received two threatening phone calls. And worst of all, in the Laundrorama, a visit from Edward Coolidge himself. He and Rena had had words, and she regretted the conversation.

Arthur gave his wife one final stern look, then picked up his lunch pail and left.

* * *

WHEN fifteen-year-old Danny Paquette slept that late morning, the banshee screams of the wind played in his dreams. He was growing and groggy like most adolescent boys. There was a hedonistic reflex to stay warm under the cotton sheets and wool blankets while the cold world swirled around the house. He was grateful his mother had let him sleep in.

When he awoke, though, he became startled. He could clearly see the hands on the clock. It was after ten.

I've missed my dentist appointment, he realized. *Why didn't Mom wake me up?*

Danny went down to the kitchen and found she had made breakfast for his dad and brother, Victor. But his mother was nowhere in sight. He went from room to room, calling for her, but the house was empty. Danny dashed over to the freezing barn to see if she had looked in on the cows, but she wasn't there either. He doubled back to the house, again going rapidly through each room. He yelled out her name. Nothing came back. He looked under beds. He looked in closets.

Danny stood in the kitchen, uncertain what to do next. Eventually, he picked up the phone and called his aunt, who lived nearby. "I can't find my mother. She was supposed to wake me up. She's not in the house."

"I'll send your uncle Charlie right over," she said. Charles Robinson was Arthur's brother-in-law and a cop in Manchester. Robinson was off duty that day and rushed over to the farm. It was only about ten degrees outside. He figured Rena couldn't be far away.

"Uncle Charlie, what are we going to do?" Danny asked him.

"Easy, Danny. We'll find her. Take me to the barn," his uncle said.

The pair stumbled through the barn, calling out Rena's name. They searched each stall for her. Perhaps she had slipped on the ice. Perhaps she'd had a heart attack. Robinson either didn't know about the tip Rena had given the police or wasn't thinking of it at the time. He was sure her disappearance was related to some random misfortune.

"Look at that!" Danny pointed to the far end of the Paquette property. In the distance, a column of smoke was rising into the chilly sky from the direction of the pigsty, about a half-mile from the farmhouse.

Danny and his uncle ran through the bright sun and cold winds punishing the land. Tall weeds, long dead from winter, poked out of the snow and whipped their legs as they ran by. The small pigsty was in sight. Robinson remembered his brother-in-law saying that the smell of the hogs was too much for any of them, which was why he'd built the sty on the back of the land. It was a rectangular shacklike structure with a slanted roof, and there was smoke coming from inside the building. Robinson made it to the door first. He grabbed hold and began to tug on it. It wouldn't open; a log was propped up on the outside like a buttress, blocking the way. Robinson kicked it away, then ripped the door open and stepped inside. His mouth fell open in horror.

"No, Danny!" he commanded his nephew. "Turn away!"

"No!" The boy had already stepped inside the sty. "Mom!" he cried.

His uncle pushed him out before he could see more.

Robinson took a step into the pigsty. On the floor lay Rena Paquette's smoldering body. She was still wearing her morning coat and slippers and lay on her back, sprawled out as if taking a nap—although her body was blackened by fire.

By all accounts, Danny Paquette was never the same after that moment.

* * *

SEVERAL hours later, the backside of the Paquette farm had become a circus. Sixteen-year-old Victor Paquette watched as firefighters came and went, police came and went, reporters came and went. The whole time, Victor sat on a log, the same log that had been used to wedge the sty door closed. When the men in uniforms were done, a priest from the local church came to administer last rites. Victor then watched a group of men in sharp hats and camel-hair coats inspect the scene. The uniformed men displayed deference to these gentlemen.

One of the finely dressed men noticed Victor sitting on the log. He came over to the boy. "Don't worry, kid," the man said. "This will all work out for you."

Victor took his eyes off his mother's body, still smoldering in the sty after the fire department had doused her with water, and looked at the guy in the trench coat like he wanted to punch him in the teeth.

"You got a cigarette?" the boy asked instead.

The man reached into his pocket and gave him a cigarette. He blocked the steady wind with his hands and lit the end with a lighter.

Victor sat and watched the smoke trail from the butt in the cold morning air.

* * *

TWENTY-ONE years later, in 1985, following family prayers at the funeral home, a light blue and silver hearse took Danny Paquette's body to St. Francis of Assisi Church, the same church where his mother's funeral had been in 1964.

Victor was not among the six pallbearers, who were mainly friends of Danny's. One wore his uniform from the army. Another wore his dress blues from the marines.

The family knew the priest saying the mass. He was the same one who had performed last rites on Rena in the pigsty. "Danny has attained the goal and purpose of his life," he offered in his homily. "He now possesses God. No more pain, no more suffering, no more tears. Just a complete and total happiness. He has attained before us what we also hope to attain."

Outside of St. Francis, police were copying down the license-plate numbers of those in attendance. The church was packed for the service. The list of mourners filled ten pages in the funeral book. Victor stood beside his sisters and older brother in the front pew. He turned and scanned the room, surprised to see, in the back, a face he hadn't expected: Billy "the Knife" Couteau, Jimma Bolduc's boss.

Danny Paquette was buried in the Pine Grove Cemetery in Manchester at 11:00 a.m.

— 7 —

Bad Blood

No one from Denise Messier Paquette's family attended her ex-husband's funeral, not even Danny's daughters. There was too much bad blood from their divorce, and Denise had left for Alaska with the girls three years earlier. It certainly didn't seem right to attend the mass, to pray for Danny Paquette's soul, when so many of them thought he got what he deserved, and maybe even wished he was in hell.

Over the previous few months, the Messier family had been thinking a lot about Danny Paquette. They'd been conspiring to keep a secret from him at all costs. And they demonstrated that they were willing to go to great lengths to maintain that secret.

They didn't want Danny to learn that his stepdaughter, Melanie, had returned to New Hampshire and was attending high school about fifteen miles away in Hopkinton.

* * *

WHILE Danny had been in the state mental hospital in 1981, Denise had tried to keep a low profile. She'd had a good job at a circuit-board manufacturer in the accounting department, and her crazy ex-husband was no longer showing up to bother her.

Then one night, the phone rang in her kitchen after an otherwise uneventful dinner and the subsequent dismissal of the children to bed. Denise did not recognize the voice on the other end.

"Who is this?" she asked.

The caller identified himself as a caseworker from New Hampshire Hospital, where Danny was being treated. He said that although Danny had been there for nearly a year, he was not getting any better. In fact, he confided, Danny's violent streak seemed to be getting worse.

"His year is almost up, and we can't keep him here any longer. If I were you, I'd consider moving far away from him," the caseworker told her.

Denise was shaken, but she didn't act immediately. When Danny was later released from the state mental hospital, he began visitation with their three girls at his home in Hooksett. Denise's empty apartment, calm and quiet in the absence of her children while they were visiting Danny, was a guilty pleasure for her. During those times, her sister Pauline, or her mother, Loretta, would often visit.

On one of these visits, Denise and her mother were sitting at the kitchen table when the phone rang. On the other end of the line was eleven-year-old Melanie, crying that she wanted to come home.

Denise reassured her daughter, but when she hung up, Loretta Messier asked whether it was the first time Melanie had called her mother from Danny's house like that. Denise admitted it wasn't.

"Well," Loretta said, "she's called your father. Same thing. Asking her grandfather to pick her up and take her home."

Denise began to wonder if there was something sinister going on, if Danny had done something to Melanie. Something awful and abhorrent. Something a mother might never forgive herself for allowing to happen.

* * *

ONE summer night, while the day's heat lingered as long as the trailing sun, Denise gathered her three daughters in the living room of their apartment. Audrey and Caroline, both toddlers, were too young to understand what was happening, so she addressed only her oldest.

"Melanie," she began, "we're going on a trip."

"What do you mean?" the girl asked.

"We're going someplace new. Someplace far away from Daddy. But it's a secret. We can't tell anyone what we're doing or where we're going."

"Where are we going, Mommy?"

She exhaled deeply, then forced a smile. "Back to Alaska."

"When are we going?"

"Tonight. Now. We have to pack our things. But it's going to be like a camping trip, and we'll just take what we really need. We're going to leave the rest here."

Melanie and the other girls enjoyed the game of packing. They grabbed stuffed animals and precious keepsakes, packing them before items unimportant to little girls, like socks or underwear. The game was going well when a knock came at the door.

Denise shushed the children, and all activity stopped. Even the baby was quiet. Denise peered through the peephole and saw it was Danny in the doorway. The very man they were fleeing from had chosen this night to make an unexpected visit.

She quickly and quietly huddled the children together. "Girls, don't say anything about our trip to Daddy. It's a secret, OK?"

All the girls nodded. Denise gathered herself at the door, then turned the knob to let Danny in. He walked into the apartment to find his two daughters and adopted stepdaughter still awake and in the living room staring blankly back at him.

"What's all this?" he asked.

Denise improvised. "The girls couldn't sleep."

"They're not in their pajamas."

"They don't want to go to bed." Denise turned to the girls and batted her hands to indicate they should run along. "Go to your rooms, girls. Mommy will be there in a few minutes."

The girls scurried from the living room. Audrey and Caroline simply began playing in their room, but Melanie stood breathlessly at the door, her ear pressed tight to the wall. Danny had come to discuss money. He had received some cash in a settlement from Harley-Davidson, a result of his accident in the White Mountains. He gave half to his ex-wife. She took the money and thanked him, then showed him the door. Danny left the apartment and didn't return.

Denise summoned the children and inspected what they had packed. Then she gathered their things and led them outside to her car to begin their long journey north.

* * *

KATHLEEN McGuire didn't hear the news about Danny Paquette's death until Sunday morning, November 10, 1985, after a series of phone calls among the Messier family. Her sister-in-law, Pauline, had read about the shooting on the front page of the *New Hampshire Sunday News* and called her mother-in-law, Loretta Messier, who then called Kathleen's husband, Philip Messier.

The sudden departure of Daniel Paquette from this earth solved a lot of problems, not only for exiled Denise, still in Alaska, but also for Melanie, who had been living with her aunt Kathleen and uncle Philip while going to high school, making friends, and trying to escape detection by her stepfather. It was a secret the family had gone to lengths to keep.

But Danny's death also posed a new set of problems for the homicide prosecutor.

"I'm going to get dragged into this case; I know it." Kathleen had only been working for the attorney general's office for two months. She would have to go to the attorney general and tell him about her connection to the victim, an embarrassing prospect for such a proud woman. *It's a conflict of interest. It's a scandal.* Although she knew her colleagues would be duty-bound to wall her off from the investigation, she also knew just how many rocks they would be willing to look under. She and Philip were housing Danny's stepdaughter, Melanie, who had moved back to New Hampshire over the summer. There was no avoiding the fact that Detective Roland Lamy and his state police investigators would be showing up at her house in Hopkinton.

* * *

KATHLEEN McGuire was born in Manchester in 1948 and graduated from the University of New Hampshire with a degree in history. She met and fell in love with the dashing Philip Messier, a U.S. Air Force pilot, and the couple married in 1970. (Somewhat unusually for the era, Kathleen never formally took the Messier name.) Philip's job meant the couple moved around the country several times during the first years of their marriage. By the time her sister-in-law Denise was marrying Danny Paquette, in 1974, Kathleen McGuire was getting her master's degree at the University of Florida and teaching history to teenagers.

When Philip Messier retired from the military in 1981, the couple returned to New Hampshire, where he took a job as an airline pilot for Delta. He flew planes right over the old neighborhood he'd grown up in on Brown Avenue, up the street from the Paquette farm. There was predictability for the first time in their marriage, and soon there was also a baby boy, born in 1982. But Kathleen wasn't content to be a housewife like many of the other pampered women of Hopkinton, New Hampshire. She instead decided to make a career change and become a lawyer.

After graduating from Boston College Law School, Kathleen clerked for Justice Chuck Douglas of the New Hampshire Supreme Court. From there, she landed at the New Hampshire Department of Justice. Instead of toiling away in one of the other divisions, like Consumer Protection or Charitable Trusts, Kathleen landed in the high-profile Criminal Bureau, prosecuting homicide cases. There wasn't as much money in it as there would be in private practice, but it was where Kathleen felt like she belonged. She wanted to move up, become chief of the Criminal Bureau some day. There was nothing stopping her from dreaming of becoming New Hampshire Attorney General. The current attorney general, Stephen Merrill, had designs on the governorship. As the great New Hampshire statesman Daniel Webster said, "There's always room at the top."

After hearing about Danny's death, Kathleen made a mental list of the things she'd have to do to make things right at work. Before Kathleen spoke to Attorney General Merrill, however, she first had to let Melanie know about her adopted father's death.

But Melanie was away at the moment. She had just left for a field trip to Quebec with her French class. That gave Kathleen at least three days to figure out how she'd tell Melanie that the man she'd been hiding from was dead.

* * *

ON Tuesday following the shooting, Corporal John Barthelmes interviewed Kathleen McGuire at the attorney general's office. Kathleen was told that the reason was to discuss allegations of an incestuous relationship between the deceased and his adopted daughter. The police had pieced together information gathered from interviews of Paquette's neighbors and members of the Messier family whom they'd questioned in the first days of the inquiry.

Kathleen McGuire was clearly uncomfortable, but Barthelmes noted that he believed her to be forthcoming about what she knew.

Though Kathleen McGuire and Philip Messier had been married since 1970, they hadn't returned to live in New Hampshire until after Denise and Danny had already divorced. "I don't know much about Denise and Danny's relationship," Kathleen told the state police investigator, but she confessed that based on what she'd heard from her sister-in-law, she believed Melanie had indeed been molested by her stepfather before the family had fled the state. She said the girl didn't talk about the sexual abuse with anyone and became upset whenever it was mentioned. Kathleen also confirmed that Denise had expressed fear of Danny Paquette.

Kathleen told Barthelmes that Denise Paquette's financial situation in Alaska was desperate, and there were problems in the mother-daughter relationship. The previous summer, Melanie had come out to visit their Hopkinton home for three weeks, but Philip had convinced his sister to let the girl move in with them and their toddler. Danny still didn't know where his family was hiding, and everyone agreed it would be best if they kept Melanie's return a secret. Perhaps even change her last name.

The assistant attorney general also told the corporal she had no idea who might want to kill Danny Paquette.

* * *

BEFORE sending investigators to speak to Louis Messier, Denise and Philip's father, Corporal John Barthelmes did some snooping around into his background. Messier had been a cop in Manchester, and he retired with the rank of sergeant. He had actually made lieutenant, but following some sort of internal department investigation, he had been busted down to "zebra" and asked to retire. The details of why Messier was asked to quit were never made public. Colleagues described the elder Messier as meek and mild-mannered. Barthelmes was given the names of some of Messier's friends at the sailboat club on Lake Massabesic. He remembered that Victor Paquette had chortled about Louis Messier when he'd asked him about Danny's relationship with his former in-laws. Victor had said he'd always been suspicious of how a city police officer could afford a sailboat.

Louis Messier told investigators that his daughter-in-law, Assistant Attorney General Kathleen McGuire, was the one who'd told him about Danny Paquette's death. He told Sergeant Frank Beliveau, of the Hooksett Police Department, and Sergeant Thomas Winn, of the New Hampshire State Police, that his former son-in-law would threaten his granddaughter Melanie to keep her quiet about the abuse. He also confirmed that his daughter had been struggling to get by in Alaska. He said he'd given her one thousand dollars, and he was sure that her brother Philip had given her a couple hundred dollars, too. Messier said there had been no discussions in the family about whether Denise should return to New Hampshire.

"How did Denise seem when you told her about Danny's death?" they asked.

"Relieved," he said, "but she was also upset."

As the interview went on, Messier became extremely nervous, but by the end of the questioning, he had calmed down. The officers wrote in their report they didn't know what had caused him to become so anxious.

The investigators asked if they could speak to Messier's wife, Loretta. "She's very excitable," he told them. "I don't think that would be a good idea at this time."

* * *

TWO weeks after the shooting, Sergeant Tom Winn visited Melanie Paquette at her aunt and uncle's home. He asked a plainclothes female state trooper to come along.

Melanie was fifteen years old, with delicate features and short dark hair. She was tomboyish, with a quiet demeanor.

"I never liked Danny," she said, her eyes focused on some invisible spot on the floor. "He was very strict and mean. He would belittle my mother." Melanie told the troopers that Danny would badger her mother about how the house was kept, but that he would never help her. Melanie said her mother had been held responsible for not only the housekeeping, but all the plumbing, carpentry, and electrical work inside the Whitehall Road house.

Even after the divorce, Danny would still pester Denise. Melanie had seen him physically abuse her mother. It got so bad, she said, her mother moved the whole family to Wasilla, Alaska, a city that Melanie did not care to live in.

When the discussion got around to her relationship with her stepfather, Melanie indicated that she would be more comfortable talking to the female trooper alone. Winn excused himself from the room. With some gentle probing from the woman, Melanie admitted that Danny had raped her. She also said she was sure Danny had molested another girl from the neighborhood, one who used to come over to play with her when she was a child.

When Winn returned to the interview, he asked Melanie where she'd been on the morning Danny died. She told him she'd gone to a field hockey game with a boy named Eric before leaving on her field trip to Quebec. The game was in Plymouth, sixty miles north of Hooksett.

Winn asked Melanie if she knew anyone who would want to kill Danny. She said that she did not.

* * *

AFTER Christmas, Victor Paquette showed up at the Hooksett Police Department. Frank Beliveau, now a lieutenant, sat down with him.

"I was thinking over the holidays," he began, "that Kathy McGuire might have had Danny killed."

It was a serious allegation about a member of the attorney general's office. "What makes you say that?"

"There was a custody battle. Between Danny and McGuire. She and her husband wanted guardianship of Melanie. But Danny didn't know that."

Victor learned that, at Denise's request, Philip Messier had applied to become the administrator of Danny's estate. Danny had no will and had not designated anyone to take care of his affairs, so the probate court granted Messier's request. He worked with a law firm to sell off the last of Danny's possessions: his welding tools, his old cars, his property. Messier said the money would go to Danny's children, his heirs. Victor saw it a different way. He added the guardianship to the inheritance and came up with a motive for murder.

* * *

CORPORAL John Barthelmes went back to Kathleen McGuire and asked about the custody case. She told him that she and her husband had begun the paperwork to be named Melanie's guardians months earlier, but when they'd learned that Danny would be notified about the proceedings, they'd dropped it. Now that Danny was dead, they were undecided about whether or not to refile.

Kathleen also revealed to Barthelmes that her niece had told a psychological counselor about the abuse. The counselor filed a report with the state's Department of Health and Human Services to investigate Danny. At the time of his death, no one from the Family Services Division had yet spoken with him.

* * *

THE investigative team for case I-85-147 decided they needed to talk to everyone in the Messier family. There was reason to believe that Melanie's sexual abuse and Denise's exile from New England were motive enough for any of them to kill Danny Paquette.

Hooksett Police Department lieutenant Frank Beliveau and officer Steve Agrafiotis questioned Denise's other brother, Richard Messier. He ran an auto dealership and repair shop in Manchester. The Hooksett officers sat around a table in his office.

"I've known Danny Paquette since I was eleven years old," he told them. "We'd play around in his father's farm equipment." He told the investigators Danny wasn't ever the same after his mother's death.

Richard Messier said that his brother, Philip, was the golden boy of the family. As far as his parents and siblings were concerned, Philip could do no wrong.

"What about his wife, Kathleen?"

"Kathy's a do-gooder," he replied. "She holds herself above everybody else."

Richard Messier said his dealership had once employed Tom Benzel, Denise's first husband and Melanie's biological father. He had given Benzel a job as a salesman after he left Dunkin' Donuts. Messier had lost touch with him when Benzel left the dealership more than a decade earlier, though he told the cops they'd had lunch once, that past summer. Messier said he'd tried to discuss Denise and Melanie, but Benzel had taken little interest in his ex-wife's troubles.

Messier said he had a business relationship with a motorcycle shop in the city, and he'd sometimes see Danny's welding truck at this shop. The owner told Richard Messier that when Denise left the area, Victor Paquette asked the shop owner if he knew where his brother's ex had gone. He wanted to tell Danny.

"I was in that shop a week ago, and they said that Victor had come in and left a message for me."

"What was the message?" Agrafiotis asked.

"The message was, 'Fuck you.'"

* * *

WHEN Tom Benzel spoke to Agrafiotis and Trooper Colon Forbes about his ex-wife and biological daughter, he was dispassionate. He'd spent the previous twelve years working as a project specialist for a plastics manufacturer, and he had been married to a schoolteacher for the past eight years. They were childless. He had long moved on from that girl at Dunkin' Donuts who had married him, had his child, and then broken his heart.

"I knew Danny Paquette in high school. We weren't friends, just knew each other casually," Benzel said.

He told the officers that in 1973, two years after Denise had left for Alaska the first time and cut off contact, she called him up and asked if they could talk over coffee.

"I've been back for a little while," she told him. "And I've been seeing Danny Paquette."

Benzel knew the couple's history, the baby boy they had together and gave up for adoption. He wasn't upset that Denise was with Danny.

"How is Melanie?" he asked her.

"She's great. She's almost three."

"I'd like to see her. If I could."

Denise agreed at first. But before a meeting could be arranged, she changed her mind. Benzel thought it was one thing if Denise wanted to refuse his offers of child support, but he felt he still had a right to see his daughter.

Benzel went to court to get visitation rights to see Melanie and settle the issue of support payments. A week later, Denise showed up at his door with legal documents of her own.

"Danny wants to adopt Melanie," she told him.

Benzel was crestfallen, but he decided not to interfere with the adoption proceedings. He had no further contact with Denise or Melanie for nearly a decade.

In 1981, Denise called Benzel and said Melanie had been asking lots of questions about her real father.

"She wants to meet you, Tom."

"What about Danny?"

Denise paused. "Danny and I are divorced." She made no other mention about problems in the family.

The couple met in a restaurant in Derry to talk about their daughter. Afterward, Denise instructed Benzel to follow her to her apartment.

The reunion was not as tender or life affirming as adolescent Melanie probably envisioned it would be. There were hugs and smiles, soft voices afraid to shatter the gossamer bond they both hoped might form, but to Benzel, father and daughter felt every bit like the strangers they were. He and Melanie took turns talking about themselves, introducing themselves to each other. Yet, though awkward, the meeting was hardly painful or regrettable. Melanie asked if Benzel would visit again. He said that he would.

Benzel visited Melanie every two or three weeks. His wife began to complain that he was spending too much time with this young girl, perhaps upset that it meant prolonged contact with his first wife, too.

After Denise fled with the girls to Alaska, Melanie kept in contact with Benzel by telephone and letters. At first she wrote often, but then the letters and calls tapered off, finally stopping all together.

"I was only doing it for Melanie," Benzel told the cops. "She wanted the contact and the connection. But Denise and Melanie . . . they were from another time in my life. And that time was over." Agrafiotis wrote in his notes that Benzel said he no longer had any feelings for his ex-wife and daughter.

Benzel said he had received a phone call from Denise's mother, Loretta Messier, over the summer telling him that Melanie was planning on returning to New Hampshire. She asked if he would be willing to help pay for Melanie's ticket home. Other members of the family were putting money toward bringing Melanie home, she said. Benzel thought the request was odd, but he agreed to have lunch with his former brother-in-law, Richard Messier, to discuss it. The officers confirmed that this was the same lunch that Messier had mentioned during their interview with him.

The former in-laws and ex-colleagues met at a Chinese restaurant on South Willow Street in Manchester. Benzel said he was polite to Messier but not inclined to put any money toward bringing Melanie back to New Hampshire. That was the last Benzel ever heard about it.

"I still haven't heard if she ever made it back to New Hampshire," he said to the officers.

The investigators nodded, made notes, and then proceeded to ask a series of prearranged questions.

"Did you kill Danny?"

Benzel seemed ready for the question. "No."

"Do you know who did?"

"No."

"Do you own any guns?"

"No."

"Did you know that Danny had ever assaulted Denise?"

"No."

"Did you know that Danny had sexually abused Melanie?"

Tom Benzel looked shocked, puzzled. "No."

* * *

TROOPER Colon Forbes and Lieutenant Frank Beliveau visited the elder Messier's home to speak with Denise's mother, Loretta. They found her feisty and full of opinions. She said that while working as a bookkeeper in Alaska, Denise was having trouble making ends meet. Her daughter had a good job, but the cost of living in Wasilla was high.

"Denise couldn't [afford to] dress Melanie like all the other children in school," she told them. "She's having a hard time."

Loretta Messier said she was the one who broke the news of Danny Paquette's death to Denise. She claimed she'd called her daughter in Alaska and that Denise had cried. Loretta said her daughter had been in shock.

"Did you know that people had sent Denise money?" the sergeant asked Loretta.

"I don't know of such things."

"Did you know that your husband, Louis, sent her a thousand dollars?"

The older woman got nervous. She wouldn't look at the cops. She stammered and finally mumbled that Denise was going to pay him back.

On the day of the shooting, Mrs. Messier said, she had been grocery shopping by herself in the morning. She had been home the rest of the day.

"The way he died was too easy," Danny Paquette's former mother-in-law said, pointing a finger at both officers. "He should have suffered first."

— 8 —

You Can't Go Home Again

SERGEANT Roland Lamy made arrangements with a detective in the Alaska State Police to question Denise Paquette. A cassette tape and transcript of the interview were sent back to Officer Steve Agrafiotis in Hooksett, New Hampshire, for safekeeping.

In the accompanying letter, Sergeant Edward Stauber of the Alaska State Troopers said Mrs. Paquette "was cooperative and appeared sincere during the interview."

"Who would you vouch for being above suspicion?" Stauber asked her.

"My family," she told him. "Let me tell you ... Danny was a person who could make enemies so quickly. He was sharp with his remarks. He was cruel. He was running a business at home, and very often he would kick people right out of the yard. Sometimes physically. He frightened me many times. One time he did it to a police officer who came to the door. Took him by the shirt and shoved him right outside. He was an incredible human being. No fear whatsoever of repercussion. Didn't even consider whether he needed to be liked."

Denise told the Alaska State Trooper that she didn't truly learn the extent of Danny's abuse of Melanie until a year and a half after they had moved away. She said Melanie had been near suicidal, not handling it well.

Denise described her financial situation as "horrible." She

said that when her brother Philip learned of her dire straits, he'd offered to bring Melanie back to New Hampshire. He could buy her clothes, buy her shoes. He could put her through college.

"Did you have any hesitation about her going back to that area knowing that . . ." Trooper Stauber began.

"Oh, much, much," she said. "And we talked about it at great lengths. I tried to impress upon my brother that it was important to keep a low profile. We talked even of having her use their name. I didn't feel real comfortable about what might happen."

Stauber asked what they would've done if Danny had discovered that Melanie was living in New Hampshire.

"Bring her right back to Alaska without hesitation."

"What kind of person is your brother?"

"Philip? He's my favorite brother. I love him. I'm closer to him I think than anyone else in the family." She sighed ruefully. "We're not a very close family."

Stauber probed deeper. He said that Philip, who was attached to his niece and who knew that Danny had abused her, would seem a likely suspect. Those circumstances were a powerful motive toward revenge.

"Phil hasn't revenge in him," Denise said confidently. "He felt he could protect Melanie. He wanted her to have counseling and get through school and go to college. He is intelligent enough to know that it serves no purpose to go out and shoot someone."

* * *

SERGEANT Tom Winn had originally interviewed Melanie Paquette on November 22, the day after Thanksgiving. On New Year's Eve, Sergeant Winn and Officer Steve Agrafiotis returned to Hopkinton to interview Eric Windhurst, the boy Melanie said she'd been with at a field hockey game on the morning Danny Paquette was shot.

Eric Windhurst was a handsome boy, tall and athletic, with a thick tuft of hair. He seemed relaxed and helpful when talking to the cops.

"I got friendly with Melanie because she plays on the soccer team with me," he told them.

"The *boys'* soccer team?" Agrafiotis asked.

"Yeah. First girl ever to do it," he said. "We don't have a girl's team."

Eric said they were not dating but that he had invited her to come with him to the high school field hockey championships at Plymouth State College. He said he'd picked her up at 9:00 a.m. at her aunt's house, drove to the game, and left when the game was over at noon. They stopped in Concord to get burgers at McDonald's, then he dropped Melanie off at 2:00 p.m. so she could pack for the school trip to Canada.

The cops gave the kid their business cards and left. Sergeant Winn made a note in his report that "the above information is substantially the same as given by Melanie Paquette when she was interviewed."

When he returned to the Hooksett Police Department, Officer Agrafiotis received a phone call from John Windhurst, the boy's father, who said he had additional information about the Paquette case. Windhurst said that after the police had left, Eric had told his father a few more things that the police should be aware of.

"At some point, Melanie told my son that her father had beat her mother and had molested her. Melanie also told Eric that her father had molested a neighbor's child."

* * *

"THE only problem I ever had with Danny was when we were teenagers," Denise Paquette's sister, Pauline Gates, told Hooksett Police Department lieutenant Frank Beliveau. Pauline said that Danny had made sexual advances toward her when they were teens.

"When Denise and Danny were having problems, no one from my family was allowed to go to their home on Whitehall Road," she added.

Pauline said that after the divorce, Denise confided in her about Melanie's molestation and said her sister had considered running away to California, where she could get free tuition for college. But in the end, Denise had decided to return to Alaska. She knew Danny didn't wander far outside his family circle and didn't think he'd follow her to the Land of the Midnight Sun.

Once Denise left the state, Pauline sold all of the belongings that her sister had left behind, then she sold all of her own belongings and moved to Wasilla with them. Pauline, who had been separated from her husband since 1981, liked the idea of starting a new life, too.

Pauline could see that Denise was having a difficult time making ends meet. There was credit card debt and other money problems. At one point, Denise went to a financial counselor. Denise met an Eskimo named Willie Crow* who had been living on workman's compensation for an industrial accident that mangled his hand. Denise and Willie started to date, even though he was considerably younger than she was. But she soon grew unhappy with the relationship.

Pauline told Lieutenant Beliveau she decided to return to New Hampshire after only a few months. She also said that *she* was now Willie Crow's girlfriend and that he had moved in with her after recently visiting her in New Hampshire. The couple now shared a small rented home with another couple.

Pauline could tell that her niece Melanie had struggled to fit in up in Alaska, and she told Beliveau that she knew that Melanie was now back in New Hampshire, and knew to keep it a secret.

"I didn't know that Philip and Kathy were trying to become Melanie's guardians," she claimed of her brother and sister-in-law. "I didn't find that out until four days ago. I don't really get along with them."

Pauline said that Melanie was also afraid of Danny's brother, Victor Paquette. She said something had happened at Christmas, just weeks after Danny's death, that Victor tried to bring some gifts to Philip and Kathy's home in Hopkinton, and harsh words were exchanged at the front door. She didn't know what was said, only that Melanie was scared of her stepfather's brother.

* * *

NOT long after Lieutenant Frank Beliveau quizzed her, Pauline Gates called for a family meeting. Her tone with everyone was

---

* Denotes pseudonym

somber and serious. "There's something I need to tell you all," she said. The family agreed to meet at the parents' house in Manchester.

Virtually everyone in the Messier clan had gathered at Louis and Loretta's home that January evening. Pauline's brothers, Philip and Richard, were there with their wives. Her sister Suzanne was accompanied by her husband, John Perley. The only one missing (besides Denise, who was still in Alaska) was her sister Linda, whose husband wanted nothing to do with that side of the family.

When everyone was settled, Pauline made a shocking confession. "I stole money from work, and I'm in a real jam." She was a bookkeeper, and she admitted to her family that she had been pocketing business receipts from the satellite TV installation shop over a period of several months. Pauline had quit the job a month earlier, and when asked if she had been fired for the embezzlement, she said no. She told them after she quit, the boss discovered more than $24,000 was missing, but he had told her that if she could pay him back $15,000, he wouldn't go to the police. Then Pauline admitted that she had almost none of the cash.

John Perley spoke up. Pauline's brother-in-law was a vice president at a local bank. He said Pauline had already approached him about a loan, but neither he nor the bank could give her that kind of money. It was soon clear that Pauline wasn't going to find a quick way out of this mess.

The scope of Pauline's actions washed over the family. They thought back to the extravagant purchases she had been making, claiming she was getting performance bonuses at work. There had been new clothes, furniture, a color TV, bicycles, and a piano. They had all been duped.

One can only imagine what went through the mind of Kathleen McGuire while she heard this. Her relationship with her sister-in-law Pauline had already been strained. As an assistant attorney general, Kathleen also knew what stealing $24,000 meant in New Hampshire: a class-A felony with seven to fifteen years in prison if convicted. She was already entangled in the Danny Paquette investigation because of one sister-in-law, and now another sister-in-law was likely going to be charged with a felony.

The family did not pay Pauline's way out of the pickle. But at the end of the family meeting, Richard Messier offered to get her a good attorney.

* * *

A week later, Sergeant Roland Lamy got a call from one of the assistant attorneys general working on case I-85-147. It was a tip about a coworker, and it needed to be handled delicately. The assistant attorney general told Lamy that Kathleen McGuire's other sister-in-law, Denise Messier's sister Pauline Gates, had recently embezzled thousands of dollars from her employer.

Detective Lamy did not much like Kathleen McGuire to begin with. She'd rubbed him the wrong way more than once, and though she hadn't been with the attorney general's office long, she and Lamy had already had arguments. That's why Lamy had sent Corporal Barthelmes to question her the first time.

At 8:30 in the morning, the secretary informed McGuire that three officers were there to see her. At the New Hampshire Department of Justice, it wasn't an unusual occurrence.

Sergeant Lamy sent Corporal John Barthelmes, Lieutenant Frank Beliveau, and Officer Steve Agrafiotis, and Kathleen told the cops all about the Messier family meeting the previous Thursday.

After the discussion, Kathleen emphasized that she wanted the information she had given them to remain confidential.

* * *

THAT afternoon, the trio of investigators drove from the state capitol to a small workshop on a back road in Manchester. There was a pair of large satellite dishes pointing skyward. This was the main office of Uplink TV*, and the men asked to speak to the manager.

Gary Nebeker* told them that Pauline Gates had worked for him from May of 1984 to November of 1985. Nebeker said he never thought of Pauline as a bad employee, but she was

---

* Denotes pseudonym

quick-tempered and emotional. Whenever she got into customer disputes on the telephone, he would have to step in and tell Pauline to keep her voice down.

"In the past year, I hired an accountant to help me with finances," Nebeker told the investigators, sliding a fresh cigarette into the corner of his mouth. "That's when I started to suspect I had a problem with Pauline. The guy just couldn't get the books to balance."

Nebeker's accountant did an in-depth audit for the whole of 1985. "How much did she take?" Beliveau asked. Nebeker pulled out a neatly typed piece of paper. At the bottom, circled in red pencil, was the figure $23,782.74.

"If you didn't fire her, why did she leave?"

Nebeker explained that he'd hired a new girl on November 5, 1985. She tried to balance the books from the day before and was $100 short. Her first day on the job, the kid was really upset. Pauline later told the girl she found the $100 in her own pocketbook, that she must have put it there by accident.

"It was on that same day that [Pauline] gave me a two-week notice."

"Did Ms. Gates ever mention anything about her brother-in-law, Danny Paquette?"

Nebeker took a long drag on the cigarette. "One time, my normal welder was sick and couldn't do a dish install for me. He said he could get a Paquette to come over and do it. Pauline said if Danny Paquette came over, she would leave. She said she was afraid of him."

"Anything else?"

"She couldn't stop reading the newspaper articles about him getting shot," Nebeker said. "The Monday after it happened, she talked about it all day."

"What did she say about it?"

"That she was happy for her sister," he said. "That now her sister could finally come back to New Hampshire."

* * *

THE next day, Lieutenant Frank Beliveau took the rookie, Officer Steve Agrafiotis, with him to interview Willie Crow, Pauline Gates's boyfriend. Agrafiotis had terrible handwriting, almost indecipherable, but he excelled at taking the senior officers' notes and typing up complete reports.

"You learning a lot on this case, kid?" Beliveau asked him.

"Yes," said Agrafiotis enthusiastically.

The Hooksett officers rang the bell to a rented house in Auburn. Willie Crow opened the door and invited them in. Crow said he lived there with Pauline and three other people. The cops noticed that the home seemed nicely furnished and clean.

Crow said he'd met Pauline in 1983 while dating her sister in Alaska. At first their friendship was platonic; then in January of 1985, Crow visited Pauline in New Hampshire, and a romance blossomed. Crow had been on the East Coast, in Boston, to get the first of two reconstructive surgeries on his crushed hand.

"Look," he said, slowly flexing his hand for them. "I'm getting better."

"What can you tell us about Pauline?"

"She has not been doing well. Not for the past year. Both physically and mentally. She's having a tough time."

Crow said that what seemed to give Pauline the greatest amount of joy was seeing her niece, Melanie. Every other weekend, Melanie would spend the day at Pauline's house. Crow said Kathleen McGuire had strict rules about when Melanie had to be home, and Pauline wasn't good about getting the teenager back to Hopkinton on time. This caused a lot of friction between Pauline and Kathleen.

Agrafiotis asked if Crow knew whether Pauline was involved in any illegal activities. At first he hesitated, but then he revealed that he knew about her embezzlement from Uplink TV. "I knew she had all this money," Crow said. "She told me an old man from the Jordan Marsh department store was giving it to her. Then she later told me the truth."

Crow said he knew that Pauline had confessed the deed to her family at a meeting last week and that her brother Richard had hired her a lawyer.

"Does Denise know about the embezzlement?" Agrafiotis asked.

"I don't know," Crow said. Then after a minute, he offered,

"Do you think Pauline knew something about money being sent to Denise to use as a hit on Danny?"

Beliveau and Agrafiotis did not answer. Neither of them had said anything about Danny's shooting or the possibility that the embezzlement money had been used to finance a hit.

* * *

CORPORAL John Barthelmes called Gary Nebeker at Uplink TV and asked if he knew of any criminals or shady characters associated with Pauline Gates. Nebeker said there was one sketchy guy they might want to look into.

Hugo Pinsky* owned a satellite television business in Vermont. Business was good in the Green Mountains, where cable TV was still largely unavailable. Pinsky would contact Uplink TV to get equipment. Often he'd bounce a check or come up short on his payment to Nebeker. Each time it happened, Pauline would cover it.

Pinsky may have looked like so many of the liberal hippies who lived in Vermont, but this hippie did not exude peace and love; he had an aura of something more sinister.

Barthelmes and Lamy tracked Pinsky down in his timber frame home in the Vermont woods. He invited the plainclothes state police detectives inside. Pinsky sat casually at his kitchen table. Sergeant Roland Lamy stood over him and questioned him; Barthelmes wandered around the room.

"Do you have any guns?" Lamy asked.

"Used to have a shotgun," Pinsky riffed. "My wife made me get rid of it."

"Was that because you got arrested for firing it in the air?"

"It went off by accident," he laughed, not caring if they believed him or not. "These bad dudes were walking up my driveway. I just wanted to scare them off."

"Yeah? You deal with a lot of bad dudes, do you?"

"Heh, heh. Don't you, officer?"

"How do you know Pauline Gates?" Barthelmes asked from the far corner of the room.

"She's a nice working-class girl. I like her. I even sold her

---

* Denotes pseudonym

a dog. Did you see the kennels when you came in? I raise chows."

"That's kind of a faggoty dog, isn't it, Hugo?" Lamy said. "Why is Pauline covering your debts with Gary Nebeker?"

"She likes me, too."

"Did you ever sell drugs to her?"

Pinsky just laughed.

"Where were you on Saturday, November 9, Hugo?"

Lamy towered over the hippie. The guy just smirked back at him. "Can't say that I recall," he said. "But if you gave me enough time, I'm sure I could think of something."

— 9 —

It Will All Work Out

THE probe into the embezzlement case of Pauline Gates and its possible connection to Danny Paquette's murder continued through the end of January 1986. On January 28, work on the case—and work all over New Hampshire—came to a halt, just as it was scheduled to. In offices and classrooms statewide, people gathered around televisions to witness a historic event they'd long been anticipating: New Hampshire teacher Christa McAuliffe was about to become the first civilian in space. She taught at Concord High School, which Kathleen McGuire passed on the back route from her Hopkinton farmhouse to the attorney general's office. McAuliffe's husband, Stephen, was a local attorney, and many of the cops knew him, too.

Everyone planned to go back to his or her regularly scheduled duties after the *Challenger*'s liftoff. But few were able to, after the shuttle's tragic end.

Once they were able to focus their minds on work again, detectives took another look at Pauline Gates. She was not cooperating with investigators, who were trying to connect her embezzlement to the murder of her former brother-in-law, Danny Paquette. Willie Crow, however, made an itemized list of what Pauline had spent the $23,782.74 on. There were guitars, furniture, electronics, a mattress and box springs, an upright piano, and an all-terrain vehicle. There were dinners and lunches and dresses and shoes. But even with values rounded up to the nearest $100, it still didn't account for all $23,782.74 of the embezzled money. Crow's list could only account for about half of it.

Pauline had retained an attorney through her brother, Richard. The lawyer, Gary Lenehan, called Lieutenant Frank Beliveau to request that his client not be questioned by police. He then followed up the phone call with a letter spelling it out for them.

"In the event that you have an arrest warrant for Pauline Gates, please contact me and I will make her available to your department," the letter stated. "To be clear, I do not wish my client questioned at any time in regard to any investigation. This letter serves as an assertion of my client's Fifth and Sixth Amendment Rights."

Sergeant Roland Lamy was perplexed. "Any" investigation, it read. Surely this was more than an embezzlement case. There was more than $10,000 of that money that was unaccounted for. It was more than enough cash to pay someone to kill a child molester.

Lamy had a theory about the case: Pauline Gates had embezzled the money and paid for the hit on Danny Paquette not to avenge the molestation of Melanie, but to pave the way for her sister, Denise Paquette, to return home to New Hampshire. He thought Hugo Pinsky, the hippie who seemed to owe Pauline a favor, could have been the trigger man, but it was also possible that Pinsky had hired one of those "bad dudes" he knew for the job.

* * *

WITH no other avenue to get around the attorney and talk to Pauline, the I-85-147 investigative team instead spoke to her siblings again. While Lamy called Denise in Wasilla, Alaska, Beliveau visited Richard at his auto dealership. No one approached Assistant Attorney General Kathleen McGuire.

Beliveau candidly explained to Richard that the missing money was highly suspicious. The gap of nearly $10,000 was hard to reconcile. He said they weren't interested in the embezzlement, only the death of Danny Paquette. If Pauline had nothing to do with the murder, then she had nothing to fear from them. But she needed to explain the money trail more clearly if detectives were going to be satisfied.

Richard understood the cops' plight. His sister had her faults, but he did not believe she was willing to participate in or capable of pulling off an assassination.

"Pauline has not been well," he admitted. "She can't eat. She can't sleep. She's suicidal." Beliveau noted that those conditions didn't exonerate someone as a murder suspect; they actually made her look guiltier. He also told the cops that these investigations had caused problems for Kathleen McGuire at work.

"Can you get Pauline to talk to us?"

Richard agreed to go to Pauline and try to convince her to cooperate with the murder investigation.

But Pauline Gates would not talk to New Hampshire State Police or Hooksett police investigators. Her attorney, Gary Lenehan, sent another letter to the state police, reiterating that Pauline had invoked her right to remain silent and that any further questions should be directed to him.

Seeing no other option, the state police recommended that the Hillsborough County Attorney press charges against Pauline Gates for embezzling $23,782.74.

* * *

ROOKIE patrolman Steve Agrafiotis finally got a return phone call from the only Messier sibling whom they hadn't been able to contact. Linda Messier was the one sibling other than Denise who'd missed the family meeting in which Pauline confessed to the embezzlement. Linda told Agrafiotis that Pauline hadn't been completely forthcoming with them.

According to the police report, Linda said her sister Pauline and Willie Crow were drug users. She said she'd seen her sister on many occasions with large baggies of marijuana. She said she knew Pauline had also purchased cocaine. Although Linda could not offer any solid proof of Pauline's alleged bad acts, she felt pretty sure that Pauline had spent that extra money on drugs.

* * *

PAULINE Gates's embezzlement trial was scheduled for May.

The rest of the work done on the Paquette case was slapdash. Officers tracked down people like Ruth Szeleste's sons, as well as Billy "the Knife" Couteau, and Jimma Bolduc, but there was nothing substantial to link any of them to the shooting. The police also looked closely at the rest of the Messiers, to determine if any of them had the means to engineer the killing; they even looked at whether Victor Paquette could have done it.

Victor said he had no beef with his little brother. He admitted he had different ideas about welding than Danny did and they'd sometimes bitch at each other if they worked on the same welding project, but none of the ill will ever lasted past quitting time. The brothers were close: Victor had once needed money to buy a car, and when he'd asked Danny to loan him two thousand dollars, Danny had driven straight to the bank, and come back with a fistful of cash. Victor had paid him back with interest.

There seemed to be no other lead as promising as Pauline Gates. She emerged as the unofficial prime suspect. But the day before Pauline's embezzlement trial, the county moved for a continuance. The witnesses were told that they weren't needed to testify.

A senior state police investigator came to the Hooksett Police Department for an update on the Paquette case. The local officers who had been working for six months on I-85-147 were prepared to walk the investigator through their evidence, but instead, the senior investigator took the floor.

"This is a hunting accident," he told them. "We have nothing to pin on any individual. This was a hunting accident."

The Hooksett cops looked at one another. "This could have been a lot of things, but there's no way this was a hunting accident."

"You've never been able to prove that bullet wasn't a stray. For now, the case will remain open and undetermined. The state police personnel assigned to this case have other cases they need to focus on."

The senior investigator got up from the table and left the station, effectively shutting down investigation number I-85-147.

* * *

THE task of explaining the new posture of the case to Victor Paquette fell to Detective Sergeant Roland Lamy. Victor, who never hesitated to call Lamy directly, dialed the detective about his brother's case when he learned that Pauline Gates's embezzlement trial was on hold.

"Unless we develop some new leads, this is going to be classified as a hunting accident," Lamy informed him.

"No!" Victor roared. It didn't make sense. "That was no fucking accident. Somebody took him out! I saw his dead body with my own eyes! No stray bullet could have done that!"

Lamy listened to Victor rant on the other end of the phone, and then repeated that unless any new leads came up, the case would stay as it was.

Victor was certain that the embezzlement case's continuance was Kathleen McGuire's doing, that the attorney general's office was trying to sweep the whole mess under the rug.

"The attorney general's office has not interfered with the conduct of this investigation," Lamy said.

"Fuck you!" Victor shouted, and hung up.

* * *

VICTOR Paquette felt like he had when his mother was killed: helpless, frustrated, and angry. He could still remember that bitterly cold day in February of 1964. The day his mother died, and all that the police had done was give him a cigarette.

Sitting on that log on the backside of the Paquette farm that subfreezing afternoon, Victor Paquette fervently believed that Edward Coolidge had murdered his mother. Rena had fingered him as Pamela Jean Mason and Sandra Valade's killer, and she'd confronted him directly about his role in the slayings. Now, her incinerated body had been discovered in the same pigsty she'd claimed Coolidge's mother had told her he'd used to kill one of the girls.

"*This will all work out for you*," some guy in a suit had told him that day, implying that life would bring him better times to come.

Word of Rena Paquette's death had spread through a city already in an uproar over the murder of two young women. Arthur Paquette and other relatives were quick to offer reporters the detail that Rena had been following the Pamela Mason investigation and that authorities had just questioned her about what she knew. *The killer strikes again*, the city said. *None of us are safe*.

In 1964, the attorney general still had to go out and face the press directly, and that afternoon's briefing with Attorney General William Maynard, a man who bore a striking resemblance to Dwight Eisenhower, was especially vigorous and sharp. Reporters were hounding Maynard, absolutely punishing him for withholding details, berating him for not spilling what he knew.

"Until the autopsy is complete, we will not know the cause of her death," Maynard told the press corps regarding Rena Paquette. The body was being taken to Moore General Hospital, where a physician from Harvard University could examine it. But the scribes continued to push hard on this point, asking again and again how Rena had died. Maynard eventually relented and gave the reporters their headline.

The front page of that evening's Manchester *Union Leader* featured a large picture of the pigsty with an *X* drawn at the door where Rena's body was discovered, taken by staff photographer George Naum (who, twenty years later, would also take the pictures at Danny Paquette's funeral).

The headline spanned six columns above the fold. "*FAIL TO LINK PYRE DEATH TO PAM CASE*," it read.

"What is this?" a puzzled and grieving Arthur Paquette said, clutching the afternoon paper.

The attorney general had told reporters that investigators did not think the death of Rena Paquette was related to the murders of Pamela Mason or Sandra Valade. They didn't think Mrs. Paquette's death was a murder at all. They believed Rena Paquette had committed suicide.

"What?" Arthur yelled while reading aloud from the paper. Relatives were at his side trying to calm him.

He read on. Asked by reporters why she would have killed herself by self-immolation, Maynard offered up the theory that Mrs. Paquette was despondent over the recent assassination of President Kennedy.

The Paquettes told the reporters who later interviewed them that Maynard was wrong. Beyond the utter lack of evidence to support Maynard's theory, Rena Paquette had been a devout Catholic, who would never have taken her own life.

Nevertheless, Rena's death certificate listed "suicide" as the cause of death. When the Paquette family returned home after Rena's funeral days later, they noticed a plume of smoke rising from the backside of the farm. While they were gone, someone had set another fire in the pigsty where Rena's body had been burned.

One week after the death of Rena Paquette, police arrested bakery deliveryman Edward Coolidge and charged him with the murders of Pamela Mason and Sandra Valade. Despite the mounting circumstantial evidence also linking Rena's death to the killer, Attorney General Maynard refused to reconsider his findings in her case.

* * *

VICTOR Paquette slammed the phone down hard after speaking with Sergeant Roland Lamy. It felt like it was happening again. *A hunting accident? A fucking hunting accident? No one will ever be held accountable for killing my brother.*

Victor stumbled into the bathroom and splashed some cold water on his face. He looked at his reflection, ran a hand over his bald head, and looked deep into his own eyes.

After his mother's death, Victor developed a deep distrust of authority, especially the police and the attorney general's office. Now they were proving him right. It was happening all over again.

The words of that man in the trench coat from 1964 came back to him. *"Don't worry, kid. This will all work out for you."*

This will all work out for me, he thought, staring at his reflection. It hadn't worked out so far. But if Victor Paquette had his way, he'd see that justice would be served, both for his mother and for Danny. And he would never stop until someone paid for what he or she had done.

Part Two

THE WHITE KNIGHT

In the middle of the journey of our life
I came to myself in a dark wood
where the straight way was lost.

—Dante Alighieri, *The Divine Comedy*

— 10 —

The New Girl

MELANIE Paquette had been running for hours, or at least that's what it felt like to her. At the end of practice, the coach of the Hopkinton Hawks varsity soccer team was making the players run fifteen-minute drills followed by brutal wind sprints. As the only girl on the team, Melanie was working hard to keep up with the boys, but to make it worse, she'd been battling a sore throat all day. That morning she'd woken up with white spots on her tonsils, and running in the early September rain wasn't making her feel any better. But the petite sophomore had something to prove. Although the school was waiting for a legal opinion on the issue of whether a girl could play on the boy's team for the first time, she wanted there to be no doubt that she belonged there. But today, she just couldn't keep up.

"Hey, Melanie!" Eric Windhurst, a junior and captain of the Hawks, called her to the bleachers. "Get over here right now, and tell us what's wrong!"

Melanie trotted over to sit with Eric and the boys who'd been injured in the first game of the season, the day before. It was a game the boys felt strongly they should have won.

At Eric's urging, she told the guys she was bummed because she couldn't keep up and that she wasn't even sure that the school was going to let her play on the team at all. She then told them that she was thinking about quitting altogether.

All the boys started talking at once. One said he'd already made his opinion about the situation known, having gone to the coach with a teammate and pleaded Melanie's case for twenty minutes. The other boys nodded, telling her stories about other kids who'd tried out but weren't good enough. They'd simply ignored those kids until they went away, they explained. They weren't ignoring Melanie. They really wanted her on the team.

Melanie thought she'd never met a bunch of guys as nice as these. She was brand-new to the school, having only just moved back to New Hampshire to live with her aunt and uncle a week earlier, but she felt ready to take on the world.

It was September 5, 1985, two months before her stepfather would die.

* * *

MELANIE Paquette moved to Hopkinton, New Hampshire, from Wasilla, Alaska, on August 27, 1985. Her uncle, Philip Messier, had convinced her mother, Denise, that Melanie had enjoyed her summer visit to Hopkinton so much that it seemed moving there might be good for her. Hopkinton had one of the best high schools in the state, and a lot of good kids for Melanie to hang around with. Though her uncle Philip had a three-year-old son with his wife, Kathleen McGuire, they also had a nanny and few financial woes. They lived a lifestyle totally different than what Melanie was used to in Alaska. There, her mother often resorted to making Melanie school clothes, copying the stylish outfits that the better-off girls wore.

Melanie's uncle Phil and aunt Kathy's house, the inaptly named Hopkinton Poor Farm, was a local landmark, a historic white colonial that sat on the main thoroughfare that led to Hopkinton Village proper. From 1834 to 1872, the land had been the town's "poor farm," but by 1985, there were no signs of poverty, and the only vestiges of farming that remained were the Christmas trees Phil grew on the land behind the house. During the holidays, the Poor Farm was a popular place for townspeople who desired to decorate their homes with balsam firs and Black Hill spruces of the "cut-your-own" variety. The business was a sideline for Phil, who worked as a commercial airline pilot.

Two days after her arrival, on Thursday, August 29, 1985, Melanie attended soccer tryouts at her new high school. Despite her skill in the sport, she was nervous. Her uncle Phil had told her that the Hopkinton Hawks had won the state championships for the past two seasons and what a big deal it was for the town. On the way home from the state finals, the team bus drove through town followed by a parade of cars driven by parents and other students who'd attended the game. The cars honked their horns all the way through the town's two villages, Hopkinton Village and Contoocook, announcing the Hawk's victory to sleeping residents, who welcomed the cacophony.

At first, Melanie felt her nerves at tryouts were well-founded. There was only one other girl there, and the boys seemed intent on ignoring them both. But then Melanie gained confidence as she played around the field, using the footwork she'd practiced barefoot in her backyard for years. She took a chance and kicked for the goal, making the shot and scoring on the team's goalie, Drew Jordan. After that, the boys told her she was good and made a point to tell her they weren't too offended by her goal, or by her gender, for that matter.

After tryouts the team held a scrimmage, and Melanie opted not to play. It was only her first day, and it seemed to her that the boys on the team really wanted time on the field. Later that night, her aunt Kathy gave her a hard time about having opted out, not understanding her niece's reasoning for choosing the sidelines when she clearly had the skill to engage the boys. This upset Melanie, who felt her aunt had no sympathy for why she didn't strive to be Pelé at her first day at practice, surrounded by boys she didn't know.

She felt her uncle Phil, however, understood where she was coming from. It wasn't the last time she'd feel this sense of comfort with her uncle. He was blood, after all. Her aunt, however, was another story.

* * *

THE days before the start of the school year were a whirlwind for Melanie. Her aunt and uncle took her shopping more often than she'd ever been, buying her new clothes, many pairs of shoes, and brand-new soccer gear. Phil also began decorating her room, painting the ceiling and hanging fresh new wallpaper.

"I'm beginning to feel a little bit guilty for buying so much stuff," Melanie wrote to her mother. Melanie felt obligated to repay them and would do jobs like weed the vegetable garden without being asked. The idea that her aunt and uncle would give her so much just because she was living with them wasn't something she could easily absorb.

Despite their generosity, however, things with Melanie and her aunt Kathy were tense. Melanie perceived her aunt as uptight, not receptive to the needs and feelings of a teenage girl. Though she and her mother had their problems, their relationship was more like that of girlfriends, and to Melanie, the authoritarian role Kathy played felt foreign.

The clothes Kathy chose for her niece were too "vogue," according to Melanie, a testament to the fact she didn't ever seem to understand Melanie's teenage taste or point of view. When the first day of school rolled around, Melanie chose to wear a pair of stirrup pants and a sweatshirt that her mother had made for her instead of one of the new outfits her aunt had purchased. It probably would have irked Kathy McGuire to no end, but she wasn't there to see it. Philip and Kathy had just left on a weeklong trip to London, one last hurrah before she started her new job at the attorney general's office. They left Melanie and their young son in the care of Wendy Smith, the twenty-eight-year-old live-in nanny who stayed in the apartment above the garage.

At school, Melanie found making friends was easier than she'd expected. Girls approached her and introduced themselves, oohing and aahing over Melanie's status as the first girl to ever play on the boys' soccer team. The only reason the school didn't have a girls team, they told her, was because there weren't enough girls to play both soccer and field hockey.

Back in Alaska, Denise received long letters from Melanie about her first days in her new town. Melanie gushed endlessly about her new clothes, her teachers, and *Catcher in the Rye*, which she'd recently begun reading. "I really can relate to this guy," she wrote. Melanie complained of her lack of synchronicity with her aunt, and she expressed gratitude for her friendship with Wendy Smith, the nanny she had bonded with in her aunt and uncle's absence.

Overall, Melanie's letters to Denise told a story of a girl adjusting well to life in a new town. At the end of one, she proudly wrote her new address with bold strokes as a reminder for her mother to write back. The only clue that anything was not what it seemed—just a girl going to live with well-off relatives to go to a good school—was a postscript she added below the Poor Farm's zip code.

"I'm keeping my name." Melanie wrote in answer to an unasked question. Melanie was not going to change her last name to "Messier" to further her effort to hide from her stepfather.

* * *

ONE thing Melanie wondered if she'd ever get used to was how much her new high school revolved around its sports teams. Wednesday, September 4, was the Hawks first soccer game of the season. Melanie later wrote to Denise that the team had been dismissed from school early to ride the bus to Pittsfield, a town more than thirty miles away. Though the decision hadn't yet been made to allow Melanie to play in games, she had technically made the team, so she was allowed to attend the game and sit on the bench.

The game didn't go the way the team had hoped, ending in a 1-0 loss. To Melanie, the team's reaction to the loss was surprising. The very boys whose enthusiasm and humor had made her long to be accepted were now sullen and silent. Melanie was also taken aback by how much *she* was affected by the loss. She'd only known the guys for a week, yet she marched with them onto the bus in solidarity. No one said a word during the fifty-minute ride back to Hopkinton. Melanie sat with the goalie, Drew Jordan, and held his hand. She was sure he was about to cry.

When the team arrived back at school, Melanie took off her shoes and kicked the ball around with Drew to try and cheer him up. The other boys gathered around, expressing surprise that Melanie could play even better without her shoes on. They probably didn't realize that Melanie hadn't been able to buy many pairs of soccer shoes in her lifetime. "It was pretty cool," she later wrote to Denise. "I like it here."

* * *

THE following day was Thursday. Melanie's sore throat made practice particularly rough for her, especially given that so many boys had been injured in the season opening game, so those who were left were on the field nonstop. But when Eric Windhurst asked Melanie what the matter was, and then led the team in telling her how much she mattered, how much they wanted her, she realized she was now one of them. It was likely the first time she felt she belonged anywhere.

On Friday, Melanie joined the ranks of injured players— she'd sprained her ankle in gym class, and by the time practice rolled around, it was too swollen to put her shoe on. That night, Wendy took Melanie to the emergency room at Concord Hospital, and the crutches they gave her to use for the weekend meant that she had to miss a party she'd been invited to by the guys on the team. Melanie wasn't used to being invited to parties, something she expressed to Denise in writing.

"Do you think it's OK for me to go to parties, Mom? I mean, if I went to one of these parties I would probably drink and stay out late. Is it OK to do that?"

To anyone reading Melanie's words, it would have been clear that she was desperate for some direction, begging for adult guidance. Yet given the number of times Melanie pleaded with Denise to write her back in her many letters, it's not clear whether she ever received that guidance from her mother.

Melanie chafed at that same support and guidance when it came from other sources, however. When her aunt Kathy and uncle Phil arrived home from their London trip that Sunday with bags full of souvenirs, the cool adult-free lifestyle Melanie had experienced over the first week of school clashed with the Messiers' sudden barrage of parenting, something she expressed in another letter to Denise.

> *Monday morning they just screwed up everything. "Don't forget to eat breakfast, make your bed, pack a lunch, did you do your homework" was all I heard. Then they made me catch the bus outside the house when the bus stop was down the road, just so [her] stupid precious little [son] could watch me get on the bus! I hate it when they treat me*

like I'm two. I hate it! . . . He never did get to see me on the bus because the bus just went right past me. . . . As if it wasn't embarrassing enough to have the bus go right past you, Aunt Kathy has to call the school to complain. PLEASE HELP ME LORD! . . . I mean something has got to change here and FAST.

Just days before, Melanie had felt a part of something new, something exhilaratingly close to real happiness. "I'm supposed to be so cool because I'm on the guys' soccer team and every time I turn around one of my relatives is embarrassing me to tears. *I'm ready for my own apartment!*"

Melanie was finally allowed to start playing in soccer games, but the "cool" she felt while on the field, wearing the uniform with the number 20, would often fade when her aunt showed up on the sidelines with her baby cousin and their family dog, Sadie, who would try to run onto the field. Melanie took solace in the school's cheerleaders, who yelled loudly for her, and in her teammates on whom she'd begun to rely as her primary support system.

* * *

AS September passed, Melanie struggled to find a balance between her life at a new home and her life at a new school. She was surprised when Kathy and Phil granted instant permission for her to attend the annual French-class trip to Quebec in November, although it seemed Aunt Kathy and Uncle Phil were supportive of everything Melanie wanted to do, as long as it embedded her further into the Hopkinton idea of normal.

On Thursday, September 12, Melanie had a normal school day, followed by soccer practice. After practice, she goofed around with the guys, who'd already fully integrated her into their tribe. It had gotten late, and Melanie didn't have a way home; her aunt and uncle had gone to Boston for the day. She was grateful when team captain Eric Windhurst offered her a ride.

Climbing into Eric's Volkswagen Rabbit, Melanie probably felt a little overwhelmed. "The guys" had become her instant family, Eric included, but the junior stood apart from the pack. For one, he was the leader, not just on the field, but off it as well. Eric wasn't always attached at the hip to one particular buddy, like many of the other boys were. Though he merged easily into any group he chose, he traveled just as easily alone. Melanie must have also noticed Eric's good looks—he was 5 feet 10 inches, with a slim but naturally strong build, and his dark, wavy hair and steely blue eyes easily ranked him as one of the best-looking boys in school. He was also charming, dynamic, and a great storyteller. She wrote about him to her mother:

> *Eric gave me a ride home. Eric is a very nice guy and I like him a lot. He took me on a tour of Hopkinton and showed me all the land he owns. He practically owns Hopkinton. . . . He wants to do something this weekend if it's nice. I'm willing to if UP+AK don't schedule my whole week.*

Melanie played it cool with her mother, but there was one secret she couldn't bring herself to write in her letters. She was falling in love with Eric Windhurst. It seemed every girl in school was her rival for his affections, but she didn't mind. Though she accepted the request for dates from other boys, all the time she really wanted to be with Eric. No boy had ever treated her as well as he did. She had been blessed to play soccer well enough to be with Eric nearly every afternoon. But it was also a curse, as she knew Eric would never see her as anything other than a kid sister.

As the leaves fell and the weeks passed, Melanie tried harder to get along with her aunt. The Poor Farm sometimes felt more like a prison with an open door, and the girl often turned to Wendy Smith for advice. She felt like she could tell the nanny anything.

But the new room and the new clothes and the new friends were not a tonic that could soothe the troubles in Melanie's mind, her nightmares, her sadness. It would be nearly twenty years before the troubled woman would reveal the real demons that tormented her.

— 11 —

The Captain

ERIC Windhurst wasn't one of Hopkinton's "rich kids," and it bothered him when the friends he rode ATVs with on the weekends lumped him into that group. Sure, his mother had money, and he certainly knew all about the property she owned, but it wasn't as if he drove a fancy car like Ricky Patenaude, whose parents owned Pat's Peak, the local ski resort. He didn't have the kind of parents who gave their kids spending money or bought them expensive cars. He was more likely to get other kinds of things from them, like the hunting rifle his father had given him for his birthday. Other than that, he had to work for what he got, just like his ATV buddies did. There is a great difference between being "money rich" and being merely "land rich."

Eric took a certain pride in not being seen as snobbish, a Yankee self-deprecation of sorts that ran in his family. But he was also a teenage boy, and the temptation of the privilege he did have because of his family's holdings could sometimes be too hard to resist. He had friends to impress, boys like Craig Metzger, Davis "Dee" Clark, Mark Hoevler, and Eric Prescott. And then there was Matt Quinn, probably his closest friend. Ricky Patenaude had a whole ski mountain to offer the gang, but as a Windhurst, Eric had something to offer, too. Namely, the Kimball Cabins.

It was widely known around Hopkinton High that the cabins,

especially perpetually vacant cabins 9 and 10, were one of the two main places in town to party. The other was the sand pits, which lay on Hopkinton's rural west side. At the pits, Eric was always at the center of things, building the bonfires and making sure there was enough beer. But because his family owned the Kimball Cabins and the secluded property they were on, there Eric played court master, carefully screening who was and wasn't allowed to come to the gatherings he hosted.

Eric's mother, Barbara, was thought of by a few people around town as a "character," less politely as "nuts." She was the sole heir of land baron John Shackford Kimball, who in the nineteenth century began a legacy of purchases and development that would shape the very town of Hopkinton. Besides the Kimball Cabins, there were the enormous Rollins Road tract (the place he had taken Melanie when he offered her a ride home for the first time), the large four-family home the Windhursts occupied next to the elementary school, and other undeveloped acreage more vast than many townspeople realized. Bridges, ponds, lakes, and farms all bore the Kimball name in Hopkinton, the legacy of Barbara's forefathers. Even Eric Windhurst himself bore it; his middle name was "Kimball."

When Barbara Kimball married John Windhurst, she brought with her two young daughters from a previous marriage, Kimberly and Lisa. John, an accomplished carpenter several years her senior, had three adult children of his own. Of the three children from his first marriage, only John's son, "Trapper John," remained in Hopkinton. (The junior Windhurst got his moniker not from the *M*A*S*H* character of the same name but because he was literally an accomplished hunter and trapper.) Together, John and Barbara reared two boys of their own: Scott and Eric, the youngest.

Throughout the years, Barbara's vast land holdings would be the source of much conflict within the Windhurst clan. Trapper John married a woman named Martha in 1981, and they lived together in one of the Kimball Cabins, owned by Barbara. It was said that the elder Windhursts felt Martha had expected a grander lifestyle when she married Trapper, because his father was so well off. If that were the case, then it was likely Martha didn't truly know the Windhurst family very well when she married into it. According to family members, it was Barbara who controlled the purse strings. Eric said that Barbara was known for parceling out her assets according to whoever might be in her favor at any particular time, even if it meant reneging on promises she'd made to others who had been in favor before them.

Another story that was shared by some was that many years later, Barbara would sell the land on which Martha and Trapper's cabin had once stood (the cabin had long since burned down in a fire) to a developer, who built a neighborhood of high-end homes within view of Kimball Lake. This transaction incensed Eric, who claimed his mother had promised the land to him and his brother for development, so that they could build spec houses on it and sell them for a profit. Another piece of land, which Scott purchased from Barbara to build his own home on, became the cause of a power struggle between Barbara and her elder son. It caused a screaming match so epic that Scott's version of the fight (the story went that he'd slammed her dishwasher door so hard that it broke) was talked about around town for weeks.

* * *

GROWING up, Eric found himself spending far more time with his much older brother Trapper than he did with his father. Around town they were often mistaken for uncle and nephew, in part because the half brothers were so disparate in age (Trapper was in his forties when Eric hit his teens).

As a young boy, Eric was often spotted following in Trapper's wake, copying the man's every move. Eric, who felt misunderstood at home, turned to Trapper as both a role model and a confidant. Trapper taught Eric everything he knew about hunting, fishing, and tracking. He also taught Eric some things about being a man, like when to speak up, and when to keep quiet.

Trapper's wife, Martha, tolerated her husband's close relationship with his youngest half brother, though she herself greatly preferred the company of Eric's older brother, Scott. She regarded Scott as a sweet and outgoing boy, while she saw Eric as guarded, quiet, and strange. Still, she understood that the boys' life at home with Barbara and the elder John was difficult, and she appreciated that the brothers saw her and Trapper as authority figures of sorts.

Trapper was a war hero, a Vietnam veteran who had served in the U.S. Marine Corps as a Scout Sniper, an elite and highly trained position that entailed going on reconnaissance missions in teams of two, with standing orders to take out enemy commanders. When he returned from the war, he suffered from many of the ills that befell Vietnam veterans, including post-traumatic stress. For a while, Trapper had lived away from Hopkinton, working as a bartender at an upstate New York lounge. When he returned, he told people that he had dated a beautiful lounge singer named Lynda who he'd met at the place he worked, and that his lounge singer had gone on to a successful acting career, playing Wonder Woman on television. Whether the Lynda Carter story was true or not, Trapper's eventual town-legend status in Hopkinton was well earned. He was the ultimate outdoorsman, always bagging the largest deer, always telling the most colorful stories. Everyone knew he was troubled, that both he and his wife, Martha, struggled with alcohol, and that he bore deep emotional scars from his time in Vietnam. But in every circle he was a part of (and he was welcomed by most), Trapper was well liked for his charisma and for his salt-of-the-earth kindness.

* * *

IN the fall of 1985, Eric was spending a lot of time around the cabins. He was a junior, captain of the Hawks soccer team, and, for the first time, the only Windhurst boy at Hopkinton High. There was no football team at Hopkinton, so captain of the soccer team was Big Man on Campus. Scott was two years older and had been a star baseball player, a student that teachers loved. Eric was anxious to establish his own reputation and create a role for himself beyond being "Scott's little brother."

Eric's gang spent a lot of time hanging out in cabins 9 and 10. The group varied day by day, but the core gang consisted of Eric, Matt Quinn, Craig Metzger, Davis "Dee" Clark, and Mark Hoevler. The boys could often be found hanging out with their friends, shooting the shit or shooting target practice at the range Trapper had helped Eric build. On the periphery were other boys, like Eric Prescott, Ricky Patenaude, and the other boys from the soccer team.

Eric's friendship with Ricky in particular was complicated. Ricky had long been the target of bullying at school, and he looked to Eric for protection, at one point even offering to pay Eric to keep a particular boy from beating him up, an offer Ricky said Eric ignored. Eric would later acknowledge that he at first befriended Ricky much the same way a pretty and popular cheerleader befriends the homely cheerleader wannabe, because it made him feel good that Ricky needed him. He did stand up for him to an extent, because being friends with Ricky had major perks, like free lift rides at his family's ski resort. But he turned his back on him, too, a fact Ricky would later confirm.

In late 1985, a new friend entered Eric's orbit: the new girl in town, Melanie Paquette. Shortly after meeting Melanie, the two grew extremely close, a relationship Eric told his friends and brother Trapper was not romantic but more like "brother and sister." Melanie dated other boys that fall, including a boy named Andrew Cheney, but she suddenly broke up with Andrew in early November, around the time she got the news that her stepfather, Danny Paquette, had been shot while welding a bulldozer in nearby Hooksett.

* * *

ON New Year's Eve day, 1985, Eric Windhurst knocked on the door of Trapper and Martha's cabin on Kimball Lake. Although it wasn't unusual for Eric to stop in to say hello, it wasn't like him to remain standing just inside the door the way he did when Trapper let him in that day.

It was obvious Eric wanted to talk to Trapper alone, but Martha stayed where she was, in her husband's favorite chair.

"I have something to tell you," Eric began. He was clearly upset, clearly troubled. Martha later said she'd never seen him this way, that she was accustomed to his more closed-off demeanor.

"Remember that guy in Hooksett who got shot? Danny Paquette? Melanie's stepdad?" he said. "Well, I did it."

* * *

EARLIER that morning, young Hooksett police officer Steve Agrafiotis had come with another cop to Hopkinton to interview

Eric about the day of the shooting. Melanie, who had been interviewed around Thanksgiving, had told the officers that on the morning of November 9, she and Eric had driven together to the field hockey championship game at Plymouth State. The police were following up on her alibi, and Eric had confirmed it to them.

But now Eric was telling his brother and sister-in-law where he and Melanie had actually gone that November morning.

Trapper and Martha listened to Eric's story, Trapper asking a lot of questions. After a time, Martha asked him one of her own.

"Do your parents know?"

* * *

TRAPPER and Martha could have walked the short distance to the Windhursts' home, but in late December, the weather in New Hampshire isn't exactly welcoming.

John and Barbara Windhurst occupied the largest apartment in the four-family home they owned in the heart of Hopkinton Village, next to the entrance of the Harold Martin Elementary School. This living arrangement was one that few in town understood: why, when the Windhursts owned so much, they chose to live alongside their tenants in an income property.

Trapper and Martha sat down at the Windhurst kitchen table with John. Barbara leaned against the sink with her arms crossed.

"We have something to tell you," Trapper said.

Trapper had recounted what Eric had told him and Martha earlier that day. Barbara reacted harshly, denying that her boy could be capable of such a thing. What struck Martha about the exchange, though, was her father-in-law John Windhurst's reaction. Although the old man seemed surprised, he didn't express any visible disbelief at what his son had allegedly done.

It was a short conversation. And when it was over, Martha and Trapper went home to their cabin.

* * *

JUST before three o'clock in the afternoon on New Year's Eve, 1985, Officer Steve Agrafiotis received a telephone call at the Hooksett Police Department from John Windhurst, Eric's father.

During the call, John claimed that after the police had interviewed Eric that morning, his son had told him additional information. He told Agrafiotis that according to Melanie, Danny Paquette had beaten his wife and had molested his stepdaughter.

It is possible that at the point John Windhurst made the call, he had not yet heard from Trapper that his son Eric had, in fact, committed the crime that the police were investigating. It is possible that Eric had told his father about the officers' visit, and did, in fact, give him details about Danny's relationship with Melanie that his father felt might aid police in their investigation.

But it is also possible that the phone call to Agrafiotis occurred after Trapper and Martha's visit, in which case John Windhurst had just learned that his youngest child was Danny Paquette's killer.

No one spoke much about the murder after New Year's, though Martha later said she had a vague understanding that Trapper took the gun Eric had used to shoot Danny Paquette and destroyed it. The secret was out within the Windhurst clan, but like other family troubles, it seemed content to stay where it lay—at least for now.

* * *

THE remainder of his junior year was a whirlwind for Eric. His secret now revealed to his family, he felt bound to his family, but at the same time, more distant than he had before. But he had his buddies, the nights they spent carousing at the cabins, and the messes they got into with girls. In addition to Melanie, there was also one boy in Eric's inner circle, Matt Quinn, who knew the entire story of what happened on November 9. There were others who vaguely knew that Eric had done something bad that they were not supposed to talk about. In the way of high school rumors, these rumblings turned into hallway whispers. "Did you hear Eric was in a hunting accident?" "Did you hear that Eric once stabbed someone?"

Ricky Patenaude remembered sitting in study hall with

some students he didn't know. "I heard that Eric Windhurst is really dangerous," one of the kids said.

"Nah, he's a pussycat," said Patenaude, unaware of Eric's role in the shooting.

But as the school year drew to a close, the whispers died down. Spring moved into summer, and summer into fall.

In the autumn of 1986, Eric began his senior year at Hopkinton High School, with a brand-new chance to capture the state soccer championship that had eluded the team the previous year. The new girl, his "little sister" Melanie, had left town over the summer, moved back to Alaska to live with her mother. But life went on. The boys—Eric Windhurst, Matt Quinn, Craig Metzger, Davis "Dee" Clark, Mark Hoevler, and Ricky Patenaude—kept living as they always had: going to school and playing sports during the week, throwing parties on the weekends.

It probably looked to most people like nothing had changed, and that Eric had merely taken over for his older brother Scott as the star Windhurst in town. But despite the routine of teenage life in Hopkinton, all was not well within the young captain. The events set in motion a year prior had changed him, and the more time passed without consequence for those events, the more difficult it became for Eric to keep his fractured feelings inside. Those feelings turned into behaviors that transformed the way people saw him, and the way he saw himself.

Eric, who had long been known as mischievous, elevated himself to "troublemaker" status. One day, he and some friends discovered an old book of blank checks a tenant had left behind on one of the Windhurst properties. Later they'd "forget" whose idea it had been to use the checks at the Burton Snowboard factory store in Manchester, Vermont, but the boys got in big trouble for it. Eric's father, John, however, chalked up the mess to "boys being boys."

Eric spent less and less time at home, often sleeping on friends' couches or at the Kimball cabins. When his half-sister Lisa had run away from home while in high school, his mother, Barbara, had sent police after her to bring her home. But the leash was long with Eric, either because his parents didn't care or because he didn't care if they did. Or perhaps it was just because he was the youngest, and as is often the way with the youngest, he simply got away with more. Eric's friends' parents felt bad for him, in part because they were aware of his mother's volatile reputation, and in part, simply because they liked him.

Teenage Eric Windhurst's reputation as a wild card was cemented at the end of his senior year, just two days before graduation. On the night of the senior banquet, he threw one last party on Kimball Lake, in an open area of sand not far from the cabins. Though he said the party was open to "everyone," what he meant was it was open to everyone who was a student at Hopkinton High School.

A female classmate with a dubious reputation for smoking pot and snorting coke showed up at the party with a drug-dealing boy from neighboring Concord High School. Eric threatened the girl, telling her to get her friend to leave the party immediately, but what made the threat particularly memorable to everyone in attendance was the way Eric made it—while pointing a shotgun at the stoned girl's face.

* * *

IN June of 1987, Eric Windhurst and the kids he'd grown up with graduated from Hopkinton High School. It was a time to say good-bye and to pursue new beginnings. But Eric wasn't like the other graduates, at least not in the way they were able to put high school behind them and move on to new things, a clean slate ahead. Eric's slate wasn't clean at all, far from it. And as he was about to learn, though no legal consequence had befallen him, the deed he'd done had not been forgotten.

Twenty miles south, a man named Victor Paquette was steeling himself for a fight for the truth, knowing that it might take years. But right here where Eric lived, in Hopkinton, New Hampshire, the seeds had also been sown for a different kind of consequence, a personal price he'd find himself paying for many years to come.

— 12 —

Bury the Truth

VICTOR Paquette, two of his sisters, and his oldest brother stood next to each other in a light drizzle at Pine Grove Cemetery in Manchester. This time, Victor was not wearing a dark suit and uncomfortable necktie. He wore his leather jacket with the sleeves pushed up to his elbows, tight jeans, and sported his gold earrings. He head was uncovered and his remaining hair was shorn to the scalp. The only hair on his head was his graying eyebrows and his black mustache. Joanne had an umbrella for them, but Victor preferred to stand in the open and take the punishment.

It was November 13, 1991, nearly six years to the day since the family had gathered in this graveyard to bury their youngest brother, Danny. Victor's six-foot frame had gotten tougher, more rugged, but the past few years showed mostly on his face. He watched the backhoe as it cut into the hardened turf, but his eyes were not really focusing on the work of the machinery. Victor was staring off into space, seeing beyond the metal arm swinging and scooping and going down deeper in front of the gravestone marked "Paquette."

Someone put a supportive hand on his shoulder and snapped Victor out of his trance. It was Richard Baron, a childhood friend of his and Danny's.

"We've come this far," Baron said to Victor.

"Yeah. Thanks to you."

"Now we'll finally learn the truth."

Both Victor and his friend looked over at the police officers waiting at a respectful distance away, standing alongside the hearse that was to transport the body to the State Medical Examiner's Office in Concord.

There was a quiet *ting* when the backhoe struck something approximately six feet down. The other cemetery workers scurried to get some straps to hoist the casket out of the hole. They moved quickly but solemnly.

Victor rejoined his siblings under umbrellas as the mechanical arm pulled the box from the earth. His sister reached for his hand, but when Victor didn't respond, she settled for placing her hand on his bare forearm, where Victor had recently gotten a tattoo.

It was a playing card, the ace of spades.

The tattoo had one other feature: a bullet, passing through the card, with drops of inked blood trailing in its wake.

* * *

KATHLEEN McGuire was no longer with the attorney general's office. In September of 1988, she had become chief of the Criminal Bureau. That made her a senior assistant attorney general and put her in charge of the homicide unit. Within three years of her arrival at the attorney general's office, not too long after she graduated from law school, Kathleen McGuire had become the top prosecutor in the state of New Hampshire.

Her time as criminal bureau chief was even shorter. In August 1989, Governor Judd Gregg nominated forty-one-year-old Kathy McGuire to become a superior court justice. "She's prosecuted more major criminal cases in New Hampshire than any other [lawyer]," Gregg said proudly. The executive council confirmed McGuire's nomination three weeks later.

* * *

THE first years following the death of his brother were especially tough for Victor. He was edgy and jittery. He kept a gun and a knife with him most of the time. People avoided him in public, even in Manchester's seediest bars, where almost anything went.

Only one man reached out to Victor to check on him periodically. Richard Baron had been a schoolmate of Victor's and Danny's. Baron was not a biker, nor a welder, not very much like either of the Paquette boys at all. He was, however, faithful to them and had remained their friend despite the different paths their lives had taken.

Baron was a graphic designer and a printer. Business cards and brochures were his bailiwick. He also had a keen imagination, an ability to write well, and the guts to do what he thought needed to be done. The last quality was what endeared him to Victor.

"How are you doing?" Baron would ask Victor. The slow-talking, baritone-voiced man would usually mumble something about the day being different, but the shit remaining the same.

"I have a theory about Danny's death," Baron confessed.

"Well, go ahead and tell me," Victor said. "It couldn't be any stupider than a stray bullet from a hunting accident."

"I think Danny's murder is related to your mother's."

The idea was bold. Victor had considered the two deaths were only tied together in the stars or among the Fates. Of the many theories espoused and rejected, that the killings were connected in a real way was one he hadn't thought about.

"How could that be?"

Baron told him what he thought. Then he said he was going to investigate the crimes on his own and write a book.

* * *

WHEN Manchester police arrested Edward Coolidge on February 19, 1964, it was as if a great weight was lifted from the city. People walked into churches, interrupting the services, to announce aloud the news that Pamela Mason's killer had finally been caught.

In the later days of the investigation, two men told investigators that on the night Pamela went missing, they'd offered help to the driver of a 1951 Pontiac that was pulled over on the side of the road, near where Pamela's body was found. A neighbor reported that Coolidge, who owned a 1951 Pontiac sedan, was away for six hours during the evening of the blizzard. The cops quizzed Coolidge on January 28, approximately the same time Rena had contacted police with the tip but before their visit to her at the farm, and asked him to take a lie detector test on Sunday, February 2. During that polygraph, the suspect said he'd been shopping in a neighboring town and confessed to stealing some money from his employer. The results of the lie detector were inconclusive. The cops let Coolidge go on the morning of February 3, the day Rena Paquette was killed.

The morning after the arrest, Manchester District Court was a madhouse, full of reporters, photographers, and angry citizens. Edward Coolidge was hustled out of the small brick building by his two new attorneys. The evidence against him included a .22 Mossberg rifle, some ammunition, and some of Pamela's bloodstained clothes, which had been found in his car. Coolidge had to keep his head down to shield himself from all the flashbulbs exploding around him.

A grand jury indicted Edward Coolidge on two counts of first-degree murder, one for Pamela Mason and one for Sandra Valade. Despite the daily protestations in the paper by Arthur Paquette, Maynard did not seek to charge Coolidge with Rena Paquette's death. Coolidge went to trial in June 1965 on the first indictment: the killing of Mason. When the jury was shown the bloody items recovered from his car, it was all but over. Coolidge was found guilty and given a life sentence. Believing that Coolidge would spend the rest of his life behind bars, Maynard didn't bother to bring forth the remaining indictment for the Valade slaying.

"Already got him for one," he told people. "No need to get him for two."

* * *

EDWARD Coolidge's attorneys appealed the conviction on the grounds that the search of his car was unconstitutional. It took six years, but on January 12, 1971, the U.S. Supreme Court agreed to hear *Coolidge v. New Hampshire*. It was to become a landmark case. Arguing on behalf of the petitioner was Archibald Cox, President John F. Kennedy's solicitor general and the man who would be the first Watergate special prosecutor.

In June 1971, in a 5–4 decision, the Court ruled that the search of Coolidge's car had indeed violated the Fourth Amendment. The warrant to search the 1951 two-door Pontiac had been drawn up by the police chief, but it had been signed not by a judge, but by Attorney General William Maynard. Under New Hampshire law, any justice of the peace could sign a search warrant. But the justices ruled that Maynard, who was the lead investigator and prosecutor in the case, was not a "neutral and detached magistrate" as required by the Constitution. Coolidge's conviction was overturned, and the case was remanded back to New Hampshire.

On retrial, the option of capital punishment was not available to the prosecution, and two key witnesses had since died. Faced with the prospect of trying him without any admissible evidence, the state offered Coolidge a plea. He copped to the second-degree murder of Pamela Mason and was given twenty-five to forty years in jail, with credit for the years already spent in prison.

With time off for good behavior, Coolidge was scheduled for release in 1991.

* * *

STATE Medical Examiner Roger Fossum waited patiently that November day in 1991 for the body to arrive at the morgue at Concord Hospital. The office of state medical examiner was still relatively new, and the medical examiner didn't have facilities of his own. After the high-profile investigations of Danny Paquette and the unidentified bodies found in Bear Brook State Park, a real push had been on for New Hampshire to hire its own medical examiner. Fossum had worked at the Dallas Medical Examiner's Office.

The Paquette exhumation had been planned for some time, but something was missing. "Did you ever get the paperwork from the original case?" Fossum's secretary, Joy Cadarette, asked him the day before.

"No. It's a cold case. Where would it be?"

For years, officials had relied on local doctors and medical school professors to conduct exams and submit the paperwork. "I hate to say it, but it's probably buried in the state archives building."

"Ugh," Fossum groaned. "We'll never find it there."

Cadarette came to work the next day in some rugged clothes

and drove over to the state archives. The caretaker pointed her toward the dozens and dozens of boxes holding copies of past autopsies. One by one, she searched through the boxes looking for "Paquette." She spent several hours breathing in the must of old paper, brushing dust off her clothes.

"Finally!" she exclaimed. "Here it is."

Like finding a needle in a haystack, Cadarette had at last found the casework for the body being transported to the morgue.

The file read "Rena Paquette, Feb. 1964."

* * *

IN 1990, just months before Edward Coolidge's scheduled early release from prison, Richard Baron went to the media advocating that Coolidge should be investigated for Rena Paquette's unsolved murder. Baron had played amateur sleuth and dug up his own new evidence on the twenty-seven-year-old case, finding a retired Manchester police officer who had been a first responder to the original crime scene on the Paquette farm.

"We were working in that area of town on the Mason case when we got a call over the radio," former inspector David Lord told Baron. "Three or four of us went to the pigsty and found the body. There was a log bracing the gate. There was no way she could have opened it. There was no way she could have braced it herself."

"So you all assumed it was a murder right from the start?"

"Yes. Then the thing came down that she 'committed suicide' and we said 'no way' but we were told to forget it."

"Who told you to forget it?" Baron asked.

Lord said he believed the order came from the attorney general, William Maynard. "It was discussed quite a bit amongst us. But when your boss tells you to forget it, your hands are kind of tied."

* * *

BARON'S theory was that Danny's death might be connected to Rena's killing twenty years earlier. Both mother and son had died under mysterious circumstances. Danny had said he'd recovered memories of the day his mother died—memories of her arguing with a man in a white uniform. Coolidge, a bakery delivery man, had worn such an outfit. Danny said he was going to write to Coolidge in prison and confront him at his next parole hearing. But before he could do so, Danny was killed.

The veracity of this recovered memory is uncertain. Young Danny had told police in 1964 he had overslept the morning his mother died, so it was unclear when he would have seen this confrontation. But the "clue" was enough to convince Baron and the Paquettes of a possible link between the slayings. They went on a media whistle-stop, telling Rena's and Danny's story to anyone with a notebook. The biggest attention that they got for the case was from the NBC show *Unsolved Mysteries*. The crew came to New Hampshire to film reenactments of the deaths of both Paquettes.

The day the crew had returned to 898 Whitehall Road to film Danny's death was extremely emotional for Victor. The actor who played Danny looked just like him, right down to his mustache. Gil Daigle brought his old Case 450 bulldozer back. Court Burton played himself. Even neighbor Kevin Cote, who ran to give Danny CPR, got to re-create his part. Victor got to play himself and pretended to ride motorcycles with his "brother." It was not the real thing, but for a moment it felt like it was.

The episode aired on Wednesday night, October 24, 1990. The national exposure to the unsolved case generated a few leads but nothing substantial. However, the high profile of the network show lent gravitas to the Paquettes' generational struggle to resolve the case. Yet despite the maelstrom of innuendo and public outrage, ultimately no official took up the investigation into whether Danny Paquette had been killed by an associate of Edward Coolidge to shut him up about the 1964 case.

The final years of Coolidge's prison sentence were tranquil for the inmate, even as mention of his name drew seething reactions from the public. Coolidge had adjusted well to life behind bars. Although his first wife had divorced him, Coolidge had a second, jailhouse wedding in 1979, marrying a woman from Concord. On several occasions he nearly won early release, but sympathetic parole board members were eviscerated in the press.

Coolidge was transferred to the James River Correctional Center in Goochland, Virginia, to serve out the remainder of his sentence. He was released on March 16, 1991. Coolidge walked out of the facility wearing a red shirt and blue jeans. He carried a portable television and a plastic bag filled with all his worldly possessions. No one was there to meet him when he stepped through the gates. He was fifty-three years old.

* * *

AFTER Coolidge's release, Victor Paquette and Richard Baron approached the attorney general's office about reopening Rena's case. They spoke with a pretty assistant attorney general named Tina Nadeau.

"There is very little we could do at this point," she told the men. Much of the physical evidence was missing or destroyed. Witnesses were dead now.

"What if new evidence came to light?" Baron asked.

She said it would have to be more than a cop saying someone told him to shut up. It would have to be something significant, something that proved she was murdered.

"We don't even have the autopsy report," Victor said. "My father asked for it many times, but Maynard refused to give it to him."

Baron spoke up again. "What if you exhumed Rena's body? If you found something . . . say a gunshot wound or a crushed skull . . . would that be evidence?"

Nadeau agreed, but cautioned even if something like that were found, it wouldn't change the fact there was almost no way to prosecute the case.

"It would mean something to me," Victor said. "All my life, people told me my mother was nuts. That she offed herself. That she sparked herself up. I never believed it. It would mean a hell of lot to me and my family."

Nadeau further cautioned that it was unlikely the state would pay for such an exhumation. The men sat quietly, feeling like the wind had left their sails. The Paquettes never liked their odds when it came to getting special favors. Victor knew the state was not going to pay for it.

"I'll pay for it."

Nadeau was stunned. So was Victor.

Baron had his hand up, like a schoolchild. "I'll pay for the exhumation."

* * *

THE body of Rena Paquette was transferred to Dr. Fossum's exam table. When she was laid to rest in 1964, Rena's remains had been placed in a black body bag, then into a sealed casket and vault. Arthur Paquette Sr. had done so specifically, because he believed that someday another examination would be made.

Fossum cross-checked the yellowed paperwork his secretary had found. There were several things that troubled him about the original findings.

From the first examination, Fossum did not believe that Rena's death was suicide by fire. Aside from being an exceedingly rare manner of death, the evidence did not support it.

There were no matches or lighters found in the pigsty, nor was there any lighter fluid or other combustible materials. Rena didn't smoke and had a known fear of fire. Although the body had been badly burned, the flames had not spread to the rest of the very flammable wooden structure filled with hay.

Rena was found lying on her back, in an almost peaceful repose. Fossum knew that in those rare cases of self-immolation, the bodies had been contorted, twisted from the excruciating pain of the burns and smoke inhalation in the moments before death.

Lastly, there was a notation from the original autopsy that semen had been found in the corpse. No one ever questioned Arthur Sr. about whether he and his fifty-four-year-old wife had made love that morning, and the family patriarch was now dead. Samples of semen were not maintained, but Fossum had serious concerns that Rena might have been raped before her death.

Fossum concurred with the original findings that the *cause* of death was the fire, but he did not necessarily agree that Rena was conscious when her body was ignited. However, there were no wounds or other physical trauma on the corpse, nothing that would indicate she was beaten, shot, or stabbed. He did inform the family, however, that he was going to make a change to the death certificate as to the *manner* of death.

"I don't see how this could have been a suicide," Fossum said to a newspaper following the case. "I mean, I can't rule it out completely, but it would be the most bizarre suicide I'd ever have seen."

"So she was murdered?" the journalist asked.

"My suspicion is yes, but I have no conclusive proof of that. It would require additional police work to say the manner of death is homicide."

"So what happens now?"

"I am going to remove 'suicide' from the death certificate," Fossum said. "Instead, it'll be listed as 'indeterminate.' That's the best I can do for now."

When Victor heard the manner of death was going to be changed, he was relieved. Even if this didn't solve the mystery, it proved to the world that his mother had not died by her own hand.

"If you saw all the same stuff that the doctor in 1964 saw," the reporter asked, "how come he came to a different conclusion?"

"The doctor who did Mrs. Paquette's first autopsy did solid work. He didn't mess anything up," Fossum said. "In fact, when he was done, he didn't make a ruling on the manner of death or how she came to die by fire."

"Then how did 'suicide' get on the death certificate?"

Fossum said he had no idea. That night he went home and told his wife it was the most troubling case he'd ever had.

* * *

AFTER the cemetery workers re-interred Rena's body at St. Joseph's Cemetery, the Paquette family stayed behind for some time. Victor asked Baron to stay with the relatives.

"I won't forget what you did for me and my family." Victor whispered to his friend. Victor wondered if now his mother could rest in peace. He looked over at the other Paquette grave and unconsciously rubbed the ace of spades tattoo on his forearm. Someday, he hoped, his brother would rest in peace, too.

— 13 —

Everyone Comes Home . . . Eventually

Eric Windhurst wanted two things from life: to get out of Hopkinton, New Hampshire, and to be a real man, just like his brother Trapper John. Trapper had been Eric's idol since as far back as he could remember, and being like him meant becoming a U.S. Marine.

The Marines called to Eric; their commercials boasted about "the Few and the Proud," something he desired to be. He knew he could handle the trials of boot camp and hoped that his skill with a rifle might set him apart from other recruits there. Plus, enlisting would get Eric the hell out of town, far away from the things that still haunted him.

Even so, it took more than a year for Eric to actually enlist. After graduation, he stayed in town when many of his high school friends left, continuing to work odd jobs as a handyman and fixing motorcycle engines. That year was a virtual fifth year at Hopkinton High for Eric; not only was he dating Thea Koonz, a pretty high school senior, but his "little sister," Melanie Paquette, had returned to town after spending a year back in Alaska with her mother. She was now back on the boys' soccer team, too, and wearing the number 18 on her jersey, the same number Eric had worn in high school.

Thea believed that Melanie had feelings for Eric, as Melanie would often do things like showing up places she knew he would be. Eric, knowing Thea was jealous, would keep his time spent with Melanie a secret from his girlfriend, often lying to her of times spent "with the guys"—times that actually had included Melanie Paquette.

Eric was jealous and possessive himself, Thea said, and many years later she would label him "very controlling." Eric would often accuse her of cheating on him, something Thea insisted she never did. Soon, their relationship degraded into one defined by tempestuous arguments, with brief periods of peace between them. It was clear that Eric's family didn't approve of the relationship; Thea Koonz was never invited to the Windhurst home, and Eric's mother would even refuse to call him to the phone when Thea rang. Nevertheless, they dated for more than a year, well into Thea's freshman year at the University of New Hampshire, which Melanie was also attending.

* * *

IN the fall of 1987, Eric enlisted in the U.S. Marine Corps, and was sent to Parris Island, South Carolina, for boot camp. Each day, the "boots" would recite the creed of their rifle.

This is my rifle. There are many like it, but this one is mine . . .

Each day on the range while qualifying, Private Windhurst would line up the sight of his rifle with the target shaped like a head and shoulders popping out of a foxhole.

My rifle is my best friend. It is my life. I must master it as I master my life . . .

Mentally, he would go through the drill Trapper had ingrained in him. Breathe, relax, aim, squeeze.

My rifle without me is useless. Without my rifle, I am useless . . .

The drill instructors would bark at him while marching, while dressing, while making his bed. But on the range, the sergeants were helpful and encouraging. They wanted him to qualify—not as a marksman or sharpshooter—but as an "expert." Every marine is a killer. They said they wanted to turn him into a killer.

I must fire my rifle true. I must shoot straighter than my enemy who is trying to kill me . . .

After the shot, the target would retract, like someone falling to the ground. Three hundred yards away, a marine "pulling butts" would stick a light-colored cork in the hole so the distant shooter could mark his score. Eric already knew his shots cut a clean hole in the center of the distant figures, exactly where he imagined a heart would be. He might have been thinking of a long-ago shot he'd made just like it in the recesses of his mind.

I must shoot him before he shoots me. I will . . .

Before he could graduate from boot camp, a red ant bit Eric, and he began to swell up with an immediate allergic reaction. They told him marines get in the shit; they can't have a marine who was allergic to ants. Eric was released from the U.S. Marine Corps on a medical discharge, just a couple of weeks before graduation. His dream to follow Trapper as a Scout Sniper was over. He was crushed.

* * *

RETURNING to Hopkinton, Eric felt trapped in a role he'd hoped he'd never play—that of a townie. Most of his high school friends had gone away to school, including the ones who had been seniors the previous year. Eric continued to keep busy working odd jobs, making excuses for still being around, telling hardly anyone the real story behind his military discharge.

He was still dating Thea Koonz, then a freshman at the University of New Hampshire, but the relationship was as unhealthy as it had been before he left for boot camp. Eric was still possessive and accusatory, even as he continued to hide details about his friendship with Melanie from her. Once, he drove to the university to give Melanie a ride back to Hopkinton, never even letting Thea know he'd been on campus. Later, in the spring of 1988, Eric did cheat on Thea, prompting a fight that led her to end the relationship for good.

* * *

ON Memorial Day weekend in 1990, Ricky Patenaude was driving his truck back to New Hampshire from Lyme Rock, Connecticut, where he and a few friends had spent the weekend camping before attending an auto race at the local track. Patenaude had invited his old high school friend Matt Quinn, who agreed to go for the camping and beer but had no interest in automobile racing. Quinn rode shotgun with him, the two men quiet, still nursing hangovers from the night before.

"So," Patenaude suddenly said, "what do you think is going to happen with Eric and Melanie killing her stepfather?"

Quinn wasn't taken aback by the question. He figured Patenaude had heard the story long before now, maybe even back while they were all still in high school. More likely the rumors had grown out of a particular post–high school party where a drunken Eric had spilled his guts—both literally and figuratively—on the bathroom floor. Friends and strangers alike had all heard Eric Windhurst blabber about how he had shot someone.

"Rick, you know I told him not to do it," Quinn said, crestfallen. "I fucking told him not to do it, and he didn't listen to me."

Ricky Patenaude nodded solemnly, trying to act as though this was old news to him, not probing any further. But the truth was Patenaude had only heard the rumor thirdhand, never from Eric himself. His question for Matt Quinn, casually posed at the end of a long weekend together, had been designed to confirm his suspicions and fuel his confusion at why he was never told.

* * *

FRUSTRATED with his dead-end life in Hopkinton, Eric moved to Breckenridge, Colorado, in 1989 to live with high school friends who'd relocated there. While there, Eric continued to work odd jobs and lived like a snowboard bum. He partied hard with his friends and fell in love with the landscape; it was a lot like being in New Hampshire but without the nagging angst of his family issues or the daily reminders of his secret past.

In the summer of 1990, Eric was out late one night in downtown Breckenridge. He passed a restaurant under renovation, its windows covered only with a clear plastic construction tarp. Eric took a peek behind the tarp and noticed several cases of beer stacked on the restaurant's floor. It was late, and Eric had been out drinking with his roommates. It didn't seem like a big deal to him to steal what had been so carelessly left out in the open.

Later, while under arrest for the crime, he'd find out what a big deal it was; second-degree burglary was a felony in Colorado. His bond was set at twenty-five hundred dollars, and after calling his parents for money and help obtaining a lawyer, he pleaded guilty to the offense in exchange for a small fine and six months informal probation. As part of his probation, he was required to attend weekly Alcoholics Anonymous meetings for a period of six months.

Terrified of being on probation in Colorado and subjecting himself to further legal troubles, Eric returned home to New Hampshire in the fall of 1990, where his Alcoholics Anonymous attendance was reported to the Colorado court.

* * *

BACK in Hopkinton, Eric, now twenty-two, reconnected with Ricky Patenaude, who had learned of Eric's darkest secret months prior but decided never to discuss what he now knew with his old friend.

Eric also reconnected with a woman named Tracy Donahue, who had been a classmate in Hopkinton High School. Though they had never dated in school (Tracy's gang was mostly made up of kids from neighboring Concord), they had old friends and memories in common, and soon, they began a casual relationship.

In early 1991, Ricky Patenaude and Eric embarked on a road trip to visit their high school friend Mark Hoevler, then living in Florida. Ricky had just broken up with his girlfriend and insisted on turning songs off the radio that reminded him of her. On the way down South, they stopped for an overnight visit with Eric's half-sister Lisa, by that time married and living in Williamsburg, Virginia.

When the young men arrived in Florida, they met some of Mark's friends, including a young blond girl named Elizabeth, who caught Ricky Patenaude's eye. He, Mark, and Eric stayed with the girls for a couple of days before returning to New Hampshire.

When they got back to Hopkinton, Elizabeth's dad called both Ricky Patenaude's and Eric's fathers, saying that his daughter's Rolex watch was missing. He suspected it had been stolen by one of the boys. Both boys denied it, and John Windhurst vehemently defended Eric. Conveniently omitting Eric's Colorado conviction, John declared, "My son is not a thief."

A few days later, Ricky was getting dressed and picked up the dress shoes he'd last worn on the trip with Eric. One of the shoes felt funny to him, kind of stiff. He reached inside and discovered the missing Rolex watch.

When he called Elizabeth to tell her that the watch had been located, she responded very suspiciously, insinuating that one of them—perhaps Eric—had planted the watch in Patenaude's shoe after being accused of stealing it. He told the girl he'd send it back to her right away.

When Eric learned that Ricky had not been more vigorous in defending him on the phone, he was furious. To him, it was the same as Ricky calling him a criminal. The two had words, and the friendship fractured. According to friends who knew them both, the fight brought a deep anger out in Eric and sent Ricky into a depression that lasted for weeks.

* * *

THE watch incident made Eric remember why he'd wanted to leave Hopkinton in the first place. In his hometown, it seemed that things never changed, that nothing was ever easy. Remembering how happy he'd been living in Colorado, he decided to head out west once again, this time enrolling at the Motorcycle Mechanics Institute in Phoenix, Arizona. Eric vowed it would be different, that he'd finally learn a trade he could be proud of and start a new life in a new place. After graduating from the institute, he moved back to Breckenridge, Colorado, where he began working as a mechanic at a successful snowmobile dealership.

Eric at last felt that his life was truly starting. He was making something of himself in a place he loved, far away from the things that haunted him in Hopkinton. While in Colorado, he roomed with his old friend Craig Metzger. He made new friends, people who knew him only as Eric from New Hampshire, not as a Windhurst, or a Kimball, or that kid who once took out a shotgun at a high school party.

During the week, Eric worked hard in the shop, impressing his boss with his easy way with customers and his skill with the tools of the trade. On the weekends, he'd snowboard, or if it was warm, he'd go for hikes with the guys, searching for cliffs to jump off of into frigid mountain streams. Life was about as good as it got for him, and Eric began to change in positive ways, growing into a man with mature principles, values not based on his family name or high school status but the decency of honest work and communion with nature.

Still, Eric struggled. With the blossoming of maturity came something else, a feeling in his gut that something inside of him was all wrong. It hurt physically sometimes, and Eric would take long walks at dusk, thinking that fresh air would rid him of the nauseous feeling that dogged him more and more as the weeks turned into months.

Near where Eric lived was a small white church, and as he would turn around to head home each night, he'd often pause to look at the light on in the rectory window, at the silhouetted figure bent over the desk, probably the minister writing the sermon for the upcoming Sunday service. Eric wasn't religious and never had been. But every night he paused and thought about knocking on that door, asking the man inside if he could talk. On one of these nights, he realized with the force of an avalanche what it was that wasn't right inside him. The feeling he had wasn't nausea, or homesickness for New Hampshire.

The feeling was unbearable, soul-eating guilt.

The boy who had just begun to grow into a man thought truthfully about what it was that he had done all those years ago, about what it really meant, not just to him and Melanie, but to everyone else. To his family. To Melanie's family. To Danny's family. To God.

Eric had known all along that vigilante justice was not the same as courtroom justice. But he'd had bravado, truly believing that he'd done something good in protecting a friend. He'd thought himself a hero of sorts, an image easily fueled by a turbulent chemistry of testosterone and the alcohol-soaked lifestyle of his late teens and early twenties. Mostly, though, he was afraid of the consequences, and all of these years, he'd been running in fear from the plain truth.

I took a man's life, Eric thought. It was like he'd suddenly woken up from a reverie, the high-flying dream of an invincible adolescent. And he'd woken up into an adult nightmare.

God, what have I done?

* * *

ERIC'S boss couldn't have been happier with his new mechanic. He was a model employee, meticulous in his work, never late.

In mid-May 1992, Eric got a personal call at the dealership, something that hadn't happened in the entire time he worked there. His boss walked solemnly to the service area, personally seeking Eric out to hand him the phone. He didn't look angry, just concerned. The caller had said he was John Windhurst, Eric's father, calling from New Hampshire. His tone sounded like it might be bad news.

Eric took the handset, nodding in apology for the interruption in the workday.

"Dad?" he said. "What's going on?"

"You've got to come home, son," the voice on the other end of the phone said, all stern business. "The police are poking around again. They have a letter. It's pretty damning."

Eric kept it short, promising his father he'd call him back after work. Walking with the phone to the front of the dealership, he thought about how to tell his employers that he had to quit and return to New Hampshire. This had been the start of something, probably the best chance he'd had at building a life untainted by the past or the complexities of being a Windhurst in Hopkinton.

He thought of something he heard once, back in high school. Eric couldn't remember if it was a teacher or a coach who'd chuckled when he expressed his plans to leave the town after graduation, how he hoped to never return.

"You can't pretend your home isn't where it is, Eric," he was told. "Everyone comes home . . . eventually."

Eric returned to New Hampshire immediately, claiming to his boss and his friends in Colorado that the reason he had to go home was because he missed his old girlfriend, Tracy Donahue.

The couple did resume dating when he returned, and more than four years later, in September of 1996, they were married. The marriage lasted six years, dissolving in April 2002.

— 14 —

The Letters

IN April of 1992, Richard Baron and the Paquettes appeared on a local daytime talk show hosted by Cathy Burnham, a former Miss New Hampshire. During the show, they restated the case that Rena's unsolved death was tied to Danny's shooting. Under the hot, white lights, the family looked washed out and sad. Even mighty Victor looked sad. They pleaded with the 4:00 p.m. television audience that if anyone had information about the case, he or she should contact them.

Within a week, two anonymous letters arrived.

Despite the fact that Lisa Brown styled her hair like Diane Sawyer, she couldn't hide the fact she had the bite of a bulldog. That was the image she was trying to portray. Brown, a local New Hampshire TV reporter, didn't have the subtle touch of certain interviewers; she didn't try to draw flies with honey-laden questions. Women in TV news had to be tough to be taken seriously. Brown had always worked hard, constantly aspiring to prove herself to her professors, her colleagues, and, ultimately, her viewers.

Brown had spent several years trying to work her way up to the major markets, the big stations in the big cities. It meant living a gypsylike existence, trying to get hired at small-town TV stations in places she wouldn't otherwise choose to live. One news director had offered her a job if she would come back to his office after hours. She decided to look elsewhere.

In 1992, Brown was a co-anchor for *WNDS Up Front*, an hour-long newsmagazine that ran each evening. She was fascinated by crime and loved television that was "real." She was always looking for a great story.

A call came through the WNDS switchboard one evening while Brown was preparing for her live broadcast. "My name's Richard Baron. I have information about an unsolved murder that you might be able to help solve."

Brown was intrigued. "Go on."

"It's about the Danny Paquette murder . . ."

"The guy shot in Hooksett? Yes, I think I've seen it on *Unsolved Mysteries*. And the Cathy Burnham show."

"So you're familiar with the case."

"Sure. But it's been done," she noted. "What do you have that we haven't heard before?"

Richard Baron replied, "How about the name of the killer?"

* * *

LISA Brown met with Richard Baron and Victor Paquette at the Derry studios of WNDS. It was late spring of 1992. The cinderblock building was tucked at the end of an industrial road, wild grass climbing to tickle the undersides of transmission dishes erected in the adjacent field.

"For many years, we believed that Danny's death had something to do with the death of his mother," Baron explained. "But we don't believe that now."

"Why not?"

"Because of these two letters I received since our last television appearance," Baron said, producing the documents.

"Can I read them?" Brown probed.

Baron turned to Victor who nodded, as if the decision to share the letters hadn't been made until that moment. Baron slid a postcard across the table to Brown.

The postcard was filled on one side from top to bottom with words produced on a Remington typewriter. With the exception of a faint trace of red through all the letters from a two-tone ribbon, the document was flawless. Brown held the postcard carefully at the edges, as she imagined a detective would hold a valuable piece of evidence.

The card read:

> *It is common knowledge in Hopkinton that a young man named Eric Windhurst shot Paquette with his father's .270 rifle to avenge abuse to Paquette's daughter, a friend of Windhurst. Windhurst arranged an alibi from the Quinn boy. Eric Windhurst's brother, Scott, told Mr. Windhurst so he is aware of what happened.*
>
> *I am dumbfounded as to why the case is still unsolved. It is a bad example to the many young people who know the facts about this murder. They look at it as a "justified murder" because of the alleged abuse. This is not healthy.*
>
> *Windhurst has a long history of shady dealings in this Village including check forgery. Nonetheless he has misled the police very successfully.*
>
> *He is obsessed with guns and is a crackerjack shooter. It is said that he keeps his friends mum on his dealings through charm, through intimidation and through threats. I can understand why, can't you?*
>
> *A Former Neighbor*

Though brief, the postcard spoke volumes about the case. Paquette's murder was a revenge killing. Brown was stunned. She no longer held the postcard delicately; she instead pinched the edges with white fingers. She looked up and tried to speak through a suddenly dry mouth.

"Can I," she said, "read the other one?"

The second letter was two pages long. It was also typewritten, but filled with misspellings and misplaced punctuation. There was something wrong with the typewriter's ribbon, as the tops and bottoms of letters in the composition were often cut off. It left the impression to all that these two letters were written by separate people.

> *Dear Mr. Baron,*
>
> *I am grateful I was watching the Kathy [sic] Burnham Show about the Paquettes on April 30th. Something has been eating away at me but I have been afraid to step forward. Seeing the pain the family is suffering persuaded me to do so.*
>
> *The family is wrong to conclude that Danny Paquette's*

death is connected to his mother's death. Melanie Paquette, Danny's daughter told me Eric Windhearst [sic] (who was going to Hopkington [sic] High School with her) shot and killed her father.

She and Eric had talked alot [sic] about how she hated her father because he had sexually abused her. Eric wanted to blow him away (he is an expert marksman). He had gotten away with all kinds of crimes before. Once he and some of his friends had taken some checks from a cabin his father rented out and forged them to buy things. He never got caught. I know she thought Eric was cool at the time, he was alot [sic] older than she.

She said Eric took his father's 270 rifle. They drove to her fathers [sic] house in Hooksett, parked on a road near the house and walked through the woods where they could see the house. She pointed out her father working in the yard. Then Eric told her to go back to the car. He shot him and ran back to the car.

I don't know why but the police questioned Eric about the murder. However, he had gotton [sic] one of his friends who knew about everything (a Matt) to give him an alibi. Eric's father was friends with the police, plus Eric himself is so cool, clean cut and charming, nobody would ever expect he'd do a thing like that. So they didn't question him again.

I hope this information will help you and the family. I know it is incredible to think it happened this way but it did. It will be hard for you to reach Eric because he had [sic] been lying low out West since he graduated.

May God Bless the Pauqette [sic] family.

Brown was thunderstruck. Here was a juicy story being handed to her on a platter. The letters had everything: the culprit, the motive, the method, and the accomplices. Who sent these letters? Was it really "common knowledge in Hopkinton" that Eric Windhurst had committed this crime?

All she had to do to get a career-changing story was prove it was true.

* * *

LISA Brown began thumbing through the Hopkinton phone book, cross-checking names against the 1987 yearbook. Richard Baron said he'd verified the letters by calling Eric Windhurst's classmates, pretending to be someone else. He said that some of them had indeed verified the story. As much as she wanted to believe Baron, Brown knew she had to hear it for herself.

Brown called the homes of people in the yearbook pretending to be working on a story about high school cliques. She quizzed people about their own high school memories.

"Who was the most popular kid in school?"

"It would probably have been Eric," one girl said. "Eric Windhurst was the captain of the soccer team. He had a group of really tight friends who hung out with him."

"What were their names?"

"Well, there was Matt Quinn. They were really tight."

Brown noted that both letters said a friend had helped Windhurst with an alibi. One said it was "a Matt"; the other said it was "the Quinn boy."

"There were a few others. Dee Clark. Ricky Patenaude. Mark Hoevler. Some of them played soccer. They all had cars. They all drank together at Eric's cabin in the woods."

"Did they ever get into any trouble?"

"One time there was this party in the woods, at the cabins that Eric's family owned. It was the night of the senior banquet before graduation. I think most of the senior class was there. This girl in our class showed up at the party with some kids from Concord High who weren't invited."

Brown scribbled notes. "What happened?"

"Eric pulled out a shotgun and pointed it at the girl's face. Told her and the Concord kids to get out. It freaked everyone out. They left. That was the end of it."

* * *

DAYS later, while Lisa Brown was typing up scripts in the newsroom, a call for her was pushed through from the switchboard. She grabbed the receiver and tucked it under her chin, still punishing the keys on the IBM clone with two fingers. "Who is this?"

The voice was that of a man. He didn't identify himself. "You know that story you're working on?"

"Which one?" She had many stories she was working on.
"Stop it."
"What?"
"Stop calling around Hopkinton and asking about things that don't concern you."

The tapping on the computer keyboard stopped. "Who is this?"

"Don't do the story about Danny Paquette. No good will come of it."

Brown had not mentioned Paquette's name to anyone. "Is this a threat?"

The line clicked and went dead.

* * *

BROWN was intrigued by the fact that the girl implicated in the letters had been living in the house of a homicide prosecutor who later became a judge. She also grew suspicious of the fact Kathleen McGuire and Philip Messier had petitioned the court to be Melanie's guardians a week before Danny died. Could insurance money have been the motive?

Brown went to Merrimack County Probate Court and asked for the file. When she was told it was under seal, Brown wrote a motion by hand to have the files opened. "In my own research, I have obtained information which could assist the state in determining if Mr. Paquette's death was a homicide, rather than an accident." In the motion, she implied that Kathy McGuire might be implicated in the death.

The probate court notified the interested parties: the Messiers, the attorney general, and Melanie Paquette. The clerk had little luck finding Melanie, her family having moved around the country so much. The attorney general took no position on whether the file should be opened or not. The Messiers stated that they were no longer Melanie's guardians—they said they hadn't heard from her in some time—and didn't object to the files being opened. They did point out that there were several passages in their filing of a "personal nature" regarding Melanie, and they requested that those passages be redacted before distribution.

After several weeks, Brown won her motion. In the file were typical legal documents and estate summaries. The money

Danny Paquette's daughters got was modest: around twenty thousand dollars each. There was nothing in the file that looked suspicious. Nothing in the file that implicated Melanie or the Messiers. There was no smoking gun.

* * *

LISA Brown finally aired a report on the Danny Paquette shooting. With no corroborated evidence, the reporter could not name names. Instead she reported on the existence of some anonymous letters that suggested a conspiracy among a group of teenagers in Hopkinton. It was not the career-changing story she had hoped to deliver.

Brown forwarded the letters and a report of her investigative findings to Sergeant Roland Lamy at the New Hampshire State Police (NHSP). She still felt she was on the right track even if she couldn't prove anything.

What she didn't know was that Lamy already had copies of the letters, obtained from Richard Baron. And although they knew all the same information as the reporter, the NHSP would not seriously follow up on the leads for another year.

— 15 —

Persons of Interest

New Hampshire State Police sergeant Roland Lamy would get an annual phone call from Victor Paquette right around the November anniversary of the shooting.

"What are you doing to solve my brother's murder?" the gruff biker would always ask the detective.

"I assure you, Victor, we have not forgotten about your brother's case. We will investigate any new leads that become available." Lamy would always hear Victor mumble a dissatisfied "Fuck you" right before the receiver slammed down and cut the connection.

On May 5, 1992, Lamy received a call from Victor's friend, Richard Baron, asking to meet him at an ice-cream stand. Baron passed the first of two anonymous letters he received to Lamy. He scanned it meticulously. The name Eric Windhurst rang a bell.

"The writer of this letter called me yesterday," Baron said.

Lamy looked up from the typewritten note. "Who was it?"

"It was a young woman. She didn't give me her name. But she said that Melanie bragged to her about getting Windhurst to do the shooting."

Lamy thought back to those months following the November 1985 death, chasing down every piece of ass Danny Paquette ever nailed, looking at every hoodlum Victor ever got into a beef with. To that day, they were still unable to clear

Pauline Gates as a suspect, with all of her embezzled money that went God knows where. This letter was different. It was a solid lead.

"I called the Windhurst house last night," Baron boasted.

"Why the hell would you do that?" Lamy cried.

"I said I was a friend from high school looking for Eric. He's out of town. He's currently living out west."

Lamy rolled the pages between his fingers. "We will investigate this letter and its contents as all other leads are handled," he said flatly.

Two days later, Baron called to say a typewritten postcard had arrived making more of the same claims. Lamy asked Baron to give him the postcard also.

* * *

THE following week—as Victor and Baron were giving copies of the letters to reporter Lisa Brown—Sergeant Lamy asked Eric's father, John Windhurst, to come to New Hampshire State Police Headquarters and discuss the letters. The old man walked kind of slowly, but he was friendly to the detective, small-town congenial. John Windhurst told Lamy that he was a union carpenter, now retired from Local 538. They sat in an interrogation room for privacy.

"My son Eric is in Colorado right now. He's living out there with some friends. He just completed motorcycle repair school. I expect him back home in New Hampshire in a couple of weeks."

Lamy slid the letters across the table and asked Windhurst to read them. "They both depict a certain plot involving your son Eric. Could you comment on their substance?"

Mr. Windhurst read them carefully, shaking his head at times. "I bet I know who wrote these."

Lamy reached for his pen. "Who?"

"Ricky Patenaude. He and Eric had a falling out sometime back. Something about Eric stealing a Rolex watch. Ricky's always accusing Eric of doing the bad deeds that he does himself."

"Is that right?" Investigators were working under the assumption that the two letters had separate authors.

"Yes. The thing in this letter about the check forging, that never happened. Ricky is very jealous of Eric. They used to be best friends. He's very unstable."

"Did your son kill Danny Paquette?"

"No, of course not," the elder Windhurst said.

"What about the claim your other son told you about the crime."

"That never happened."

"What do you remember about that time?"

"I remember that Eric said Melanie was going around telling everyone in high school that Danny had sex with her and that he was still molesting kids in the neighborhood." Windhurst sighed disapprovingly. "My oldest son, Trapper, knew Danny. They had worked together at Continental Can Company in Londonderry for a while. They'd go out to that restaurant at the traffic circle with coworkers for drinks."

"What do you know about Melanie's whereabouts?"

"Only that she left the state and called her math teacher to say she was getting married."

Lamy put his pen down on the table. "I assume that's what I asked you to bring in? The only one you have?"

Windhurst nodded and reached over to the bag he brought in. Lamy inspected its contents and gave him a receipt. It listed the item as a Winchester Model 70 .270 rifle belonging to John Windhurst. Of course he had other firearms, but this was the only .270 he owned. The weapon was sent to the crime lab for comparison to the bullet recovered from the telephone wire.

After the meeting with Lamy, John Windhurst called Eric in Colorado and told him he needed to get home right away.

* * *

FIVE days later, a one-page report landed on Roland Lamy's desk. It was from the forensics laboratory.

"Based on its general rifling characteristics," the supervising technician wrote about John Windhurst's rifle, "specimen RPL-1 could not have discharged the bullet in exhibit HPD-1."

* * *

SERGEANT Lamy located Melanie Paquette living in California. She was married and now had the last name Cooper. The detective spoke with her twice on the telephone, asking to interview her about the anonymous letters. Twice she demurred, explaining that she was a busy mother taking care of a houseful of young children and that there just wasn't time to answer the questions.

"I don't really remember a lot about that portion of my life," Melanie said. "I've tried to block a lot of it out. Because of the abuse. I'm afraid I wouldn't be able to focus on what you were asking." She offered a compromise. "Maybe if you wrote down the questions?"

Lamy needed Melanie to clear up some of these allegations. It was unorthodox, but he agreed to write up some questions and mail them to her.

* * *

ON July 23, 1992, Sergeant Lamy spent an entire day typing up five pages of questions he wanted to ask Melanie Cooper. There were twenty-seven questions, but several included subquestions and follow-ups. It took a week, but Melanie returned a five-page letter, neatly tabbed and typed, answering the investigator.

> Q: In regards to the sexual abuse that was inflicted upon you, do you know if any police agency ever questioned Danny on the issue?
>
> A: To my knowledge . . . no.
>
> Q: Could Pauline Gates have become emotionally involved in the guardianship issues to the point she could have become involved in this shooting, either planning it, hiring someone to do it, or physically taking part?
>
> A: In my opinion . . . absolutely not.

Lamy thumbed through the responses, mostly frustrated with the answers about her relatives. Melanie had little recollection of people like Victor or what might have been said around kitchen tables when her stepfather's name came up.

> Q: In regards to the attached letters and consistent with my telephone conversation with you, could you please

comment on each issue in the letters as to any truth or possible reality.

A: As far as the letters go, I'll confirm the things I know to be true. First, I did talk to Eric about the abuse although I can't recall how much. I remember hearing something about the forged checks, but there were so many rumors in the town that I don't know how much truth there is to the whole thing. Mostly Eric and his friends liked to be cool so they probably made up the whole story and spread the rumor themselves. I did think Eric was cool at the time and he was older than me. At least when I knew him, he was "cool, clean-cut, and charming." He was really into guns and hunting as were many of his friends.

Q: Please describe your relationship with Eric Windhurst. Was he ever your boyfriend? Did you ever tell him anything that is reflected in these letters?

A: Eric and I got to be friends when I played on the high school soccer team. I always thought he was so cool. I practically worshipped the ground he walked on—one of those stupid high school things girls do. Anyway, after soccer season we really didn't hang out anymore. I always wanted to be his girlfriend but I never was. He treated me like a younger sister. He was just a high school infatuation of mine and he always played "Mr. cool." I told him about the abuse.

Q: Do you have an opinion of whether or not Eric Windhurst would have a reason to shoot Danny?

A: In my opinion, he did not have any reason to shoot Danny.

Well there it was, Lamy thought. *Or there it wasn't.* If she was going to finger Eric Windhurst for the shooting, that's when she would have done it. Without the murder weapon, there seemed to be no way to prove this theory of the crime without corroborating testimony.

Melanie made two things clear in her questionnaire. Her family was sick of talking about Danny's death. And they just hoped the whole thing would go away.

Q: Philip Messier tells the police in his 12-27-85 interview that Melanie was extremely afraid of Danny Paquette. Is that true?

A: I was extremely afraid of Danny. He haunted us for a long time. He had tried killing my mother. He abused me (not just sexually). He was a monster and I was very afraid of him.

* * *

NOTHING more happened in case I-85-147 for more than a year.

On August 23, 1993, Sergeant Roland Lamy and his partner, Sergeant Arthur Wiggin, drove to Hopkinton to question the Windhurst family. They arrived at the Windhurst home around eight o'clock in the evening. A beautiful woman named Christine met them at the door. She introduced herself as Scott Windhurst's wife; they had been married for about a year. She was woozy from a medical procedure she'd had earlier in the day.

The woman summoned her husband, who came to the door with a suspicious gleam in his eyes. Scott Windhurst was a workman with the electric company. He stood on the porch with the plainclothes detectives, his arms folded defensively across his chest.

"I've heard all those rumors for years, and there are no facts whatsoever that substantiate that Eric had anything to do with the Paquette shooting," he complained. "Ricky Patenaude's got it in for Eric. He's probably been the one spreading these rumors."

Wiggin asked Scott if he owned any rifles. He replied he was more into archery and liked to fire a crossbow. But he had two rifles: a .243 Bicentennial rifle that had been in the family for years and a Ruger Model 77 muzzleloader. Neither were precision weapons or capable of firing a .270.

As the four stood on the front porch in the descending dusk, a set of headlights swung off the main road and up the driveway. John Windhurst Sr. stumbled out of the car and slammed the door. He pointed a finger at the large, bald-headed cop leaning on the front post.

"You!" he said to Lamy. "I know about you now. You know what my lawyer said about you?"

"No, what?" Lamy was curious.

"That you're an asshole. That you're a scumbag."

Windhurst kept swearing at the cop, shaking his fists. Lamy and Wiggin took great pains to remain polite. They made notes about John's behavior but did not mention whether his wife, Barbara, was present for his tirade.

"He says you are a treacherous cop and can't be trusted," Windhurst continued. "He said we are not to talk to the cops and especially not to Lamy."

John Windhurst plopped down on the front steps. Lamy's report noted that Windhurst had been drinking, and his exchange with the detectives had worn him out. He sat there breathing heavily, the whole group staring at him.

"I'm sorry," he said. "I lost my composure. I wasn't expecting to see you here. I apologize, Sergeant Lamy."

"That's all right, Mr. Windhurst."

"But, it is true what my lawyer said to me."

"That I'm an asshole scumbag?"

"That I shouldn't talk to the police."

"Look," Wiggin said, turning his attention to include Scott and Christine. "You're right that these are just rumors, and they may have been around for many years. There might not be anything to them. But we can't prove or disprove any of it unless we talk to Eric."

"He has attorneys now," his father said. "They should be consulted."

Lamy agreed and offered to facilitate a meeting. "There are documents, investigative notes we can share with his lawyers. To get to the bottom of this, clear his name."

"Who is representing him?" Wiggin asked.

"Mark Sisti," Windhurst replied.

* * *

ATTORNEY Mark Sisti, along with his partner, Paul Twomey, were superstars in the New Hampshire legal community. They were famous, not just around the courthouse, but throughout the Granite State. Sisti and Twomey represented the defense in one of New Hampshire's most sensational crimes: Pam Smart, a teacher from Derry, accused of enticing her teenage lover and his friends into killing her husband. In the days before Court TV, mainstream media coverage of the salacious trial was intense. Larry Drake, the actor who played developmentally disabled Benny on *L.A. Law*, played a self-assured, confident Mark Sisti in the CBS TV movie about the crime, and later the story was the inspiration for the fictional *To Die For*, a film starring Nicole Kidman. Pam Smart was convicted, but Sisti and Twomey won their reputation as the go-to defense team in the state.

Sisti promised Lamy he would discuss the possibility of an interview with his client. A short time later, he informed the detective in writing that Eric Kimball Windhurst would not submit to any questioning from police.

"You may consider this," he said in a letter, "an indication of Mr. Windhurst's right to remain silent and his right to retain counsel."

* * *

SERGEANTS Lamy and Wiggin took another crack at talking to friends who had been in Eric's circle. They interviewed Mark Hoevler and his parents. Mark said he had no knowledge of Eric Windhurst having been involved in any kind of crime. His parents said they resented being contacted by Lisa Brown and the media asking for information on a crime they knew nothing about. Mark also said the rumors about Eric had been around since high school and were regarded by most people as ridiculous.

Matt Quinn told Lamy and Wiggin he was upset that Lisa Brown had misrepresented herself to him and his mother, claiming to be doing a story on high school reunions. Lamy told Quinn his name had appeared in a letter as part of a cover-up. The young man dismissed it, saying he had no information about any crime and that he was willing to take a polygraph test if he had to.

Eric Prescott also said that the rumors about Eric Windhurst from high school were ridiculous. Prescott prided himself as currently being a college student and, as if extolling

Eric Windhurst's innocence by extension, told the cops, "I'm not the type who would hang out with criminals."

Craig Metzger agreed that tales of Eric's crime had been circulating since high school, but no one believed a word of them. Metzger said that after high school, he'd moved to Colorado, and eventually so had Eric. They'd lived together and became ski bums. But, he said, they were no longer very close, having had a falling-out over stealing each other's girlfriends.

* * *

SERGEANT Lamy sat down with Ricky Patenaude in an interview room at the Hopkinton Police Department. Ricky sat next to Bill Simpson, a former classmate from Hopkinton High who was now a member of the local police department.

Patenaude looked sad as he sat there talking to the cops. "Lisa Brown called the house looking for me, but my sister answered the phone. She's six years older than me and never hung around with us. Everything she knows, she heard it from me. That makes it hearsay, doesn't it?"

Lamy agreed that it did.

"I miss hanging out with Eric," Patenaude said. "But there are parts of Eric that I don't understand. He lies whenever he has to. I've seen him lie to his parents, his girlfriends. He has no conscience about it."

"You two had a falling out? Over the Rolex watch thing?" Lamy added.

"Yeah. I don't know how that watch got into my shoe. I didn't put it there. Someone could have put it there after we got home, know what I mean?" Patenaude took a deep breath. "I thought I could still be Eric's friend and go along for the ride. But I knew that I couldn't anymore, and I had to pull away."

"Did he ever tell you he shot Danny Paquette?"

"No," Patenaude said. "But I heard he told some guys at a party in 1988."

"Which guys?"

"Don't know."

"Who told you this, if not Eric?"

Patenaude declined to say who told him. Lamy gave him a card with his home phone and his pager. He asked Ricky Patenaude to call him if he wanted to talk.

***

SERGEANTS Lamy and Wiggin went to the posh home of Ricky Patenaude's parents, the owners of Pat's Peak, the local ski resort. When TV reporter Lisa Brown had sought out Ricky a year earlier, his older sister Sabrina answered the phone. They chatted for a long time, and Sabrina had passed along tantalizing rumors that seemed to match some details in the anonymous letters. But the reporter could never get the woman to go on the record or explain how she knew what she knew. Aware of Brown's suspicions, the investigators now wanted to take their own crack at Sabrina Patenaude.

The detectives waited fifteen minutes for Sabrina to arrive. They sat in the living room with her parents, Sally and Wayne Patenaude.

"All of Ricky's friends are blaming him for the whole Eric mess," Sally Patenaude said. Her husband sat stoically while his wife continued. "Ricky's scared. After he spoke to you police officers, his cat mysteriously disappeared. I'm worried they're trying to get back at him."

Sabrina rushed into the room with her newborn baby in a carrier. According to the investigators' notes, she was already emotional.

"Do you know the name of the young man who has been calling Lisa Brown and threatening her at work?"

Sabrina became upset and at first refused to answer. "I can't believe you're asking me to give you the name."

"So you know it."

She became even more emotional. "Why is that even important?"

"At this point in time," Lamy told the family, "we have no factual information to connect or suspect that Eric Windhurst is guilty of a crime."

Mr. Patenaude waved his hands at the cops. "Don't you know Eric and Melanie and all their friends have had years to cover their tracks, destroy the weapon? Where have you been all these years?"

Sergeant Wiggin explained the information they now had was new, and that was why they were following up on it now.

Mr. Patenaude again waved his hands dismissively. "I can't believe how misinformed you are."

"You should talk to Craig Metzger," Sabrina said. "He has lots of facts."

"We did talk to him," Lamy responded, "and he has no facts at all."

Sabrina grew upset again. "You've obviously made up your mind that you're going to protect Eric Windhurst. I wish I never had gotten involved."

"Why, if you all feel so strongly about this, did none of you contact the police to tell them that Eric Windhurst had committed this crime?"

Sabrina sobbed. "Anyone who knows Eric knows he's capable of this."

* * *

"**NOBODY** fucking knows nothing!" Sergeant Lamy roared to Wiggin, driving back to state police headquarters. "The suspects won't talk. The families won't talk. The friends won't talk. The goddamn enemies won't talk. All they've heard are rumors."

He was furious with himself for thinking for a brief moment that they were about to arrest someone in this case.

Even with the lead they'd been given, though, there was one fact of the case that the hard-nosed detective was still trying to wrap his mind around. *Nobody could have made that shot*, Lamy thought. *Right through the heart at three hundred yards? Not Annie Oakley. Not Wyatt Earp. Not Lee Harvey Oswald. How the hell could a seventeen-year-old boy have pulled it off?*

It was late September. The days were getting shorter. Lamy knew it was only a few weeks until November. He would soon be getting his annual "fuck you" call from Victor Paquette.

— 16 —

Guilty Feelings

As New Hampshire State Police sergeant Roland Lamy began to contemplate retirement in 1993, he considered two high-profile cases left to square away. One involved the disappearance of a woman in Raymond, New Hampshire. In January 1985, Denise Bolser's husband had come home from work one day to find his wife missing. There was a note left in the kitchen reading, "We have your wife. Don't call police." Any footprints leading from the couple's house were obliterated by new snow. Bolser's truck later turned up at Boston's Logan Airport, her Social Security and charge cards left neatly on the seat.

The prevailing theory was she had been killed, perhaps outside of the home, and her body disposed of. Lamy didn't buy it. Although he had no evidence to support his theory, Lamy thought the woman was alive, living a new life somewhere far from New Hampshire. He swore he'd find her before he hung up his badge.

The sergeant also had the unfinished business of the Danny Paquette case. Though this one bugged him to no end, Lamy did not have much hope of clearing the case from his docket before retirement. Then, one night in October 1993, he got a call at home from a state trooper working in the northern part of the state. He said a man had come forward with information about the Hooksett homicide.

* * *

MICHAEL Manzo was a reporter for the *Laconia Citizen* newspaper. His beat was the tiny town of Bristol, New Hampshire, a community where not much of anything happened. Manzo had spent a year at the prestigious Deerfield Academy prep school in Massachusetts, then attended the University of New Hampshire School of Journalism. After a year he dropped out, joined the U.S. Army Reserve, and got an apartment near Lake Sunapee in central New Hampshire. On the weekends, the bored preppie would visit friends at the University of New Hampshire, crashing at his former fraternity house.

Manzo had a talent for writing, and despite the fact that he never graduated, Manzo was able to get a job as a correspondent with a small paper in northern Massachusetts, leading to jobs at other papers in New Hampshire. In 1993, after a year at the *Citizen*, Manzo was about to start a job that November with the *Union Leader*, the state's largest newspaper.

One of Manzo's last assignments for the *Citizen* was to cover a murder trial. The story revolved around a case that had gone unsolved until a witness had stepped forward to implicate the killer. Manzo was moved by the witness's bravery. He was certain that the crime would have never been solved if the witness hadn't come forward. It was a thought that struck a nerve deep within him, sparking a memory of an incident he hadn't thought about in years.

Manzo had been paying courtesy calls to all of his news contacts in the Bristol area, saying good-bye and thanking them for their past cooperation. One of the people whom the young man went to visit with was Steve Crocetti, the police chief in Danbury. "Chief" was a part-time position in the tiny town, and Manzo had known Crocetti from his second job, a part-time gig with the Bristol police.

"I have something I need to get off my chest," Manzo told him.

"What is it?"

"For five years, I've kept a secret," he said. "My former girlfriend told me she had her father murdered."

Crocetti was shocked at the confession. "Why did you keep it a secret?"

"Because I knew the guy had molested children," Manzo said. "I think all this time I've played judge and jury, because I thought Danny Paquette deserved to die."

* * *

AFTER a series of phone calls, Sergeant Lamy was able to arrange a meeting with Michael Manzo. Manzo explained that he had met Melanie Paquette while she was a freshman at the University of New Hampshire. She had told him about the murder one night while she visited him at the frat house, but Manzo never knew whether to believe it or not.

"Why not?" Lamy asked.

"Because half the time, Melanie was full of crap," he replied. "Melanie started doing weird stuff. One day she got on her bicycle and rode all the way to Manchester on a whim."

"A whim? That's a fifty-mile bike ride," Lamy snorted. "Who did she see? Someone from high school, maybe?"

"No, it was her aunt Pauline," Manzo replied.

Pauline Gates, the aunt who'd embezzled thousands of dollars from her employer, was a name Lamy hadn't heard in a while.

"And when she rode her bike back the next day, she went to the UNH athletic field house and slept on the roof. Said she wanted to be alone."

"What do you remember about what she said to you?"

Manzo closed his eyes and thought back to that night on campus.

* * *

YOUNG Mike Manzo sat on the couch in the library of the Phi Kappa Beta house with his arm around Melanie Paquette's shoulder. It was late at night, and although the house was known for round-the-clock debauchery, the library was quiet.

They had met in September 1988. He was attracted to Melanie because she was girl-next-door cute, her dark hair coming halfway down her delicate neck. She was quiet and shy most of the time, but she had a smile he thought was charming. Things went fast. They had only seen each other about three or four times, but they had already had sex once, and Manzo saw something swimming in Melanie's eyes even then. He wondered if she was falling in love with him. Tonight, the girl was emotional, upset about something.

"What is it?" he asked.

"I . . . I can't talk about it."

Manzo said the frail coed needed much coaxing to talk about what was bothering her that night. He was sure by her anxious behavior that she was about to discuss something rather big, and he wondered if his girlfriend was going to confess to being a lesbian. He was shocked when Melanie described the years of sexual and physical abuse at the hands of her stepfather. It explained her funk, her recent distance from him. Manzo certainly hadn't expected what Melanie told him next.

"I had my stepfather killed."

"What?"

"I had a friend in high school. He was going into the marines after graduation. We talked about it beforehand. I took him to my stepfather's place. It was like farmland. He was outside working on a tractor. We were hiding in the tree line, and my friend shot him with his hunting rifle. Then we ran through the woods to get away. When the police came, I tried my best to be surprised and upset."

* * *

"HOW was the relationship after she told you that?" Lamy asked Manzo, now sitting across the table from him, talking into a tape recorder.

"She seemed relieved to say it, to get it off her chest. She seemed closer to me after that, like she could open up."

"And you got closer?"

"For a while," he said. "But in the back of mind I never really knew if what she said was true or not. I wasn't from the area, so I never heard about the murder. And it wasn't like there were any cops coming around to ask me questions about it. I just never knew."

"Why are you coming forward now?"

Manzo thought about his answer. "I'd like to think I'm a different person now than I was five years ago."

Lamy made some final notes. "Did Melanie tell you anything else?"

"Just that she had a relative, an aunt, who worked for the town or something. She was a secretary or something. The police knew her aunt so Melanie was never seriously considered a suspect."

* * *

"HELLO?"

"Is Melanie Paquette home?"

"Uh, this is she."

"Hi, uh, this is going to sound kind of strange," the man fumbled. "This is Mike Manzo calling. Do you remember me?"

At the mention of the name, the female voice on the other end of the phone got brighter. "Yeah, I do. From UNH, right?"

"Yeah, from UNH!"

The former couple began to chat in the manner of old friends catching up. Michael told Melanie that he'd gotten her phone number from a private detective. (In 1993, before widespread Internet access, this wasn't an uncommon way for old friends to track each other down.) Melanie explained that she was now married and living in California. She spoke lovingly of two daughters, one who was about to turn three and the other who was eighteen months old. Melanie asked Manzo what he'd been doing for the past five years, and he responded, "A little bit of this, a little bit of that." Their discourse had all the familiar warmness of two old lovers, safe in their separation of time, space, and affection.

"This is going to sound weird," Manzo began. "I didn't think it was true at the time. But there were some things that you and I talked about that I've seen in the news lately. And it's making me nervous."

"I don't know what you're talking about really."

"You don't?" This was going to be harder than Manzo thought. "Well, it seems to me when we were going out, you told me about a possible murder in Hooksett of one of your family members and that's what the broadcast was about. You don't remember anything about that?"

"No."

He recapped that night at the frat for her. "I thought you told me that you killed him, and . . ."

"I did?" She sounded surprised.

"Yeah."

"Well, no."

"But do you have any idea who did? Or know anything about it?"

"Well, I've heard stuff," Melanie said. "But I don't . . . I didn't do it."

"I would think," he pressed back, "that you would remember something like that. You don't remember a thing about it?"

"I don't even know what kind of conversation this is, calling me up like this."

Manzo said he had lived with this secret for five years. Now he wondered if he should go to the police and tell them what he knew.

"It's nothing you have to worry about," Melanie told him.

"Well, it is."

"No, you're just blowing something out of proportion that's not even legitimate."

"Why don't you talk to the police?"

"I have," she said. "I've answered all their questions, filled out their questionnaires. Whenever something comes up, I talk to the head guy, Sergeant Lamy."

Manzo looked across the table to the burly state police detective listening to the conversation through a set of headphones. Lamy had been taking notes, passing suggested lines for Manzo. The cassette recorder between them continued to roll tape. Lamy made a motion with his hand that indicated the young man should continue talking.

"You told me that your friend had him killed or that you had asked a friend to kill him," Manzo said, smoothly reading from Lamy's hand-scratched script. "That he was shot on his farm in Hooksett. That's what you told me. And that makes me nervous knowing that."

Melanie's tone became darker. "I had a lot of problems back then."

"I know you did."

"I mean, I told a lot of people a lot of things."

"So none of it's true? When you said . . ."

"I had him killed. No."

"If the things you said to me aren't true, then why did you say them?"

"I said lots of things. I told people I was dying. I told them I had a year to live. I just wanted attention in a lot of different ways."

"Well, you're getting it," a bitter Manzo retorted. Was it possible? She told all her college friends she was dying when it wasn't true. Could she have been lying about the shooting all these years? "I've been upset before. I haven't gone and told people I killed someone. It doesn't make any sense to me."

Melanie's tone changed again. This time she was aggressive. "I'm really kind of irritated by the whole situation."

"What do you mean?"

"I'm sick of every Tom, Dick, and Harry calling me and my family to find out what the deal is."

"Melanie, I'm not trying to make your life harder or anything."

"Well you are!" she spat back. "I mean, why are you doing this? Who cares?"

"It's been eight years. The police are clueless. They don't have any idea."

"Sweetheart, not now."

Manzo and Lamy looked at each other in confusion; then they realized Melanie was not talking to Manzo at that moment. They heard a cackle of joy from a toddler who had wandered too close to the telephone. Melanie sounded like a diligent mother as she kindly redirected the child and turned her attention back to her caller.

"Yes, it's true my stepfather was a very horrible person." She had regained her temper and her composure. "He did horrible things to me growing up and to my family. There were times in my life where I did want him killed. A lot of times I fantasized about how I would have him killed. But I never, I mean never, you know." She weakly offered, "Unless someone did something without me involved."

"But it wasn't you? You didn't do it?"

"No. I did not . . ." Melanie paused and put more attention into her words. "I mean, uh, no. I didn't do it. I don't know what else there is to discuss about it."

"Didn't you tell me there was guy named Eric?"

"Him?" she said, betraying no further emotion. "He's like a big brother. He wouldn't know anything."

There was more that Manzo wanted to say to her. Not as an agent for the government, but as someone who felt blindsided by this woman. "Have you ever known something before in your life that you haven't wanted to know, but you have? And you felt like you were supposed to do something about it?"

"I just, I don't know," Melanie said. "I mean you're just making a bigger deal out of it than it needs to be."

"Oh, wait a second!" Manzo didn't sound like he was play-acting. He had gone off-script. "I'm making a bigger deal out of it than I should? Someone got murdered, Melanie!"

"Well, I realize that."

"And I feel like I know! I don't think I'm making a big deal out of anything! If ever I'm going to make a big deal out of something, this should probably be it!"

Lamy watched helplessly as the man yelled into the receiver. Again, there was a cleansing silence. From across the time zones, Melanie's voice came back, sounding strong and reasonable.

"I know that someone's dead. I don't know why you're stressing yourself out about it. I said things back then that I regret. I said things a lot just to get attention. Just to get what I felt was the love that I needed."

"And telling me you had your father killed," Manzo, now calm, replied, "got you love?"

Melanie said, "It got me attention."

* * *

SERGEANT Lamy thanked Mike Manzo for his help and wished him luck in his new job. Lamy took the Maxwell ninety-minute cassette tape, labeled it I-85-147, and then handed it to a corporal who would store it in an evidence locker. The tape would be duplicated and transcribed, with copies going to the attorney general's office. Assistant Attorney General Tina Nadeau had been the one who signed off on the warrant for the telephone intercept.

"How did it go?" John Barthelmes asked Lamy. Barthelmes, who had been Lamy's subordinate when this case began, was now a captain and on his way to running the whole state police.

"There's nothing there," Lamy said. "The only thing she admitted is being a fruitcake."

"Did she say the other kid did it? Windhurst?"

"No. Wasn't worried if Manzo talked to the police either. Just pissed that he had nerve to call her."

"So where does that leave us with this case?"

Lamy shook his head. "There's nothing but hearsay." The anonymous letters, as tantalizing as they were, were not enough to prove Eric Windhurst killed Danny Paquette. No one could back up anything that was in the letters. The story remained a rumor, and prosecutors don't get convictions out of rumors.

Roland Lamy retired in 1994, taking a job in college campus security. Every week, he'd take his elderly mother out to dinner. Years later, a former senior official at the New Hampshire State Police said, "That Paquette case, that was one Lamy let get away," adding, "He never thought anyone could make that shot."

Part Three

THE HAIL MARY

Hell is murky. . . . Yet who would have thought
the old man to have had so much blood in him?

—William Shakespeare, *Macbeth*

— 17 —

The Chief

On a fall day in 2003, Chief Stephen Agrafiotis found himself waiting in the lobby of the New Hampshire Department of Justice, tugging nervously on the lapels of his suit. When the secretary finally announced that the attorney general would see him, he was pointed to an elevator and directed to the third floor. Agrafiotis ran a palm down his torso, flattening out the necktie against his crisp white shirt.

Although he was in plainclothes on this day, Agrafiotis had always taken pride in wearing a police uniform. He had loved looking at the sharp lines in the polyester shirts and pants, the shine of the new leather belts that held the service revolvers. He loved the badge. The best years of Agrafiotis's life were spent in the dark uniform of the Hooksett Police Department.

Encouraged by his mentor, Chief James Oliver, Agrafiotis had risen through the ranks of the Hooksett Police Department. The hills surrounding the small town of Hooksett were filled with even smaller towns and villages, all of them staffing modest police forces. There were often job openings in these towns for a chief. Agrafiotis had a solid résumé, a head for budgeting, and was an excellent candidate during interviews. It was no surprise to Oliver when Lieutenant Agrafiotis told him in 1992 he was leaving to become chief of neighboring Candia. The thirty-three-year-old's salary was thirty-eight thousand dollars.

Agrafiotis remained a resident of Hooksett and would get up each morning to drive the back roads to his new job. Every day, Agrafiotis would bank a turn at the McDonald's, go past the best Chinese restaurant in the state, and get on Whitehall Road. Each morning, he would drive past the former Paquette residence on his left; each night, he'd pass the place on his right. It was no longer a home; it had been purchased by a company and was now used for maintenance and storage, the lone commercial property in a rapidly developing residential area.

Each day as he passed by, his eyes unintentionally glanced at the Paquette house. Some days, his awareness of the home was nothing more than an instinctive feeling of discomfort. Other days, he'd play back his time there as a young patrolman, sorting the names of witnesses and suspects on index cards, wondering what more the task force of I-85-147 could have done to solve the case.

What really happened there? Agrafiotis would ask himself. He still didn't believe that it was a hunting accident that had ended the life of Danny Paquette.

The institutional memory of a cop can read like Grace Metalious's *Peyton Place*, with catalogues of secret drunks, crooks, and wife beaters living in bucolic New Hampshire neighborhoods. But the nagging frustration over the Danny Paquette case, a crime that Agrafiotis believed could have been solved, resonated with him in a more profound way.

Each day, the new chief would drive to work and focus on crime in another town. But each day he would pass 898 Whitehall Road and wonder to himself, *Where did that shot come from?*

* * *

IN 1999, Hooksett police chief James Oliver announced to the Police Commission and the Town Council that he would be retiring his post. He had been in charge of the department for twenty-one years, in addition to his sixteen years with the NYPD. The news came as a surprise to some but not those in the police community. Being a chief in a small town can be a thankless job. There is an intimacy among residents, among politicians, and among subordinates that implies a sense of access. To some people, access equates to influence. This is especially the case for those townspeople of means who get into trouble. Everyone knows the chief; therefore, everyone thinks he or she can smooth things over with the chief. Oliver didn't work that way, and many had become disappointed or embittered when they couldn't get tickets fixed or relatives sprung from jail.

Oliver's retirement meant the town was searching for a new chief for the first time in a generation. There were eighty candidates when the search began. There were some strong internal candidates who wanted the job as top cop, but the Police Commission also granted an interview to an old friend. Steve Agrafiotis, who had left his job in Candia to become chief in Raymond in 1997, impressed upon the commission that his roots were in Hooksett and this is where he wanted to be.

The police department that Agrafiotis wanted to run was very different from the department he had joined when getting there in 1983. Back then, there had only been seven officers on staff. It would not have been uncommon during a holiday or a weekend night for there to be no police officer on duty; emergency calls for the town would be forwarded to the state police. By 1999, the size of the department had tripled. This reflected both a stunning growth in the town's size and in the more serious nature of the police calls the swelling community generated.

"What would your goals for the department be?" he was asked.

Agrafiotis talked about modernizing the department. He would support the construction of a new safety complex to house the police and fire departments. Communications had to be upgraded because of the many "dead spots" on police radios across the town. He'd work to implement new technologies for record keeping and investigative services.

"You may think I'm crazy," he added sheepishly, "but if I came back, I'd like to find the money to reopen the Paquette homicide case."

The commissioners couldn't hide their smiles. "I don't have to tell you, chief," one of the commissioners said kindly, "that local departments don't have the resources—or the authority—to reopen homicide cases."

"No," he replied. "It wouldn't be my first priority. But if a murder did occur in 1985, I'd want it solved."

* * *

EACH autumn, Victor Paquette still made his round of telephone calls to each of the agencies involved in case I-85-147 and asked them for a status update. The biker dutifully called the New Hampshire State Police, the attorney general's office, and the Fish and Game Department. As the years rolled on, there were fewer and fewer people at any of those agencies who had even been around in November 1985 to remember the Danny Paquette shooting. Sergeant Roland Lamy had retired from the New Hampshire State Police. Attorney General Stephen Merrill went on to become governor. Assistant Attorney General Tina Nadeau was now a superior court judge, just like Kathy McGuire had become. Victor had fewer people he knew personally to growl at. Those he did growl at seemed less concerned as the years marched by.

Victor would also call the Hooksett Police Department. Ever since he had taken over for Oliver in 1999, Chief Stephen Agrafiotis asked that Victor's calls be patched directly through to him.

"Hello, Victor," Agrafiotis would always greet him warmly.

The biker had immediately remembered the mustachioed rookie cop from the original investigation. He'd always liked the little guy, so his tone with Agrafiotis was not nearly as antagonistic as with other officials. But it wasn't all together friendly either.

"Hello, Chief. I want to know what you've been doing to solve my brother's case."

"Victor, the law is very clear. There's very little the Hooksett police can do. We cannot investigate potential homicides on our own. Only the attorney general and the state police can do that."

Victor already knew that was the case. Chief Oliver had given him the same line each year, too.

"So you haven't done nothing, then?"

Agrafiotis told him they had not and urged him to contact the state police. The chief would then inquire about Victor's family and whether the old biker and gypsy welder was finding steady work. The calls were always brief, but longer with Agrafiotis than with any other investigator.

* * *

IN 2003, Victor made his annual phone calls with some reluctance. He had been getting the same answer for nearly 20 years, and he was sure the people he talked to were going to give him the same old line. Victor contemplated not calling, then he rubbed the tattoo on his right forearm. He looked at the depiction of the ace of spades being shot dead center, and he was emboldened to pick up the phone. If he no longer had the will to solve his brother's murder, who would?

The calls were the usual "nothing new" reports from law enforcement. *The only thing that has changed in the past two decades*, Victor thought, *is that I'm now using a push-button phone to call these bastards*.

Victor finished up his task by calling the Hooksett Police Department. He asked for the chief, as he had been instructed to do in years past.

"It's me. Victor," he said as if the chief would not recognize his husky voice and slow cadence. "I want to know if you intend to do anything about solving my brother's shooting."

There was a silence on the other end of the line. Victor heard the chief hem and haw for a moment. He was searching for a way to answer the question. At first, Victor prepared for some kind of brush-off. Instead there was something in the cop's voice that grabbed his attention.

"I don't want to get your hopes up," Agrafiotis began carefully. "I can't tell you what's happening, but we are doing something. Just trust me and hang on. I can't say any more than that, Victor."

"All right," said Victor calmly. "Thank you."

Victor took the comment at face value. Someone at the Hooksett Police Department was doing something about the case. Before he allowed any emotions to build, Victor remembered the response he had heard without fail in years past. *We can't investigate a homicide. Only the state police or attorney general can. The law is very clear.*

Victor realized he might as well ask the Boy Scouts to investigate his brother's death; they had about as much authority as the Hooksett police did.

Maybe he wouldn't call Agrafiotis next year.

* * *

PETER Heed, the attorney general, greeted Chief Agrafiotis with a hearty handshake. Heed was as jovial a prosecutor as one might ever come across. Short, with blond hair and gleaming white teeth, Heed dressed like a wealthy litigator but had the attitude of a friendly barber or shopkeeper. On his days off, he paddled with a club of die-hard kayakers on New Hampshire's rivers. The attorney general was often asked to demonstrate his baritone singing voice with animated renditions of "God Bless America" or "The Star-Spangled Banner" at public events. He would lustily oblige.

Heed had spent many years as the county attorney in Monadnock County, in the southwest corner of the state. County attorney was an elected position, and Heed perpetually enjoyed bipartisan support. Heed's ease and candor was a stark contrast to his predecessor, Attorney General Philip McLaughlin, whose professorial interlocutions at the scene of homicides were less than helpful to sound-bite-hungry journalists. But when newly appointed Attorney General Heed described how an attempted rapist died of a heart attack in the middle of the act, he blithely said, "It was instant justice," to the delight of the reporters.

Heed welcomed Agrafiotis as if the small-town chief were the ranking official in the room.

"Come on in my office, Chief," he said. Then he pointed to the man already sitting in a chair. "I'm sure you know this fellow."

Of course Agrafiotis knew the man. He was the chief's co-conspirator in this scheme, but the one with all the weight. James Oliver, the retired Hooksett chief, rose to shake hands with his protégé. Oliver was now a state representative for the town of Hooksett. True, Oliver was one of more than four hundred members of the New Hampshire General Court (a legislative body whose size is second only to that of the Chinese parliament), but Oliver sat on a committee that gave him a lot of access to the attorney general. Next to Agrafiotis and retired state police detective Roland Lamy, there was no one else who knew as much about the Paquette case as Representative James Oliver.

Heed was joined by Senior Assistant Attorney General Michael Delaney, the head of the Criminal Bureau. "So you'd like us to reopen the Paquette case?" he offered as a way to start the conversation.

"Not exactly," Agrafiotis said. This puzzled the attorney general. "I know the state police doesn't have a cold-case unit. I know that there are few resources that the attorney general's office has to pursue twenty-year-old homicides."

"So, what exactly are you proposing?"

This was it. "I want you to let us do it," Agrafiotis said. "And I want to pay for it."

* * *

CHIEF Agrafiotis had concocted a Hail Mary pass to kick-start the reopening of the Paquette case. Unlike the investigative work he had done in the past, Agrafiotis's new role would be administrative and largely invisible. His plan was unorthodox, bordering on blasphemy, but creative as all hell.

Hooksett, like so many other small New Hampshire municipalities, still ran its local government by vote at town meeting—the same way their colonial forefathers did. The town had an independent Police Commission, which predated the creation of its current nine-member Town Council. The Hooksett Police Department's annual budget proposal would be drawn up, submitted to the Town Council for review, then put up for a public vote at the spring town meeting. Up until the mid-1990s, most New Hampshire towns would still gather residents in the school gym or old meetinghouse and vote up or down the requests for new fire engines, repairs to schools, and the community's operating budget. The debates would often go well into the night and become a test of stamina between the frugal and the fatigued.

Chief Agrafiotis was able to use this arcane method of municipal finance to his advantage. The Town Council could only set a final budget figure for the Hooksett Police Department; how the money would be spent was left to the independent commission and the chief.

At the end of each fiscal year, Agrafiotis would look to see if there were any funds left over. For several years there hadn't been, as there were many demands on his growing department. But at the end of the 2002–2003 year, he'd discovered some extra money on the ledger. The chief already knew what he was going to do with the surplus. But he needed the buy-in of the Police Commission.

"This is what I propose," he told Fred Bishop, one of Hooksett's three police commissioners. "I want to take another look at the Danny Paquette case. Start from scratch. Go right back to the beginning and work forward."

Bishop didn't object. He remembered that Agrafiotis had declared his intentions to solve the mystery when he was an eager job candidate. But now he was chief, and Bishop felt it was important to support him. "If we went along with it," Bishop said, "how would you make it happen? The state police has no cold-case unit."

Agrafiotis rubbed his hands like a magician. "I want us to hire our own investigator dedicated to the case. Someone not on the force. A civilian. Someone not associated with the original investigation."

"How would we do that?"

"With our budget surplus. We'd finance the investigation. Travel. Overtime. Whatever."

Bishop looked at the dollar figure on the spreadsheet in front of him. "Can we do it for this amount?"

"Yes."

"So," the commissioner said, "why don't we go for it?"

"Because we don't have the authority to conduct our own homicide investigation," Agrafiotis responded. "Yet."

* * *

ATTORNEY General Peter Heed did not interrupt Chief Agrafiotis as he laid out his plan for running and financing the cold-case investigation. The normally chipper attorney was stone-faced and serious. Delaney, the consigliere to Heed, probed for more information.

"Which suspects would you focus on?"

"All of them," Agrafiotis said. "We'd start from the beginning. Not try to finish off threads that have gone nowhere."

"There seems to be no end to the list of solid suspects," Delaney commented. "An embezzler. Biker gangs. Teenage lovers. Any number of jealous husbands, boyfriends, or fathers. And a drug-dealing hippie."

"Or," Oliver offered, "somebody we've yet to look at."

"Right now, we'd favor none over the rest," the chief added. "We'll see where the evidence leads."

"I saw the tape of the *Unsolved Mysteries* show," Delaney said. "What's the likelihood it's connected to the mother's death in the 1960s?"

"None. It's bunk," said Oliver. "We never believed that for a second."

"Could it have been an accidental shooting?"

The two cops shifted in their chairs, and Oliver spoke. "Unfortunately, we've never been able to *disprove* that. So we have to leave it on the table as a possibility. We know there were men shooting target practice in the direction the bullet came."

"Too good of a shot," Agrafiotis interrupted his former boss. "Paquette was protected on both sides by the bulldozer. The bullet got him in the heart the split second he stood up from making a weld. The odds against that are . . . are . . . in the billions."

When the discussion ended, Heed swiveled a bit in his chair. He tapped his fingertips together in concentration. Then his usual smile burst forth from his face.

"I think we should go for it."

Chief Agrafiotis let out a sigh of relief. Oliver gave him an approving look.

"But," Heed cautioned, "we still have to do this by the book. I want your investigator to give regular reports to the Major Crimes Unit. If you find anything, if you start to get close, then I want the state police to come in and actively assist you. Remember, you still don't technically have the authority to conduct a homicide investigation in New Hampshire."

"Yes, General," Agrafiotis said, vigorously shaking his hand on the way out the door.

"No, no. It's just 'Pete.'"

Agrafiotis and Oliver walked to the elevator together. Delaney promised to assemble a task force to meet after the first of the year to work out logistics. Once the elevator doors closed on them, Oliver slapped Agrafiotis on the shoulder.

"You did it, Steve. No town our size has ever been allowed to do the legwork on a homicide like this. I never thought I'd see it, but you got the ball rolling again."

Agrafiotis again ran a hand down the necktie flapping between his lapels. He was in plainclothes, but at that moment, he had never felt so proud to wear a police uniform.

Danny Paquette was shot to death while welding in his yard on November 9, 1985. At first, investigators were unsure if he had been killed by a hunter's stray bullet. VICTOR PAQUETTE

In a family of six kids, Danny (left) was closest to older brother Victor (right), who would be a tireless campaigner for justice on Danny's behalf. VICTOR PAQUETTE

Hanging above the crime scene was a decorative ace of spades that Danny had welded. This picture was taken from the telephone wire where a .270 slug was later discovered.

HOOKSETT POLICE/NEW HAMPSHIRE DEPARTMENT OF JUSTICE

Danny Paquette was working at this bulldozer when a bullet pierced his chest, killing him instantly. Authorities knew that if the shot had not been random, it had to have been the work of a skilled marksman. HOOKSETT POLICE/NEW HAMPSHIRE DEPARTMENT OF JUSTICE

This aerial shot shows Whitehall Road as it looked in 1985. The Paquette property (1) is in the middle of the picture. The shot was fired from the tree line (2), while the shooter's car was hidden in a secluded cutout farther away (3). HOOKSETT POLICE/NEW HAMPSHIRE DEPARTMENT OF JUSTICE

Some of Danny's ex-in-laws lived in Hopkinton, New Hampshire. The bucolic town would prove over the years that it could keep its secrets. COURTESY OF THE AUTHORS

Exterior of Hopkinton High School, where unbeknownst to Danny Paquette, his stepdaughter, Melanie, was going to school.
COURTESY OF THE AUTHORS

Melanie Paquette had a secret crush on Eric Windhurst. In a moment of fear, she shared her darkest secret with him.
HOPKINTON HIGH YEARBOOK 1987,
HOPKINTON SCHOOL DISTRICT

Eric Windhurst was the popular captain of the soccer team. Fun-loving but impetuous, Eric would do anything for his friends.
HOPKINTON HIGH YEARBOOK 1986,
HOPKINTON SCHOOL DISTRICT

Kathleen McGuire, Melanie Paquette's aunt, was a homicide prosecutor when Danny was killed. She later became a superior court judge. Victor Paquette accused McGuire of stonewalling the investigation.
AP/WIDE WORLD PHOTOS

Eric Windhurst's mother was the heir to the Kimball land estate. Whole tracts of land were donated to the town by the family, including the Kimball cabins seen here on Kimball Pond. These cabins were host to many of Eric's parties. COURTESY OF THE AUTHORS

Hooksett police chief Steve Agrafiotis was a rookie on the Paquette case in 1985. When he became chief in 1999, he vowed to solve the case once and for all.
COURTESY OF THE AUTHORS

Retired officer Bill Shackford, seen here holding yearbook photos of Eric Windhurst and Melanie Paquette, was an unlikely choice to restart the investigation in 2004. COURTESY OF THE AUTHORS

Senior Assistant Attorney General Jeff Strelzin was ready to prosecute Windhurst; however, Strelzin felt there were some problems with the case. COURTESY OF THE AUTHORS

Eric Windhurst in August 2006, prepared to argue he acted in self-defense of Melanie when he shot Danny Paquette.
AP/WIDE WORLD PHOTOS

Melanie Paquette Cooper looked longingly at her children in Merrimack County Superior Court in Concord, December 1, 2006. She faced charges for her part in her stepfather's murder.
AP/WIDE WORLD PHOTOS

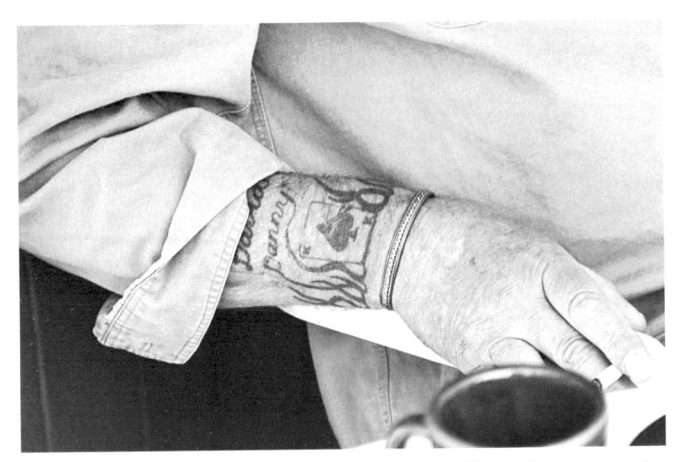

A spade being pierced by a bullet, the tattoo that Victor Paquette got in memory of his brother. Spades were a favorite design of Danny's.
COURTESY OF THE AUTHORS

Victor Paquette, Danny's hard-living biker brother, never gave up the fight to see his brother's killer brought to justice.
COURTESY OF THE AUTHORS

— 18 —

The Investigator

IT was winter 2003, more than ten years since Michael Manzo had telephoned Melanie Paquette Cooper in hopes of cracking the case. With the blessing of the attorney general, Hooksett chief of police Stephen Agrafiotis now had the task of finding someone to conduct this independent investigation. There were capable enough officers in his department, but the reality was that none of them could commit to one case. They would invariably be pulled away to do other work, investigating today's crime at the expense of yesterday's.

Agrafiotis would not have rolled the dice on his unorthodox investigation if he did not have someone in mind. But his choice was equally unorthodox.

* * *

AGRAFIOTIS had been grocery shopping one evening after work, and while pushing his carriage down the aisle, he passed a man he instantly recognized as Bill Shackford. He was examining cans, reading labels, and gently placing selections in his own carriage.

Shackford had been a member of the Hooksett Police Department in the 1970s. He retired, which for a police sleuth like Shackford meant he took a new job with another agency. He became a lieutenant with the Merrimack County Sheriff's Office, in charge of the department's criminal investigations.

He stayed in that position until 1985, when he became an investigator for the Merrimack County Attorney.

"Hello, sir." Shackford smiled and gave a friendly salute to the police chief. The two men shook hands, clearly pleased to see one another. They made an odd couple, standing and chatting among the soups and chowders. Agrafiotis adjusted his eyeglasses, which, along with his mustache, gave him the look of a short Groucho Marx. Shackford was tall and broad-shouldered, with a full head of hair that was combed, slicked, and impossibly black for his age. He was nearly eighty years old, but looked twenty or thirty years younger than that. Only the lines in his face gave it away. Shackford could have easily passed for a college football coach.

"Chief, I was wondering," Shackford asked, "is there any need for a part-time investigator at your department? I'm always looking for work to keep me busy."

Agrafiotis gave him a conspiratorial look. "Call me tomorrow at my office. I have an idea to run by you."

The next day, Shackford listened to the chief's plan to finance a new investigation into the Paquette killing. At the time of the shooting, Shackford had been working with the county and had had no role with any of the agencies lending a hand. Other than his acquaintance with Agrafiotis, Shackford had no connection to any of the original investigators; therefore, he would not be influenced by any of the theories or suspects previously developed by the I-85-147 task force. He agreed to backtrack all the evidence and start the probe all over again.

* * *

SENIOR Assistant Attorney General Michael Delaney called Agrafiotis to let him know a meeting between the Hooksett Police Department and the New Hampshire State Police (NHSP) Major Crimes Unit would be held on January 30, 2004. The attorney general's office would not be represented, but they expected a report.

"Bill, it looks like we're a go," the chief told his civilian investigator. "I want you to join me at this meeting with the state police and we'll go from there." The Hooksett Police

Commission had appropriated enough funds to pay Shackford to come in and work on the case one day a week.

"There's one thing we need to discuss," Shackford said. "What's my title going to be?" It wasn't a question of the veteran being hung up on rank or station or the other trappings of ego; it was a matter of practicality. How was he going to identify himself in person and on official documents?

This posed a sticky problem for Agrafiotis. Shackford had technically retired his badge years ago. Although he had been a lieutenant, Agrafiotis was not comfortable with part-time officers outranking full-time officers. It had been a point of controversy when he took the chief's position in Candia.

"We'll call you 'Investigator.'" For Shackford, that worked just fine.

* * *

CHIEF Steve Agrafiotis and Investigator Bill Shackford drove together on a blustery day to the office of the State Police Major Crime Unit in Concord, New Hampshire. The headquarters for the state police was in the Department of Safety Building, tucked among the other functional government facilities in a private state office park. These were largely administrative offices, where men in the forest green uniform of the NHSP mingled with Highway Safety, Fish and Game, and countless civil servants. Up until 1999, the commander of the NHSP was Colonel John Barthelmes, the trooper who had first taken over the Danny Paquette investigation.

The State Police Major Crime Unit was separated from the rest of state government apparatus. Its office was a tiny, house-shaped building at the city airport. Working there gave them access to the NHSP helicopter, but more important, it also gave them a measure of autonomy.

NHSP Lieutenant Russ Conte and Sergeant Mark Armaganian met with the Hooksett investigators and handed over the case file to Bill Shackford. He flipped through the first of about one thousand pages of documents dating back to November 1985.

"Oh," he said, turning to the chief and pointing to an old report. "Your handwriting is *terrible*."

"I know," Agrafiotis laughed. "My secretary can't read any of my notes to her."

Shackford took the copy of case file I-85-147 and brought it back to the Hooksett Police Department to review. He was troubled by what he read. Shackford had never seen an investigation like this one. The 1985 procedural seemed odd on second look. There were all sorts of holes in the work done by the detectives. He had never—ever—seen a material witness to a homicide mailed a written questionnaire.

Perhaps there really are clues to be found that the original team missed, he thought.

* * *

SHACKFORD started with a series of interviews of people from Hooksett who were around at the time of the shooting. He spent extensive time with Richard Duarte and Court Burton, the men who had been working on the property when Danny had been shot. He talked to neighbor Kevin Cote, who had rushed to perform CPR on Danny. He even tracked down Andy Myers, the telephone line repairman who'd discovered the blood-encrusted .270 bullet.

Shackford knocked on doors all around Whitehall Road, asking people if they remembered seeing anything out of the ordinary that Saturday morning twenty years earlier. It was a long shot, but much of what he was attempting to do was a long shot.

At one door, Shackford was greeted by woman in her midthirties named Lauren Gray*. He presumed she was a new home owner, someone who would not have lived there in 1985, but he was pleasantly surprised to learn the home actually belonged to the woman's parents.

"I remember the day very well. I was in junior high when that man was shot," she said. Gray invited the investigator in, and they sat at her elderly parents' kitchen table. She explained she was caretaking the house for them, as Mom and Dad were now "snowbirds" who spent the winter months in Boca Raton, Florida.

---

* Denotes pseudonym

Noting her age and the fact she'd grown up in the neighborhood, Shackford gently inquired whether she'd had any interactions with Danny Paquette.

"Not me," Gray told him. "But there were rumors about the Ouimette girls."

"What do you remember about that day?"

"I remember seeing a car parked in a suspicious place by Dube Pond that morning." Gray described a secluded dirt road that ran off the main road not far from the Paquette property. It was a cutout that had been left behind when Whitehall Road had been straightened decades earlier. There were some bushes and brush to hide the road from traffic, and it was a popular spot for underage drinkers and teen lovers.

"We'd see people park there at night, but almost never during the day," she claimed. "I told the police officer who came to my house about it. He said it was probably a hunter."

Shackford was stunned. There were pages and pages of police reports about cars parked alongside area roads, but there was no mention of any cars on this dirt cutout in the documentation. Nor was there any mention from any of the original investigators that they had interviewed this young girl.

If someone had stood at the back edge of the property line and fired at Danny Paquette, it was conceivable they would have parked at that cutout to get to that vantage point.

"Do you remember anything about the car? A plate? A model? A color?"

"All I remember was that it was a dark Volkswagen. Maybe blue or black."

Afterward, Shackford looked up whether any one of the many suspects they had drove a dark-colored Volkswagen in 1985. There was only one: Eric Windhurst.

* * *

THE next week, Investigator Bill Shackford visited the police department in Hopkinton to get some information about Eric Windhurst. When Police Chief David Wheeler heard about Shackford's inquiry, he suggested the investigator talk to Officer Bill Simpson. Simpson was out of the office on sick leave, but Wheeler suggested he call him at home.

Shackford recognized Simpson's name from Lamy's notes. He was the young cop who'd sat in on Lamy's interview of Ricky Patenaude back in 1993. Shackford used a station phone to ring up Simpson and explain his assignment. Over the phone, the officer seemed stiff, reticent about the nature of the questioning.

"I've known Eric for many years. We were in grade school and high school together. We both had an interest in guns and would target practice together." Simpson added, "He hasn't been around town much since he divorced."

He described for Shackford how Eric would make his own ammunition by hand, reloading the spent shells with gunpowder and using a press to attach the bullet. Shackford's son also made his own ammunition, and the investigator was impressed.

"What did he shoot with?"

"Eric owned a model 77 Ruger. It was a .270 caliber."

"How do you know he had this model 77 Ruger?" he asked.

"I saw him with it. It was a birthday present. From his father, I think. His father owned a .270, too." Shackford remembered the elder Windhurst's weapon. It was the Winchester model 70 that had been test-fired by the crime lab and ruled out as the rifle that launched the fatal shot. But there was no mention in any of the police reports of Eric Windhurst owning a Ruger model 77 rifle.

"Does he have a police record in town?" Shackford pressed.

"No," Simpson said flatly. "He was a wild kid as a teen, but he's never been arrested by us as an adult."

* * *

THE stray bullet theory was one that hung like an albatross around the necks of investigators: a gaggle of men shooting at bottles and cans in a sand pit to the north of the property at the time of the killing. Shackford needed a way to eliminate this red herring once and for all.

He contacted Hooksett's Forest Fire Warden, Harold Murray. For decades Murray had patrolled the town's woods and had become an expert at map and compass reading. Although Murray probably couldn't turn on his grandkid's iPod, the longtime warden was a master at Global Positioning Systems

(GPS). He felt GPS could really benefit the fire service and often gave professional seminars about the topic.

"Do you think you could help me with a special project?" Shackford asked.

Murray took GPS measurements at the sand pit: 043 degrees 04' 21.52" N, 071 degrees 26' 03.87" N. Then he added the coordinates for the Paquette residence: 043 degrees 03' 57.42" N, 071 degrees 24' 22.60" W. Then he ran the numbers.

The distance between the two points was one mile and 2,390 feet. That was still within the range of probability for a projectile to travel that far. But Murray discovered something that the 1985 investigators had failed to consider. Murray overlaid the GPS data with a topographical map and drew a straight line between the two points. The Paquette house was elevated 307 feet higher than the pit. Because the sand pit was so much lower, any shot from there would have to clear so many hills and trees that the bullet would sail far above Paquette's house. The only way a bullet could make it all the way to Whitehall Road on a straight line would be if it traveled more than one mile underground and popped out of a gopher hole before striking the victim.

Shackford felt he had finally disproved the stray bullet theory once and for all.

* * *

HOPKINTON Officer Bill Simpson was surprised to see the Hooksett police investigator he'd talked to on the phone two months earlier waiting to meet with him at the station. When Bill Shackford stood up from the table, he was as broad as a barn door.

Shackford was accompanied by a detective from the state police. Sergeant Mark Armaganian had been keeping tabs on Shackford's work, and when the investigator told him he thought he was getting close to a suspect, Armaganian thought it was time to take a more active role in case I-85-147.

"Did you ever hear rumors around town about Eric Windhurst killing a man?" Armaganian asked Officer Simpson.

"No. I never heard that."

"Were you friends with Eric in high school?" Armaganian continued.

"I did not hang out with his circle of friends."

"That would be Matt Quinn, Craig Metzger, Dee Clark, and Ricky Patenaude?"

"Yes."

"What do you know about Melanie Paquette?"

"I don't remember very much about her. She played soccer."

"Eric and Melanie had an alibi for the day of the shooting. They said they went to a field hockey game in Plymouth. No one remembers seeing them there. What do you make of that?"

"Eric Windhurst was the most popular kid in school," Simpson replied. "He was active in sports. He mingled easily with all the social cliques. If he was at that field hockey game, he would have been noticed."

"Was Windhurst a good shot?" Shackford asked.

"Yes. Probably the best in town. He always got the big buck."

"Was he talented enough to hit a small target with precision from a long distance? Could he do it from three hundred yards or more?"

"Yes, he could do that. I've seen him hit small game on the fly. He was amazing. I don't ever remember him missing." Simpson sighed. "Eric was a hell of a shot."

* * *

INVESTIGATOR Bill Shackford huddled with Chief Steve Agrafiotis and the NHSP investigators, Sergeant Mark Armaganian and Lieutenant Russ Conte. There was an awful lot of circumstantial evidence pointing at the then-teenage Eric Windhurst as being the killer of Danny Paquette.

How do we prove that Windhurst shot that bullet? they asked each other. The Ruger 77 he'd owned could not presently be located or linked to the bullet they had. Shackford arranged for a Fish and Game diver to search the bottom of Dube Pond, in hopes the shooter had thrown the murder weapon into the water while fleeing to the dirt-road cutout. The diver found nothing.

The anonymous letters suggested that his friends knew what happened, but all of them had denied that in the past.

"Twenty years is a long time," Lieutenant Conte offered. "People's attitudes change. Their loyalties change."

"We've done an awful lot of snooping in a small town the past five months," Agrafiotis said. "Sooner or later Windhurst is going to find out we're closing in on him."

The men agreed there was one rock that had been left unturned in the previous investigation, and they needed to try kicking it over. They needed to interrogate Melanie Paquette Cooper—face-to-face.

— 19 —

Tell Me the Truth

By the time Bill Shackford and the two sergeants from the New Hampshire State Police rang the doorbell to Melanie Cooper's Boise, Idaho, residence on July 14, 2004, it was already one hundred and five degrees and not even noon. All three of the men were wearing suits. One was also wearing a microphone to record anything they heard. They'd all started sweating the minute they got out of the rental car.

After the doorbell sounded, the men waited in silence. Sergeant Mark Armaganian was accompanied by Sergeant Mark Mudgett, a colleague from the State Police Major Crimes Unit who knew how to operate a polygraph. None of them spoke aloud the thought that had rumbled around in the backs of their minds for the many hours of jet flight and a layover in Milwaukee. *This is a Hail Mary pass. What do we do if she shuts the door on us? This trip will have been for nothing, and our investigation might not recover.*

After what seemed like an eternity, the door finally opened. Standing in front of the men was Melanie Paquette Cooper. There was no doubt about it. Her hair was a little longer, but despite the decades, she was still petite, with a teenager's face. Her forehead glistened with perspiration, but not from the arid summer morning. She was wearing workout clothes and had been exercising in her basement when the men arrived. Inside the house, her children were playing so quietly that the investigators didn't initially even realize they were there.

"Are you Melanie Cooper?" Armaganian asked firmly.

"Yes, I am." The woman was slightly out of breath, mopping her neck with a towel.

The state trooper smiled politely and introduced his companions. When he indicated they were from New Hampshire, the woman's gaze grew serious. "We're here looking at your stepfather's case. We still have some questions and need some information. Would you be willing to talk to us?"

This is it, they thought. *All of the work of the past six months—the past eighteen years—is coming down to this moment.*

Melanie Paquette Cooper regarded the three men on her doorstep. Her tiny body was like a barricade keeping these three interlopers from entering. Inside her house was her family, her mementos, the life she had created since leaving Hopkinton, New Hampshire. Now staring at these men, she might have realized she had not built a new life so much as she had run from the old one. She later admitted that she'd always known this day would come, that men like these would someday arrive to ask her about that time from high school, shattering everything that separated her from it.

"Sure," she said, to the utter amazement of the officers. "I'll answer your questions."

* * *

AFTER the end of her first year at Hopkinton High, in which she had been a sophomore from September 1985 to June 1986, Melanie Paquette's mood had become increasingly black. Life at the Hopkinton Poor Farm with her aunt and uncle had not gone as smoothly as she had hoped when she boarded her first plane from Alaska. Uncle Phil treated her well enough, but her perpetual friction with her aunt Kathy was wearing on her. Melanie and Kathy had tried everything, including going to therapy together. But in the end, it only accelerated the murderous path the fifteen-year-old was on.

When school ended for the summer, Denise Paquette came to visit her estranged family. It was the first time she had been back to New Hampshire since leaving five years earlier. Melanie's reunion with her mother was tearful.

"I've missed you so much, Mom."

"I missed you too, baby."

"I'm so homesick."

"Then come back to Wasilla with me."

Denise asked to speak privately with Phil and Kathy. The couple was getting ready to leave for a dinner party, and they were dressed in fine clothes for their evening out. Melanie was told to stay in her room, but instead she stood in the hall, listening over the banister to the conversation below.

The words grew heated, as Denise insisted she had Melanie's best interests at heart, while her sister-in-law asserted that Melanie would be better off staying in Hopkinton.

Twenty years later, Melanie would recall that at the climax of the fight, Kathy McGuire said something else, something that so offended Denise that she never forgave her for it.

After the Messiers left for their engagement, Denise helped her daughter throw all of her clothes in bags and boxes. There would be no letter, no notice, other than an empty room and closet for the Messiers to discover on their return. Melanie was returning to Alaska the same way she'd originally gone: secretly, swiftly, in the middle of the night.

* * *

MELANIE found that life back in Wasilla, Alaska, was darker and more unwelcoming than she remembered. Denise Paquette's finances were none the better now that her oldest daughter had returned to the fold. She'd had enough trouble taking care of her younger daughters, Audrey and Caroline, for the past year. Melanie found herself back at a large high school, just another girl who melted into the background. Here, she was just another player on the girls' soccer team; she wasn't someone special.

Her life in Alaska had begun to spin out of control, just as it had before she'd left Wasilla for Hopkinton. Twenty years later, Melanie would tell authorities that she became suicidal at the time. She ran away from home, crashing for a short time with a friend of her mother. In a bid for attention, Melanie hit herself in the face with a piece of wood and claimed to have been raped.

Among the people Melanie told about the rape was Eric Windhurst, with whom she continued to communicate through letters. She seemed to be comforted by his determination to protect her. In one letter, she also told Eric how she had been mugged at her high school soccer field, that the attacker had had a knife but she ran away. The tale got the desired response: more attention from Eric. Later, she would tell Eric she'd made up the whole story; the mugging never happened. She would tell police in 2004 that her rape story was also a fabrication.

* * *

DENISE called her brother in New Hampshire again. "Can Melanie come back?" she asked. When the weather turned warm, Melanie flew to New England and took summer courses to complete the credits she needed before senior year.

The fall of 1987, Melanie Paquette returned to the halls of Hopkinton High. She earned back her spot on the Hopkinton boy's soccer team. But she didn't wear the number 20 as she had in 1985–1986; this time she wore 18, Eric's old number.

After graduation, Melanie went on to the University of New Hampshire (UNH). She remained close with Eric Windhurst but made new friends at college, too. Among the most unlikely of her new gal-pals was Thea Koonz, who had been her high school rival for Eric's attention and who was still dating Eric long distance when Eric joined the marines and Thea arrived on campus that September. As much as she had been wary of Melanie at Hopkinton High, Thea secretly felt sympathy for the girl. Melanie was still socially awkward with those outside of the soccer clique. One night, when Melanie was turned away at the door of a high school party because the host didn't think she was cool enough to come in, Thea chased the tearful Melanie down in her car and gave her a ride home to the Poor Farm. Now UNH freshmen, the girls lived in the same dorm. Melanie sealed her friendship with Thea by making her a mix tape of her favorite songs.

When she wasn't on campus, Melanie would stay at her grandparents' home in Manchester. She thought about sticking it out another year with the Messiers, but the tension between her and Kathy had never truly dissipated.

Uninspired by any of her classes, Melanie gave up her studies and partied her way out of UNH. Her former roommate, Alice Grimes*, transferred from UNH to Brigham Young University in Provo in 1989. Alice asked Melanie if she wanted to stay in the BYU campus housing with her. Melanie was not interested in enrolling in BYU, but she was enamored with the idea of moving to Utah. At one point during their time in Alaska, Denise Paquette had made the family join the Church of Jesus Christ of Latter-day Saints (LDS). Melanie did her best to stay active in LDS, and the opportunity to move to Mormon country seemed too good to pass up. Melanie left New Hampshire for a better life out west and planned to never look back.

In Utah, Melanie's life finally began to turn around. David Cooper was an idealistic BYU student with dark hair and a warm smile. He had a very patient personality, and he made Melanie feel safe. The couple met in the fall of 1989; they quickly married in January of 1990. Their first child soon followed.

When he finished at Brigham Young, David Cooper found a job buying cars at auction. He was transferred to Southern California, and the young couple, who soon had two children, bounced around from apartment to house to apartment, depending on where the work took them. Cooper worked as a buyer until 1997, when the California economy collapsed. With a wife and now three children to feed, Cooper tried striking out on his own as a buyer in northern California, but he had little luck.

When Melanie became pregnant with her fourth child, the Coopers moved to Portland, Oregon, to live with Melanie's mother, Denise Paquette. Her daughters now grown, Denise had returned to the Lower 48, but even with Danny long gone, she stayed clear of New Hampshire. The relationship between Denise and Melanie was prickly. Time and distance hadn't made the issues between them wane. They'd both shouldered significant emotional baggage for years, and by both of their accounts, there were many things they didn't talk about.

Cooper eventually got a job as an insurance adjuster for a major company. He took the children and Melanie, now with

---

* Donates pseudonym

a fifth baby on the way, as well as his mother-in-law, Denise, and moved the whole family to Boise, Idaho. The return of a steady paycheck in their bank account was a welcome change. Cooper thought he knew a lot about cars after years of buying them, but his eyes were opened to a whole other side of the industry dealing with collision repair.

"I have an idea for a business we can run," Cooper said to his wife one day in early 2004.

He told Melanie he had been approached to open a Yamaha dealership. The franchise area would be in Wyoming. Melanie was excited; she would be a co-owner in the dealership.

"Motorcycles, huh?" She laughed at the thought. She looked around their modest Boise home. There were three daughters and two sons, from teen to toddler, clanking around the small living spaces. Melanie worried how the children would take the news about moving again, especially the older ones. Still, they would have a couple of months to worry about finding a new home while David secured floor-plan financing and built his dealership. They'd make it work, just like they always had.

* * *

SERGEANT Mark Armaganian and Investigator Bill Shackford sat down in an air-conditioned room at the Ada County Sheriff's Office at 11:50 a.m. Melanie Paquette Cooper followed them in. She had hastily made arrangements for a babysitter to watch her kids before she went with the police, driving her own car to the station. She was repeatedly told she wasn't under arrest and was free to go as she pleased.

Before they began, Armaganian asked Shackford for the keys to the rental car so he could move it out of the tow zone they'd parked in. That left the young mother alone with the old detective.

"You have three children?" he asked.

"Five."

"Five children? How wonderful." Shackford was imposing in about a hundred different ways, but he was really just a big teddy bear. "Do you know how many grandchildren that's going to be?"

"I'm hoping at least twenty-five. That's the fun part," she said proudly. Then her voiced trailed off a bit. "They're good kids. They're really good kids. I'm really enjoying them."

"I have eight grandchildren," Shackford confessed, "and eight great-grandchildren."

Armaganian returned to the room and sat down with a notebook. "Again, thank you for coming down today. This is very informal. You're helping us try to get back to 1985. So Bill and I . . ."

"So what if I didn't want to do it?" Melanie suddenly piped up. "What then?"

Armaganian took a serious and thoughtful approach, as if he hadn't until that moment considered what a terrible disservice Melanie would be doing to herself if she didn't cooperate. "We'd have to get a grand jury subpoena and ship you back to New Hampshire."

Melanie nodded in agreement. She didn't want to go through that.

"That's so impersonal it's not funny," the sergeant assured her. "So for us to incur the cost of coming out here to sit down and talk to you, I think this is a way better scenario. But, if at any point you don't want to talk to us anymore, that's fine."

After getting some of her personal information, Armaganian slowly led Melanie through a retelling of her times in Alaska and Hopkinton and about her difficulties with her mother and her aunt. When the investigator sensed the mood was right, he gently asked if she was comfortable talking about Danny.

"It's easier for me now than it was back then," she said. "I've come to grips with a lot of things."

Melanie said that she'd never liked Danny Paquette. Right from the beginning of her mother's reunion with her former sweetheart, Danny had treated Melanie differently. She saw that in the way he interacted with Jennifer, the daughter he had with his first wife, Stephanie. Though roughly the same age, Melanie detected there was a measure of warmth missing from her stepfather's interactions with her. She described a man who seemed to have two personalities: a person who would toss a ball with a child for hours, then become angry and abusive without warning. Melanie said the emotional abuse had started at a young age and grew into physical and then sexual abuse.

"I think I was nine when the sex started. I think it was around the time my mom left him and the court ordered that I had to keep going back." She said Danny never molested her sisters. Only her, the stepdaughter. "I know he was just doing it to get back at my mom. But I never told my mom what was going on. I was too afraid."

Melanie told the detectives that Danny started subtly, by trying to talk to her about the birds and the bees. The talks made her uncomfortable, but he continued. Soon, the lesson became visual, as Danny would show her his penis. Then, to demonstrate how a grown woman should feel, he would touch her. He'd invite her into the shower with him. His moves were unhurried, deliberate. The little girl had no idea something bad was being done to her.

* * *

WITH kid gloves, the sergeant guided Melanie through a rundown of where she was and what she had been doing on November 9, 1985. She answered hesitantly, saying she remembered she was at some ball game. She told them the names of her friends: Matt Quinn, Thea Koonz, and Eric Windhurst. She gave them the old alibi, not wavering much from the story they'd heard so many times before.

Melanie noticed Sergeant Armaganian and Investigator Shackford give each other looks signifying they were satisfied with what they heard. The sergeant's body language indicated he was getting ready to wrap this up.

"Now, Melanie, we have all your statements," he said. "All we have to do before we leave is verify your statements. And we do that with a polygraph. Voluntary, of course."

Melanie gave them an anxious look. "I mean, I don't know. I'm just curious all of a sudden. I haven't heard about this in so long, then all of a sudden, here it is. I mean, you don't call to get an appointment first. You just show up . . ."

Armaganian turned the wattage up on his smile, trying to soothe her. "That's the way we do business. We go and physically knock on the doors. If you still lived in Hopkinton, it would be a lot easier to do."

She looked back and forth between the men. "So how does the polygraph work?"

"We verify exactly what you told us," he said, "and then we're on a plane and out of your hair."

"They're pretty accurate?"

"Very accurate."

"Do you have a machine or something?"

"Yes. The other man who was with us will set it up."

"It's not like . . . *shots* . . . right?"

Armaganian nearly laughed out loud at the thought. "No. Oh, God no."

"It's not truth serum?" Melanie realized how naive she sounded. The cops ribbed the Mormon mother good-naturedly about the TV shows she must watch in Idaho, assuring her that a real-life polygraph was not the same as a fictionalized interrogation.

Armaganian offered Melanie the bathroom while they excused themselves to ready the polygraph. *We don't have truth serum*, he probably thought, *but sometimes I wish we did.*

* * *

NEW Hampshire State Police sergeant Mark Mudgett was a little taller than his colleague Sergeant Mark Armaganian, with the muscular build of a state trooper. His head was shorn to his skull to disguise a receding hairline. He looked tough, but he knew how not to be. Mudgett had observed the interview of Melanie Paquette Cooper on video from an adjacent room. Armaganian had done a masterful job so far guiding her to this point. Mudgett needed to match that good showing and finish the job.

Mudgett spent a lot of time explaining how the polygraph would work. He told Melanie they would talk for a long time—maybe an hour or more—before he even put the equipment on her. The detective explained that the results of the polygraph were not admissible in any New Hampshire court but anything said to him was. She was read her Miranda rights, and Mudgett reiterated that she wasn't in custody. He simply asked that if she wanted to leave that she allow him to disconnect the ten-thousand-dollars' worth of equipment from her body.

"No matter what happens here today, you get to go home and do what you need to do with your children and spend time with your husband, and all that kind of stuff," Mudgett assured her.

For the first twenty minutes of their meeting, Mudgett did all the talking. He thought he knew all the right buttons to push with Melanie: her love of her family, her faith in God, and the nagging guilt she felt. She also seemed concerned with the mysterious lie detector he brought with him.

"This whole procedure is about to determine your honesty, and if you walk out of here failing this test, there's going to be a cloud over your head. A cloud of suspicion that you had something major league to do with the death of Danny Paquette," he said. "You're a human being, just like I am. Nobody's perfect. I only know one person who was perfect, and he was here a long time ago, but his spirit lives on."

Melanie nodded at the reference, soothed by Mudgett's understanding of her faith.

"A lot of people come in here and think if they tell 98 percent of the truth they're going to pass a polygraph test. Melanie, you're an adult. You seem to have a reasonable sense of intelligence. Believe me when I say this: if you leave 2 percent of what's not the truth, it's going to be written as a lie. Because you can't change parts of how your body functions."

Melanie kept looking at the polygraph on the table.

Sergeant Mudgett continued speaking earnestly to his subject. "These investigators have flown a great distance to come talk to you, and they need your cooperation. Not 98 percent of it. We need 100 percent of it. From one parent to another, from a teacher to another. Do the right thing, tell the truth, and you'll find that the results of that will make you feel so much better when you leave here." For good measure, he added, "Life isn't always pleasant. If it were, then we wouldn't need Him to look over us, would we?"

"I guess you're right."

Mudgett leaned forward. "Melanie," he asked her, "are you going to tell me the truth?"

Melanie blanched. She rubbed her thumbs over her fingers.

"Can I have a moment alone?" she asked. "I want to say a prayer."

Mudgett agreed and left the room. He quickly joined Armaganian and Shackford, who were watching on video. There wasn't anything stopping them from talking to one another, from openly strategizing or comparing notes. Instead, they were transfixed by the picture of the baby-faced woman sitting alone in Interview 1.

Melanie stared at the polygraph left on the table, its wires strewn. Then, she clasped her hands and pressed them to her forehead. She sat in the chair for what seemed to be an eternity, unaware she was being watched by the men who had shown up on her door that morning, cracking the seams of her peaceful life. She wiped little tears from her cheeks, then rapped on the door to let Mudgett know it was fine for him to enter.

"Melanie, are you ready?"

"Yes," she said, sounding stronger than she had up to that point. "I'm ready to tell you what happened."

— 20 —

Best Friends

It was November 1985 in Hopkinton, New Hampshire. Sophomore Melanie Paquette, the new girl in school, was beginning to find her way in the unfamiliar waters of a new town. She had a few girlfriends with whom to gossip and escape lunchroom isolation. She dated a boy from her French class, then went out with a guy named Andrew Cheney. She was getting faster and tougher on the boys' soccer team. She was not a star, but she worked hard to make her captain, junior Eric Windhurst, proud.

Philip Messier and Kathleen McGuire made some phone calls to Alaska. "We want to file for Melanie's guardianship. Let us do it," Philip pleaded with his sister, Denise. "She'll be able to get health insurance. If I'm her legal guardian, she can get free airfare from the airline. She'll be able to visit you more often."

"What about Danny?" Denise Paquette asked. Her ex-husband had legally adopted Melanie when she was a baby. She wondered if he had legal standing in this.

Kathleen told her sister-in-law that she would file a motion with the probate court to keep the proceedings sealed and secret from Danny. It would require her to explain in an affidavit the reasons why Danny was a danger to Melanie. Denise Paquette understood what that meant. Assured of the secrecy of the proceedings, Denise agreed it would be in

Melanie's best interest to have them move forward with the legal guardianship.

Kathleen McGuire drafted the document herself. It ran on for five pages, making a convincing argument that the minor child had been a victim of physical and sexual abuse at the hands of Daniel Paquette. Saying Melanie's "interests would be severely and irreparably harmed," they argued that the guardianship proceedings should not include him. The assistant attorney general hoped the judge would see the important need for discretion.

But on Monday, November 5, 1985, the judge ruled that Danny did in fact have a legal standing in the guardianship hearing and denied the Messiers' motion to exclude him from the proceedings. Realizing that if they went forward Danny would be notified of Melanie's return to the state, the Messiers withdrew their guardianship request.

* * *

AT the same time as the guardianship proceeding, Kathleen McGuire decided to get her niece some counseling. Their relationship still dripped with tension and spiteful arguments. She asked around the office for the name of a counselor who worked well with kids and was given Peggy Upton's name.

Only the three people who were there know exactly what happened behind the closed doors of Peggy Upton's office. The counselor's notes of the session have been lost. But based on what Melanie Paquette Cooper would later say about the meeting, the consequences of the therapy session were murderous.

Upton spent some time alone with McGuire and then brought Melanie into the conversation. After some perfunctory biographical questions, the counselor asked the girl about her strained relationship with her aunt. Melanie acknowledged that her aunt was trying as hard as she could to bridge the gap and perhaps she was too immature to appreciate her aunt Kathy's efforts.

Sometime during the discussion, the topic of Danny Paquette came up. The name elicited such a reaction from the teenager that Upton could not fail to inquire further. Melanie pushed back; she had been under the impression the counselor didn't know about the molestation and they weren't going to discuss it. She accused her aunt of revealing the secret to Upton, a claim Kathleen and the counselor both denied.

Melanie felt ambushed, deceived. She didn't want to say anything more about the abuse. There was so much that had happened to her, so much that she wanted to forget. She wanted to forget how Danny would run his hands all over her, how he'd pull her into the shower with him, how he'd climb into her bed at night. She wanted to forget the crazy behavior he displayed, like rearranging the furniture or writing all over the walls. He would hide in the dark and jump out to scare her. She wanted to forget how Danny made her hang from a chin-up bar in the garage and then turned on his welder's torch, threatening to burn her if she let go. She saw him use that same blow torch to burn live field mice. She cried when he threatened to do the same thing to her mother. She had watched in horror as Danny killed her cat. The more she cried, the louder he laughed.

To keep Melanie quiet about the sexual abuse, Danny would put a pistol to his stepdaughter's head. It was the same pistol he had purchased when he threatened Denise before his commitment to the state hospital. Danny would rest the nozzle on Melanie's temple and pull the trigger. The girl never knew if it was loaded, not until she heard the hammer go *click*. He'd take away the gun and remind her to never discuss the things he did to her. *It's our little secret.*

Although she would recount these terrors to investigators in 2004, how much of her life she revealed in that 1985 therapy session is unknown. Melanie did, however, confirm Upton's questions about whether her stepfather had molested her. "He's a monster," Melanie told her.

Upton told Melanie and her aunt that, as a counselor, she had a professional and legal obligation to report the sexual abuse to the authorities. New Hampshire had a mandatory reporting law.

Melanie was shocked when Upton said she was going to notify the New Hampshire State Department of Children and Youth Services, who would in turn contact the Hooksett police. She begged and yelled but could not convince the counselor to keep the contents of their discussion confidential. "I won't cooperate with an investigation," she told them, a fact that Upton passed to authorities.

Melanie felt betrayed, betrayed by both her family and the system. It was not the embarrassment or stigma of being identified as a victim of sexual abuse that frightened her. She no longer feared her past as much as she feared an uncertain future.

* * *

THAT night, Melanie called Eric Windhurst and told him about the abuse. She went into the whole story. She told him about her stepfather's stay in the mental hospital, the years of abuse and molestation that had preceded their midnight exodus to Alaska, her aunt and uncle's guardianship attempt, and the debacle at the therapist's office. She then told him that, any day now, officials from the New Hampshire State Department of Health and Human Services would be contacting the Hooksett police. It was only a matter of time before Danny would learn she was secretly living in Hopkinton.

* * *

ON Wednesday, November 7, 1985—two days after the judge denied excluding Danny from the Messiers' attempted guardianship proceedings—Melanie walked past the gymnasium at Hopkinton High School during her free period. There were some students shooting hoops, the thunderous bounces reverberating off the concrete walls, amplified by the wooden bleachers that lined them. Eric was inside the gym, and he summoned her over to where he was sitting on the bleachers with Matt Quinn. "We've been talking about the situation with your stepfather," he said.

Melanie didn't appear to want to have this conversation with Matt Quinn present, but she clearly needed to talk about it. The boys watched her face as she talked about her fear that her father would find out where she was. Her fright was palpable, and it caused both boys' own hearts to pump spastically.

Twenty years later, both men would separately say they had never seen such intense fear in the eyes of one person.

Melanie would recall that Eric said the line first.

"Do you want your dad dead?" Eric asked her.

"Yeah, I want him dead," Melanie replied.

"Well, I've got connections," Eric said. "Do you? Do you want him dead?"

There was an arrogance to Eric Windhurst, a kind of pride and confidence that was rooted in his Yankee upbringing and nourished by the popularity he'd attained in school. He was also just seventeen, every emotion inflamed by the testosterone that fueled his teenage body. He thought himself to be a good person, someone who would do anything for his friends. This may have come in part from time spent with his older brother Trapper, who he saw as a John Wayne type, the kind of man he hoped to be someday. But without the nuance of experience, the maturity of years, Eric saw things without subtlety, or patience; there were only decisions and actions. There was no gray, only opaque black and translucent white.

As Eric heard the story, he watched Melanie's eyes closely as she poured her pain and fear into her words, and one thought burned into his mind. *Every adult in this girl's life has failed her.* This was something he believed to his core.

Matt Quinn's eyes bounced back and forth between Eric's and Melanie's faces. "Easy, Rambo," he said to his friend. "No one is killing anyone."

"That's right," Eric said, exhaling slowly. He now seemed deflated, his moment over. "No one's killing anyone."

* * *

BEFORE school ended for the day, Matt Quinn cornered Eric Windhurst in the bathroom. He'd felt sick since Melanie had walked up to them in the gym and spilled her guts; a knot had formed in his stomach as he realized the words Eric had spoken might be more than teen bravado. It was so bad he couldn't eat his lunch.

"Don't fucking do it," Matt confronted his friend.

"What? What are you talking about?" Eric asked.

Matt pressed on. "Whatever you're thinking about doing for her, don't fucking do it. You're seventeen; I'm sixteen," he said. "This could ruin our whole lives. Do you understand that?"

"I'm not going to do anything," Eric said. "What do you think? I'm fucking crazy?"

"I don't think you're crazy," Matt replied. "I'm scared for

Melanie, too. And that guy probably does deserve to get shot in the head. But you and I aren't going to do it."

"OK, OK. I hear you."

Quinn thought his friend answered too fast. "I'm fucking serious, Eric. Don't do it."

Eric Windhurst's charming smile returned. "I swear."

* * *

MATT Quinn thought about his bathroom confrontation with Eric and wondered if Melanie would come to the cabins that Friday night, November 8, 1985. He was still worried about Eric, concerned that he might go off on some damn foolhardy crusade like a White Knight.

Matt Quinn had known Eric Windhurst since first grade. Along with Davis "Dee" Clark, Craig Metzger, and even Ricky Patenaude, they were a tight gang of friends, and Eric Windhurst was their de facto leader. But Quinn didn't consider Eric his *best* friend; Dee Clark was Matt's closest friend in the world. In fact, when asked years later, none of the gang identified Eric as their best friend.

The party in the cabin that night was mellow. The girl's field hockey team was playing in the state finals the next morning, so the crowd was thinned out.

"I gotta whiz," Eric said to the crowd, gesturing for Matt to follow him outside.

Matt trailed Eric, who paused in the dark abscess between the two illuminated windows. Because things had been weird between them since Wednesday, he wondered if he should offer Eric a preemptive apology.

"I killed him," Eric said suddenly.

"What?" Matt sputtered, dumbfounded.

"I killed him. I killed Melanie's stepfather."

Matt grabbed Eric by the shoulder and pulled him away from the cabin, deeper into the darkness.

"When did this happen?"

"Today. I shot him."

"Keep your voice down!"

"I shot him with a pistol. Right in the head. Then I dragged his body downstairs and dumped it behind a woodpile behind his house."

Matt Quinn was thunderstruck. All he could utter was, "Holy shit."

Eric stood firm, peering into the darkness, trying to make out Quinn's reaction.

* * *

AT that moment Danny Paquette was in fact alive and well, enjoying the company of his girlfriend, Ruth Szeleste, in Hooksett. Danny planned on getting up early the next day. There was a lot to do first thing. Dick Duarte, who had been working on the 1954 Ford in Danny's garage until 10:30 p.m. that night, was coming back in the morning. Those funny Canadians were stopping by for a quick welding job. The kid, Court Burton, was starting work, and he planned to break him in by having him paint some fuel tanks. And then there was Gil Daigle's bulldozer to work on.

* * *

MATT Quinn scratched his head, unsure which way to turn. He had no reason not to believe every word coming out of his friend's mouth.

Eric continued to study him, gauging his reaction to his news.

"It's going to be OK. You were protecting Melanie," Matt said. "We'll think of something."

Eric exhaled in relief. His admiration for Matt Quinn rose exponentially. He probably felt at that moment that Matt was his best friend, someone he could count on to keep a secret safe.

— 21 —

Live Free or Die

MELANIE Paquette awoke on the morning of Saturday, November 9, 1985, to the ringing of the house phone. She'd had a fitful night's sleep. There was much on the fifteen-year-old girl's mind.

"Melanie!" Wendy Smith, the nanny, called up to her. "Telephone."

She rubbed her eyes and could see the low sun piercing the razor-thin space between the shade and the windowpane. *It's early*, she thought. *Who would be calling me?*

Melanie picked up the line on an extension in an empty room, away from adult ears, as any teenager would do. "I got it," she said into the receiver and waited for the hard, rattling click of the handset in the kitchen being placed back in the cradle. "Hello?"

"Hi, Mel." It was Eric.

"Hi." Her spirits always lifted when he called. She was dating Andrew Cheney, but she was secretly in love with Eric Windhurst.

There was an uncharacteristically long pause before Eric spoke again.

"I'm going to do it," he finally said.

Melanie knew exactly what he meant. "No, you're not," she replied.

"Yes, I am. I'm going to do it."

"No, Eric, you're not going to do it."
"Yes, I am."

Melanie thought it was Eric being silly. It seemed to her like something out of a movie. Eric was trying to be a hero, doing it to impress her. "Then I'm going with you."

"No, you're not," he came back.

"Eric, yes, I am."

"I'm not taking a girl with me."

"You don't even know where the house is," she said.

"I can find it."

"You don't even know who to shoot."

The line was silent for a moment. He was considering this.

"All right. I'm coming to get you."

* * *

ERIC picked up Melanie in front of the Hopkinton Poor Farm in his Volkswagen Rabbit. She told her aunt and uncle that she was going to the Hopkinton girl's field hockey championship game being held at Plymouth State College. The adults acknowledged that it would be a long drive there and back and cautioned Melanie that she still had to pack for the school trip to Quebec the next day.

They drove out of Hopkinton and onto the highway, traveling south past the state liquor stores and through the automatic tollbooths. It took them about twenty minutes to get to Hooksett.

Eric pulled the car into a gas station. He didn't want to run out of fuel getting out of town afterward. The attendant came to his window, and Eric asked for five dollars of regular-unleaded gas. As he pumped the gas, the man noticed a rifle in the back seat.

"Going hunting?" he asked. Eric, caught off guard, simply nodded. "It's the first day of hunting season," the man continued. "It's a good day for it."

* * *

"WHEREABOUTS?" Eric was scanning the homes on Whitehall Road. Melanie leaned forward in the seat and pointed across the road to the white house on the left.

"That's it. That's the house I grew up in."

Eric drove past. The house was on a main road that was busier than he had hoped. "Where can we park?"

"Over there," Melanie instructed. "I know a path in the woods on the back side."

Eric drove slowly, finally parking in the opening of a muddy cutout tucked behind some leafless brush.

Eric cut the engine, and the pair looked at each other for a moment. Eric made the first move, opening his door and stepping outside. Melanie followed. The boy reached into the backseat and pulled out his rifle. It was the Ruger 77 that he always shot with, the one his father had given him for his birthday. It was already loaded with .270 bullets he had manufactured himself.

Before they walked into the woods, Eric smeared his front and back license plates with mud. His effort caked the green numbers and state motto emblazoned on every plate: "Live Free or Die."

They walked along the wooded path that Melanie remembered from her days living in Hooksett. Eric was wearing drab-colored clothing. Melanie had on a bright-red coat and dress boots, not exactly the stealthiest wardrobe for what they had planned. It was as if Melanie wanted to dress up and look nice for her protector.

After a few minutes of brushing past prickly evergreen twigs, barren branches that reached out to them like bony fingers, the outbuildings of the Paquette property came into view. There were the remnants of a stone wall snaking its way through the woods next to them. They both sat on it.

Eric reached into his pocket and pulled out a pack of Trident. He offered Melanie a stick after popping one in his mouth. The girl stared at the ground and ran a hand over the nice coat, which her uncle had paid for. The boy held his rifle in the bow of his arm, the nozzle pointed away from his companion. They had come this far, and now was their last chance to chicken out.

For an eternity, they remained motionless and silent on the wall. They avoided eye contact. They were like a pair of virgin lovers unable to admit their cold feet before consummating the act.

It was a moment they both later wished they could go back to and rewrite.

* * *

SITTING in a sheriff's interview room nineteen years later, thirty-four-year-old Melanie Paquette Cooper looked into the face of the state trooper.

"We just sat there for a long time, and he was chewing gum," she said. "He just said when his gum ran out of flavor, he was going to do it."

Sergeant Mark Mudgett stopped taking notes. "When his gum ran out of flavor, he was going to do it?" He was chilled. "When he said his gum runs out of flavor, he was going to do what?"

"That he was going to shoot Danny."

* * *

ERIC Windhurst left Melanie Paquette at the stone wall and continued forward to the edge of the tree line. It was a long distance to the bulldozer where Danny Paquette and Court Burton were working. The field between him and his target was filled with high yellow grass. There was an abandoned car on blocks at the edge of the tree line. He crouched behind the front end of the vehicle and raised his weapon across the top of the engine hood, setting his sights on the yellow Case bulldozer.

There were sparks from a welder's torch blooming from the opposite side of the iron beast. *A few hundred yards*, he thought. It was a shot he had made hundreds of times in his own backyard and in the woods of Hopkinton. He could do this. The technique was instinct to him. Breathe, relax, aim, squeeze.

Breathe.

Eric found it hard to steady himself. He was breathing heavily.

Relax.

The marksman calmed himself. The tiny fluttering of his muzzle straightened out. He was ready.

Aim.

Time slowed down, and Eric was conscious of everything. The plumes of sparks stopped and the figure behind the bulldozer straightened up. With his right hand, Danny lifted the welder's mask from his face. He was framed perfectly in the outline of the machine.

Only thirty-two inches of the man was exposed in the cut-out of the seat and control area. From three hundred yards away, Eric aimed at the approximate middle of that open target: seventeen and one-half inches from the top of the man's head. That also happened to be where the heart was.

While he aimed in, there was something else he could not have failed to see. Something was dangling from the tree over the target's head. It was the ace of spades, fat as an upside-down apple, looming above like a green light for assassination.

Squeeze.

* * *

MELANIE Paquette remained motionless on the stone wall. She still didn't think Eric was going to go through with it. Even having traveled all the way from home, sneaking through the woods, and the deadly seriousness he gave the task, she didn't believe it was going to happen. Eric was just going to scare Danny. Or he'd just come back and explain why he wasn't able to do it.

Crack!

The shot echoed in the dead woods around her. Though she knew in which direction Eric had walked, she wasn't sure from which direction the report came.

The teen dug her fingernails into the dirt on the ancient stones. She peered into the woods, waiting for something to happen. She could hear branches being bent and twigs snapping quickly.

Eric Windhurst burst through nearby bushes, having improvised a new path to the stone wall. He held his rifle in front of him with two hands, running like a charging infantryman.

"Run!" he ordered.

Melanie took off up the path. Eric ran backward, keeping an eye out for anyone on the trail.

"What happened?" Melanie yelled at him.

"Keep running!"

"What happened? Is Danny chasing us?"

"Faster!"

Eric had ordered her to run faster and harder before, but that was on the soccer field. The terrain now was difficult. It was rocky. There were branches to duck and crash through. But they were athletes; they could do this.

They found the Volkswagen right where they left it, undisturbed. Eric threw the Ruger 77 in the backseat and covered it with a blanket. Melanie jumped into the passenger seat. Eric tried to drive away calmly, inconspicuously, but he revved the engine and spun the tires.

"Did you do it?" Melanie pleaded. "Did you shoot him?"

"Get your head down!" Eric grabbed the girl by the back of the neck and forced her down, pushing her to the floor of the Rabbit. They had to drive back the way they'd come, which meant passing the Paquette house again.

In the distance, they could already hear the sirens of the Hooksett Fire Rescue approaching. As they cut through the neighborhood, Eric casually looked up the elevated driveway. There was some frantic movement happening in the late morning shadows. Across the street, a woman stood by her mailbox, a hand hiding a gaping mouth. She had called the ambulance at her husband's insistence, and now she was saying a silent prayer that her neighbor would survive an apparent electrocution.

Eric reached down and put a firm hand on Melanie's head, making sure she stayed down. An ambulance, its lights and sirens blaring, rumbled by them, going the other way. He looked back at the first responders, then gripped the steering wheel tighter.

"Did you do it, Eric?" Melanie asked through growing tears.

His knuckles grew white on the wheel. "I did it," he said. But Eric didn't tell her what he was really thinking.

I never should have done that.

* * *

AN hour to the north, at Plymouth State College, the Hopkinton Lady Hawks beat the Spartans of White Mountain Regional High School to capture the class A girls field hockey championship. The Hawks, who had been ranked number one going into the tournament, won 4–2 after a stroke-off in overtime. Nearly everybody from school was there, with two notable exceptions.

* * *

ERIC and Melanie drove to a Burger King to kill time. They couldn't return too soon or her family would know that she hadn't been to Plymouth. Eric said that when the police came to talk to her, he would back up her story that they'd gone to the field hockey game together. He said he would get Matt Quinn to also verify their alibis. It was to be their little secret.

When Melanie returned home, she found everyone busy with their Saturday chores and other distractions. Melanie went to her room and packed for a Quebec trip she had no hope of taking. She assumed the police would be over any moment. But they never came. That night was quiet, with no unexpected telephone calls or knocks at the door.

The next day, Sunday, November 10, Melanie climbed on a charter bus for the seven-hour trip to Quebec. She sat in the back of the bus, seeking solitude.

Somewhere on the other side of New Hampshire's White Mountains, with the flat expanse of Canada before them, a student left his seat and slowly walked up the aisle of the half-empty bus. Melanie assumed it was someone coming to use the bathroom. The figure stopped and lurked over her. It was Matt Quinn.

"Melanie," he said. "This is serious."

Melanie didn't meet his gaze. She just looked out the window.

"Melanie. This is some deep fucking shit."

A tear rolled down her cheek. Matt turned around and returned to his seat.

* * *

WHEN Melanie returned on Wednesday, November 13, no one said anything to her about her stepfather's death when she got off the bus, hopped in her uncle's car, or returned to the house on the Poor Farm.

Kathleen McGuire and Philip Messier came into Melanie's room while the girl was unpacking. The girl sat on the edge of the bed, and her aunt kneeled before her. Tenderly, she told Melanie that her stepfather had been killed in an accident. The girl let out a sigh and allowed the tears to flow freely.

I have to put on a good show to convince them that I didn't know, Melanie thought. She did.

Kathy McGuire held her niece while she wept, and she rocked Melanie in her arms. She shared her tears. But the woman didn't cry for Danny Paquette; she cried for the child whom she'd pledged to take care of. She later told investigators that it seemed bad things kept happening to Melanie, no matter how hard they tried to protect her.

— 22 —

Everybody Dies for a Reason

MELANIE Paquette Cooper sat alone in Interview 1 at the Ada County, Idaho, Sheriff's Office spinning a soda can between her fingers. It was Wednesday, July 14, 2004. She didn't know what time it was—there was no clock on the wall—but she felt like she had been there for about six or seven hours. Soon her husband, David, would be home from work, and she would have to explain. She had confessed to him years before about how she'd had her stepfather killed. Would he agree with her decision to talk to these investigators now?

Sergeant Mark Armaganian entered the room and took a seat at the table across from Melanie. He was more than satisfied with the work his colleague Sergeant Mark Mudgett had done. Investigator Bill Shackford had stolen a few moments in another office to call Chief Steve Agrafiotis back in Hooksett, New Hampshire, to let him know their Hail Mary pass had resulted in a touchdown.

"Who did you tell about the shooting?" Armaganian asked.

"My husband knows. The only person I told at the time was the nanny who lived with us. I forget her name . . . Wendy."

"Did you tell your aunt?"

"No. I knew she could lose her job over it."

"What about your mother?"

"I had a phone call with her. It was after Danny died. I

called her and asked her if she was happy. If we could be a family again. I just kept asking her if she was happy. I never said a word, but she knew."

* * *

"IS he married?" Melanie asked of Eric Windhurst.

"I don't know his family situation right now," Armaganian said. "Because he's going through a [divorce] proceeding."

"Where does he live in New Hampshire?"

"I think he's living in Hopkinton."

Melanie responded dismissively, "Those people don't leave there."

The state trooper explained he had been on the phone with the New Hampshire attorney general's office. The prosecutor had authorized them to tape record a call from Melanie to Eric.

"When was the last time you spoke to him?" Armaganian asked.

"He called me a couple of weeks after my wedding, in 1990," she said. She remembered being surprised by the call. It had occurred to her that Eric had called just to remind her of their unspoken bond, to remind her of the blood debt she owed him.

* * *

"WHAT are the chances that I'll go to jail?" Melanie asked.

The trooper looked her in the eye. "Melanie, I don't get that sense. But I don't know for sure. I can't make you any promises. What I need to do is talk to the prosecutor."

Melanie sighed. "Do you have any Tylenol?"

"There," he said after fetching two red and yellow pills from the dispatch center.

"This room is too quiet," she said, looking physically uncomfortable. "It's so quiet in the room that it gives me a headache. I'm used to five kids, and it's giving me a headache because it's so quiet. You walk in, and it just seals you."

Mudgett stuck his head in. "We're ready in Interview 2."

She picked herself up. "OK," she said taking her can of soda with her.

* * *

MUDGETT and Shackford had hooked up a tape recorder to a sheriff's department telephone with a blocked number. Another recorder captured everything being said inside Interview 2, just as it had been recording Melanie and the interrogators for seven hours in Interview 1.

Bill Shackford joined Sergeant Mudgett, Sergeant Armaganian, and Melanie in the room. He pulled out a list of telephone numbers belonging to Eric Windhurst.

"There's no dial tone," Armaganian said mystified, the receiver of the phone in his hand.

"I'll get it," Shackford offered, assuming they'd wired something wrong.

"I can't believe this," Armaganian said. "There is a taped telemarketing advertisement on the phone right now." The trooper jiggled the plunger. The prerecorded ad wouldn't hang up.

"We must have just picked that up right when it was dialing in," Shackford said. The comedy of errors cut the room's tension.

"You get those calls here at the police station?" Melanie marveled. "They have nerve."

* * *

THE first time they called, they ran through all of Eric's numbers and got voice mail or answering machines at each. They chose not to leave messages.

The two New Hampshire State Troopers excused themselves and left Shackford with Melanie. The old man and the young mother conversed softly together. Shackford had grown up in Craig, Colorado, before moving to New Hampshire, so he was familiar with the similar Idaho climate. Melanie asked how New Hampshire had changed since she'd lived there. Shackford described the surge in building and blight that had taken over the southern cities like Nashua and Manchester. Hopkinton, for the most part, was still as it had been when she graduated in 1988.

"I used to live with my aunt, and she was a prosecuting attorney, and I remember the hours she used to spend just preparing cases."

"Yes, it's a lot of work."

Melanie's mood changed. "I wish it didn't happen this way."

"Well, there's not very many good ways for something like this to happen. But I think what you're doing is going to be good in the long run."

"It's been hard."

"This is the kind of thing that you can work through and put behind you and feel better than you have for all those years," he said.

"There's a part of you that wishes it would happen," Melanie said. "Just be done with the whole thing."

* * *

THE rest of that Tuesday, July 14, the group tried to telephone Eric Windhurst. It was now past seven thirty mountain standard time, two hours behind New Hampshire. The troopers asked Melanie whether, if they quit for the night, she would agree to return the next day to try again. She promised she would come back once she took her daughter to her eye doctor's appointment. Melanie Paquette Cooper then walked out of the Ada County Sheriff's Office, got in her car, and drove home to explain to her husband why she'd left their kids with a babysitter all day.

* * *

KA-CLICK. The cassette started to roll. It was the next morning; a new warrant had been obtained for a second phone call to New Hampshire.

"Today's date is July 15, 2004. My name is Sergeant Mark Mudgett of the New Hampshire State Police Major Crime Unit. The time according to my watch is 10:48 a.m. mountain standard time. I'm in Boise, Idaho, at the Ada County Sheriff's Office. At 10:32 mountain standard time I had a phone conversation with Michael Delaney of the attorney general's office in New Hampshire requesting authorization for a one-party intercept telephonically. I was granted permission to run a twelve-hour period for Melanie Cooper to conduct a one-party intercept with a gentleman by the name of Eric Windhurst in Hopkinton, New Hampshire."

The electronic burr of a distant phone ringing.

"Hello?"

"Hello. Is this Eric?"

"This is," he replied confidently.

"Eric, this is Melanie Paquette."

"Oh my God." He seemed pleased to be hearing from an old friend.

"I got a situation out here, and I need to talk to you." Melanie explained that the police had contacted her about Danny Paquette's death. Investigators from New Hampshire were on their way to Idaho to talk to her, and she wasn't sure whether she should cooperate or not.

"Um, should we be talking on the phone?" Eric asked.

"It's OK. I'm not home. I'm calling from my neighbor's house."

Eric said his cell phone was out in his truck. He gave her a new number, which the three New Hampshire investigators scribbled down furiously, and he told her to call back on that number.

* * *

"THEY talked to me once when we were still in high school," Eric said, without even saying hello when the call came in. "I just told them I didn't have anything to do with it."

"I don't know what to do."

"I would get a lawyer if I were you."

"That's what you'd do?" she asked.

"That's what I did. I have two lawyers. They've been on retainer for ten years."

"They want me to meet with them. They were really pushy about it."

"Of course they are. They're going to run you through the wringer. That's exactly what they're going to do."

"If I got a lawyer," Melanie said, "what do I tell him?"

"Tell the lawyer whatever you want to tell him."

"Do I tell the lawyer the truth?"

"Well, I told my lawyer exactly what happened. And that was . . . you know, that's that."

"You told them what happened with Danny?"

"Yeah, yeah."

"The whole thing?" she asked. "I'm not clear on what you said to your lawyer."

"It doesn't matter what I told my lawyer," Eric told her, ending that line of questioning. He went on a while later to say, "You know, Melanie, frankly I'm not real comfortable talking on the phone about much of this."

"I know."

"Unless you want me to jump on a plane and fly out there and I can talk to you in person."

Melanie looked over at the state troopers, asking with her eyes whether they wanted Eric to do that. Mudgett and Armaganian shook their heads and urged her to continue talking.

"You know, for crying out loud," Eric said, "you could be surrounded by five cops right now and you're in a police station as we're talking."

The investigators exchanged worried looks, but Melanie continued with the questions just as they had rehearsed.

"I don't know why this would all of a sudden be stirred up like this," Melanie said. "Who did you tell?"

"Nobody. I haven't told anybody anything." Eric explained how a decade earlier, the state police had questioned everyone in his family about his involvement in the case. "Everybody in town. Everyone got interviewed. There wasn't a single goddamned person who thought they might know anything about it they didn't interview. Jesus, every single person just about I know out here got interviewed about it. And they asked questions about me and you and whether we ever dated or whether we were involved. And that never happened. There wasn't much to tell."

Melanie sounded depressed. "I'm really sick of this."

"Yeah, well, I am, too," he said. "I mean, I tried just to live my life everyday and live it as well as I possibly can."

Melanie thought about how she, too, had lived the best possible life she could. She thought being a mother was the most important thing she had ever done, and she began to softly cry as she talked about her five kids. On the other end of the line, Eric wasn't sure if she was still there. "I don't want to do this," she sobbed.

"I don't blame you," Eric said. He said it over and over again to soothe her.

* * *

"I don't have very much money. I'm still just a carpenter. If I got to call my lawyers up and tell them they got to get active again, you know every friggin' penny I make is going to have to go to pay for these guys." It was unclear whether Eric said this to discourage Melanie from cooperating or from bringing up his name to investigators.

"But I highly suggest you get legal representation," he continued. "You're going down there and putting yourself on the line. You can just go down there and tell them you don't know anything about it."

* * *

"NO one up here has said anything," Eric assured Melanie. Then referring to the author or authors of the anonymous letters, he said, "One person, whoever the hell it is, is hell-bent to see to it I go down for this. And you know they don't have a shred of proof of anything."

The troopers continued to pass Melanie lines to say, trying different tactics to break down the wall. "So you didn't tell anyone? No one in your family knows? No one knows anything?"

"No," he assured her.*

"Well, I don't want to go to jail for something I didn't do."

"I know you didn't do it," Eric said. "That's why you have to hire a lawyer."

"What do I tell the lawyer? Do I tell him the truth?"

"We were at a friggin' goddamned field hockey game and we didn't have anything to do with it," he snapped.

"They're never going to believe that."

"How old are your kids anyhow?" Eric asked apropos of nothing.

"I've got a thirteen-year-old, eleven, nine, six, and three."

Eric was amazed and began to laugh. He'd never had children; he later claimed that a part of him thought bringing a baby into his situation would be unfair. "Jeezum crow, spread

---

* This was not actually true. Eric had told several family members, including his older brother, Trapper.

out over nine months over all those years. Do you even know what it's like *not* to be pregnant?"

"I'm just starting to get a feel for it, yeah."

"You're a regular baby machine."

"Yeah."

"How are you doing?"

"What did you ask?"

Eric's voice grew tender. "Other than what's going on now, are you OK? How's your life? Is your husband a good person? Are you all right? Are you being taken care of? I think about you all the time. I always wonder if you're OK and you're being taken care of."

The troopers had no lines to feed her for this question. "Well, it's not OK."

"You're not OK because of all this going on? Or, generally speaking, you're not OK?" Eric sounded as if he wanted her to answer that her life had been fulfilling, that his deadly decision had freed her from a life of victimization. Melanie answered the only way she could.

"I don't know."

"Well, not a day in my life goes by I don't think about all this," he came back with. "Not a day goes by I don't think about you and how you're doing."

"That's not what I want to hear." This was getting difficult for Melanie. Eric's declarations of devotion through the years weren't what she had expected. She had been trying to draw out an incriminating slip of the tongue; now she was confronted with the dilemma of saving Eric or saving herself.

"I don't think this time it's going to turn out OK, Eric. I don't want to live like this anymore. I'm tired. I'm tired of worrying about it. I'm tired of worrying about every phone call I get that's a click on the end." Then she said, "If I tell, are you going to get in trouble?"

"What do you think?" he said huffily. "Honestly, what do you think?"

* * *

THE troopers continued to pass Melanie notes, but she suddenly came up with her own idea of a line of questioning. "What if they have something?"

"Like what?"

"I don't know. What about the gun? Do they have the gun? Do they have anything?"

"I don't think they have anything," Eric responded.

"Do they have the bullet? Wasn't there something about that?"

"That was on TV or something."

"Can they trace that?"

"I don't know."

"So they can't trace it to your gun or something like that?"

"They came and took every single gun I have and [every] single gun my dad has." It was not exactly a true statement. "They checked them all."

"I'm going to go tell them the truth," Melanie claimed. "That I didn't do anything and you did. I don't trust you."

"Oh great. Thanks."

"You're way too calm," she said.

"Yeah? I've been scared about this my whole life. You know. With somebody constantly trying to hunt you down."

"Are you afraid they'll catch you?" Melanie asked. Eric denied it, and she said, "I don't understand why you're not freaking out."

"Because maybe I've lived with this so long I'm at peace with whatever happens. It's out of my hands." Eric then asked her, "Do you *really* believe in God? That He looks down on you and He knows that you're a good person and a good mother?"

"Does a good person kill someone? I don't know."

"God loves everybody," Eric said. "God doesn't have prejudice or racism or bigotry."

"Then it was wrong to kill Danny?"

"God sees everything."

"So he loves Danny?" Melanie asked.

"He loves everybody. But everybody dies for a reason. And only God knows why those people die. Only God knows why."

"Then you think God is OK with the fact that you killed Danny?"

"I can't speak for Him."

* * *

"CAN I ask you something?" Eric posed.

"What?"

"Did he really do all those things to you?"

Melanie was appalled. "Yes. Do you think I made it up?"

"No," he began. "But remember when you moved back to Alaska and you told me somebody attacked you on the soccer field walking home. And then you told me you made that up. That was the only reason I ever doubted anything you ever said."

"I don't even know what you're talking about."

"You were on the soccer field and some guy attacked you. Remember you told me that?"

"No."

"And [Danny] really did all those things to you?"

"Eric, yes. He did."

"And your little sister?" Although Melanie had not made that allegation against Danny Paquette to the authorities, it appeared as though she had made it to teenage Eric Windhurst.

"I don't know about my little sister, but I know what he did to me."

* * *

STILL fretful of Eric's coolness to the tense situation Melanie asked, "Does it affect you at all?"

"Yeah it does," he exploded. "Everything that's happened, everything I had to do with all this has affected me. Why do you think I don't have a family?"

"You're playing this on me as though it's my fault that you don't have a life and a family. Because of what you did."

"No, I made the choice not to have one. I made that choice."

"Why?" she said. Melanie wasn't picking up on Eric's deeper implication: his belief that he had sacrificed having a normal life because of this crime. "That's stupid," she said.

"How come?"

"Because it's stupid, that's why."

"You haven't changed a bit," Eric cried. "You're just as friggin' pigheaded as you've always been. Oh my God."

"So are you."

"Between all your blubbering and hysterics, Melanie comes

through. I guess people are always the same people they always are."

* * *

THE conversation, which had gone on for several hours, was losing momentum. The investigators could sense that both Melanie and Eric were ready to hang up. The suspect had not said anything that implicated him in the murder, nothing that couldn't be explained away by his high-priced lawyers. The troopers decided they needed to take another shot, but with more pointed questions next time.

"All right, I'm going to meet with an attorney now," Melanie was instructed to say. "I'll call you back afterward. What should I tell him happened?"

"Just tell them exactly what the truth is. That we went to the field hockey game and that's it. You don't remember anything else. Too long ago. Just stick with that."

"So what happens if I tell them the truth?" Melanie asked.

"Well," Eric Windhurst replied, "then we go to jail."

— 23 —

Rumor and Innuendo

THERE were less than five hours left on the team's authorization to secretly tape their telephone calls with Eric Windhurst. Sergeants Mark Mudgett and Mark Armaganian were shuffling stacks of cassette tapes, trying to separate the blank ones from the used ones. They were discussing how, if the tape ran out during the call, they could pull the phone jack out of one recorder and quickly plug it into another.

"Do you want a chair?" Mudgett noticed Melanie Paquette Cooper was sitting quietly on the floor.

"No, it's fine on the floor," she said. "Because that's where I sit when I'm upset."

Mudgett tried handing her the telephone while she was on the floor, her back literally up against the wall. He moved a few things on the table because the cord wasn't long enough to reach her. Melanie agreed to leave the phone's base on the table and pull the receiver to her ear.

* * *

"HELLO?"

"Eric?"

"Yes." It had been several hours since they last spoke.

"OK, I talked to an attorney."

"You did?"

"I told the police that I talked to an attorney. Then my husband came home, and I told him what happened. We got into a huge fight. He got really, really mad and totally left. I don't know if he's going to the police or whatever." Melanie then turned up the heat on Eric. "Why did you have to kill him? Why couldn't you have just scared him or something?"

"Your husband will be back," Eric said.

"I just wish you wouldn't have done this. If you just wouldn't have done this, this would not have happened."

"Why are you blaming me?"

"Because you killed him. Now my life is screwed up. It just would have been better to just leave it alone."

"Well, my life isn't a bowl of cherries either, you know."

"You don't think that's screwed up? What's your definition of screwed up?"

"You're right; it's screwed up," Eric said. "Stand your fucking ground! Just stand your ground! You know it's all hearsay. You know what I *didn't* do? I didn't bury my head in the sand! I stood up and I just took it! They have to absolutely—without reasonable doubt—prove all the rumors they heard from every friggin' person that got interviewed! It was hearsay. It was just rumors that they heard."

Melanie shifted uncomfortably on the floor as Eric continued laying into her.

"The only person that ever seemed to be vindictive enough to try to pin this on us," Eric said, "wrote a letter, and that person didn't have the guts to come out and say 'I wrote the letter and this is why and I have proof.'"

"This whole thing is on our heads," she replied. "Right now I don't know that I can cope with much more."

"What is your alternative? Lose your family and your husband? What are you going to do? Really, what are you going to do? Other than stand your ground, hire a lawyer, and see it through to the end."

Melanie continued to squirm on the floor as Eric unloaded his frustrations.

"You're going to meet with your lawyer, and you know what? The police are never going to be able to call you again. You're never going to hear from them until they have absolute, irrefutable, indisputable proof. Which they don't have. And every day that goes by closer to twenty friggin' years, the colder and colder [is] any information that they have ever gotten. They don't have a thing. They've got rumor, and they have innuendo. They have a totally anonymous letter that was left in a mailbox and no one to back it up. They haven't got any physical evidence whatsoever. You know what . . ."

Eric Windhurst's next words were broken off in a crackle of electricity. Sergeant Mudgett looked up from his notes to see that Melanie Cooper had just hung up on him.

* * *

"OH crap," Melanie said.

Sergeant Armaganian came back into Interview 2, his face as white as Mudgett's. There was a momentary sense of horror.

"She pulled the jack out of the wall," Mudgett explained to his partner. The telephone wires had finally given way after being stretched to Melanie's seat on the floor.

"I saw that."

"All right, that's all you did. You hung up on him," Mudgett said to a stunned Melanie. "When you call him back . . ."

"I can't do this." The woman shook her head and buried her face in her lap.

"Listen." Mudgett harkened back to his gentle tone of the day before. It was how he was able to get her to drop her guard and give up her secret. "Yeah, you can. You're doing a great job."

"No, I'm not."

"You call him back. We're going to turn right around and say this is about me dealing with this. This isn't about a lawyer anymore. I can't deal with the pressure of this any longer. All right?"

"He's not going to say anything," Melanie cried. She had hit the wall in this cerebral marathon. "He's not going to say anything."

The troopers propped up her courage. They gave her some more talking points and reinserted the phone cord in the jack.

* * *

"WHAT happened?" Eric asked after she finally called him back.

"Someone walked in the room, and I just got freaked out and hung up."

Melanie asked Eric what she should do about her husband, who, according to the police cover story, had walked out on her. Eric said her husband would come back and stick by her side, but if he didn't, then she didn't need him anyhow.

"They couldn't make an arrest then, and they can't make an arrest now. They have rumor and innuendo based on hearsay," Eric repeated. "You know what they're doing? They're terrifying a poor friggin' mother of five children. To do what? To find justice in vindicating a child rapist? You know what they are? They're cowards. They're no better than he who raped you. A little child, a little girl. That bastard. They don't have a goddamned thing. And shame on them for trying to ruin your life and my life. You didn't do anything wrong. You're a victim."

"It doesn't matter," Melanie said. "It's still wrong."

"They have nothing but rumor and innuendo," Eric said for the third time.

* * *

MELANIE Paquette Cooper then posed to Eric Windhurst the question central to this case. The question that they hadn't asked each other in November of 1985, the question investigators had privately asked themselves. In 1985, it had seemed so black and white. The teens had felt certain who the good guys and the bad guys were. Now it was gray, infinitely gray.

"Did [Danny] really deserve to die for that?" Melanie brought herself to ask. "Because I don't know."

"I don't know either," admitted Eric, the man who'd killed him.

* * *

"**I'M** only guessing," Eric said, "that you've lived a good life. I certainly can attest that I have. A good, good and honest life of hard work and honesty. I've lived a model life."

"I think about this every day. I don't feel like I can live a good life with this behind me."

"All of this has taken place in our lives," he replied. "Every aspect of everything is for a reason. It's because it's part of how our lives are supposed to unroll. The role I'm supposed to play in your life; there's a role you're supposed to play in my life. I have to believe the reason you came in my life is the reason why I've lived such a good life. I was seventeen, sixteen. I was always in trouble with one damn thing or another. And right up until I was about twenty-one I was still friggin' screwed up."

"It was wrong to kill Danny," she shot back. "You were wrong to kill Danny. It wasn't right. It just wasn't right."

"I'm going to look out for you every day, Melanie."

"How?"

"Just keeping my mouth shut. Knowing that no matter what, whether the hellfire is breathing at the back of my neck, that the only thing you and I did that day was go to a field hockey game! That's it! That's it, Melanie! That's it! That's the only thing that ever happened that day!"

Melanie was physically and emotionally exhausted. There was nothing more for her to do, to ask of him. She told him she had to hang up and check on her kids. Eric said he hoped her husband would come home soon. They both said good-bye, and Melanie placed the receiver back in the cradle.

* * *

"YOU tried," Sergeant Mudgett said to Melanie, placating her for failing to get the goods on Eric.

"I'm sorry." The tears started to roll down her cheeks.

"No, you did a good job."

Melanie mumbled something inaudible through the sobs she was trying to hold back.

"It was a very good effort, Melanie. And we're not sunk. He told you a bunch of stuff that only a coward would tell someone that was in a position like this."

Mudgett ordered Armaganian to get some tissues. Melanie refused to make eye contact with anyone.

"Melanie. Melanie. Melanie. Look at me. Do you believe what he's saying to you?"

She shook her head.

"Melanie, listen to me. Listen to me. Listen to me. You did

a great job. Eric is scared. He's not here to be able to control what you have to say. So the only thing he can tell you is to go get a lawyer. He's not going to tell you that he didn't do it. He never once told you that he didn't do it, did he?"

"No."

"He knows you know the truth. And I believe you. All the investigators here believe you."

"It doesn't matter what you guys believe."

"Are you going to give in to him?" Mudgett asked.

"Why did he have to do that?" she sobbed. "How can someone do that? Why couldn't I have been smart?"

"You don't have a crappy life, Melanie," Mudgett said, remembering her declarations to Eric of the contrary. "And you're going to get through this. You got a wonderful husband . . ."

"It doesn't make much difference in jail. My kids don't have a mom anymore."

"Listen to me, Melanie. You don't even know if anything like that is going to take place. You have friends who care a great deal about you, and you have a very supportive church."

"They're all going to think I'm horrible."

"Stop it. That's enough," Mudgett scolded her. "You be the parent that you are, and stop saying stuff like that. Because now you're being a child. You can't turn around and destroy your life over what happened twenty years ago. Come on. Stand up. We're going to take a walk outside."

Melanie looked up at the burly state trooper extending a hand to her. "I don't want . . ."

"Come on. Come on, I'm not asking you. I'm telling you. Let's get some fresh air, all right? Take this, wipe your face. Now come on. We're going to take a walk."

Melanie got up from the table, her shoulders folded in on her, and trudged to the door. She followed the men outside, looking for relief, but the hot July sun had not set and the air was humid and uncomfortable. The heat wave in Boise would continue for nearly a month. Temperatures wouldn't get out of the nineties until the first week in August.

If Melanie Cooper, walking the neighborhood with two protective state troopers and one elderly investigator, thought the path to finally escaping Danny Paquette's ghost was in front of her, she was wrong. For like so much in the nearly twenty years since that shot had been fired from the tree line to that bulldozer, nothing had been finished.

And though they all believed they were so close to uncovering the truth, nothing was quite as it seemed.

Part Four

NOTHING IS AS IT SEEMS

Genuine tragedies in the world are not conflicts
between right and wrong. They are conflicts
between two rights.

—Christian Friedrich Hebbel

— 24 —

The Gang of Five

THE sight of overall-clad, handcuffed Eric Kimball Windhurst being escorted into the Hooksett District Court on December 14, 2005 (more than a year and a half after his taped conversations with Melanie Paquette Cooper), was shocking to those Hopkinton residents who'd only learned about his past from watching the arraignment on television. Though authorities suspected there were a group of friends who knew all about the 1985 shooting, most residents only knew Eric as an honest handyman and carpenter. There were those who shook their heads trying to reconcile the crime with the gentle raconteur who held court at their barbecues, the workman who was never satisfied with imperfection, or the friendly Yankee who would drive his dog around the village in his pickup truck. One woman, who'd let Eric babysit her children, watched the screen in disbelief. "I don't know what the other guy did," she told her husband, "but if Eric killed him, it must have been *really* bad."

* * *

WHEN Victor Paquette's phone rang, he didn't catch the name of the man on the other end of the line. He remembered the guy said he was a cop, but Victor couldn't recall from where.

"We arrested Eric Windhurst today for the murder of your brother," the officer said.

Victor said, "About fucking time," then hung up the phone.

* * *

THE state attorney general's office would not have been able to go forward with an arrest and prosecution without additional witnesses to confirm what Melanie Paquette Cooper had told investigators. That meant New Hampshire State Police (NHSP) sergeants Mark Mudgett and Mark Armaganian and Hooksett Police Department civilian investigator Bill Shackford would need to track down the members of Eric Windhurst's high school clique and get them to finally admit what they knew.

Investigator Bill Shackford, the veteran detective, dubbed the innermost circle of Eric's high school–era friends the "Gang of Five." He was sure they all knew the pieces of the puzzle and how it fit together. Shackford believed the gang consisted of Matt Quinn, Craig Metzger, Dee Clark, Mark Hoevler, and Eric Prescott. In the autumn and winter of 2004, the investigators would go after them and others on their periphery whom they thought might give them information to aid in their case. They would also interview those who had been close to Eric in the two decades that had passed since graduation.

* * *

THE investigative team flew to Golden, Colorado, to talk with Craig Metzger. Shackford, Sergeant Mudgett, and Trooper Scott Gilbert (filling in for Sergeant Armaganian) stopped Metzger as he exited his apartment, which happened to be right next to the Golden Police Department. There was utter shock on Metzger's face when they introduced themselves and asked if he would consent to an interview about the Paquette case.

"I have nothing to say," Metzger claimed. "I don't know anything."

"We believe you have information, and we've traveled a great distance to talk to you," Trooper Gilbert said.

Metzger said he'd think about it and asked the officers for a business card. He called them twenty-four hours later saying his lawyer would set up a meeting the next time he was in New Hampshire, which would be around the holidays.

* * *

SERGEANT Mudgett interviewed Eric's ex-wife, Tracy, in her New Hampshire home on September 19, 2004. The couple had divorced two years prior amid rumors of infidelity, although Tracy claimed that it was Eric's poor work ethic and over-the-top temper that had ruined the marriage. They'd lived in a woodsy home in a neighboring town, their house built adjacent to the paddock where Tracy kept her horse. At night, they'd watch TV, and the horse would poke his head in the living room window and beg for carrots.

Near the end of the marriage, Eric allegedly beat up the man he suspected his wife of cheating with, but he later admitted that as a husband, he'd been "far from perfect." The divorce left Eric broke, forcing him to once again enter the family enclave and live in property owned by his mother, Barbara.

Now Tracy told investigators that Eric had never directly told her about his involvement in the crime. In the early part of their relationship, when Eric had returned from Colorado, she'd heard rumors that the police were investigating him. John Windhurst, Eric's father, dismissed the loose talk, saying that the police were just trying to frame his son. As more time passed with no arrest or serious questioning of her husband, it became easier for Tracy to forget about the cloud hanging over Eric's head.

* * *

DAVIS "Dee" Clark had also left New Hampshire after high school and had become a doctor of emergency medicine at University Hospital in Syracuse, New York. The investigators met with him in a Best Western Hotel near his home.

Clark was cooperative but apologetic. He said he'd heard the rumor at a party that Eric had killed Danny Paquette, but he'd never heard it from the suspect himself. Clark asked the troopers if he would be asked to testify at a trial, fearful of what it might mean regarding his ability to return to New Hampshire and set up a practice there.

* * *

THE team also located Mark Hoevler, the third member of the "Gang of Five," living with his wife in Portland, Oregon.

Hoevler returned the telephone calls left by the New Hampshire State Police. He promised to be cooperative and honest, just as he had been when questioned about Eric in 1993, but he said his answer hadn't changed. Although he, too, had heard rumors that Eric did the shooting, he'd never heard him say it.

* * *

SERGEANT Mudgett, Investigator Bill Shackford, and Trooper Scott Gilbert flew across the country to talk to Eric's old girlfriend, Thea Koonz, now Thea Davis. She was married and living in Long Beach, California. Thea had dated several of the boys in Eric's social circle, including Matt Quinn, Mark Hoevler, and Ricky Patenaude. She'd dated Eric for a period of time that extended into her freshman year at the University of New Hampshire (UNH), where Melanie Paquette also attended school.

Thea explained that she'd always been suspicious of her boyfriend's close relationship to Melanie, and his protestations that Melanie was like "a little sister" hadn't done much to assuage her concerns. Going so far as to befriend Melanie at UNH in an attempt to bring a rival closer, Thea described her romantic relationship with Eric as full of drama. They fought often.

Thea said that in April of 1989, Craig Metzger told her that Eric had cheated on her with Metzger's girlfriend, Kelly Olsen. This betrayal created a rift in Metzger's relationship with Eric that lasted for years. When Thea confronted Eric about his infidelity, she said Eric threatened suicide during the argument, putting the barrel of a gun in his mouth.

Furious at her boyfriend, she contacted Ricky Patenaude, with whom she'd remained friends after they'd broken up a couple of years prior. He warned her to be careful around Eric, who he said was capable of very bad things.

"What kind of things?" Thea asked Patenaude.

Though it would be years before he would confirm his own suspicions with Matt Quinn, Ricky Patenaude told her the rumor he'd heard: that Eric had shot a man while they were all still in high school.

What made Thea Koonz a compelling witness was that unlike the other schoolmates who struggled to remember what they felt and did in the 1980s, Thea had kept detailed journals of her teenage years. The investigators found her written account invaluable and a riveting peek into the past teenage lives of the characters they'd come to know so well during the course of their inquiry.

Thea read aloud her diary entry of April 16, 1989, the day that Ricky Patenaude had told her what he believed about Eric.

I want to vomit. What's the right thing to do? To live with knowing sure is worse than not knowing at all. Do I believe it? I don't know. I thought I knew him so well. I don't know. He's definitely protective. I can see it but I can't. How can I love someone capable of something like that? How? Why? How could he live with himself? I couldn't. How? Why? Deep down, I know I never want to find out. But what's right? . . . It's on my shoulders. I'm the one who has to deal with it. No one else can help. I'm going to have to live with whatever decision I make. It's so hard. I want to take the only way out and just forget about it. Assume it's just a rumor. But what if it's true? What if it's not?

The investigators were impressed with the level of detail the young woman had achieved. They were disappointed to learn that Eric never discussed the crime with Thea Koonz and that Ricky Patenaude had only said Eric "shot someone," not "murdered" someone.

* * *

INVESTIGATORS questioned Ricky Patenaude, but he told them that Eric had never at any point told him anything directly about the murder. They also decided to pay a visit to Patenaude's sister Sabrina, since police notes from 1993's volatile interview, ten years earlier, indicated that she might know more than she'd said at the time. When Investigator Bill Shackford and Trooper Scott Gilbert arrived at her home, she invited the men out onto her deck. She was very cordial.

"All and any information I had came from my brother," she insisted.

"Do you have any idea why Windhurst shot Dan Paquette?" Shackford asked.

"If you knew Eric," she said, "he wants to be the big hero and straighten the whole world."

Shackford showed Sabrina Patenaude the two anonymous letters they'd received in 1992 and asked if any of the details given jogged her memory. Her eyes lingered on the longer of the two letters, the one filled with typos, which wished God would bless the Paquette family.

"When I wrote the letter I was thinking something should be done."

The investigators looked at one another, then back to the woman.

"Then you wrote the letter," they confirmed.

"No, I didn't," she said, retracting the statement. "Did I say that?"

"You did say that. Did you write that letter?"

"No," she said, distancing herself from the comment once and for all.

Shackford made a note at the end of his report. "Was this a slip or did she in fact write one of the letters?"

* * *

DREW Jordan, who'd been the goalie on the Hopkinton soccer team back in 1985, told Sergeant Mudgett that Melanie had revealed the molestation to him during a time when they'd dated. But she'd never said she wanted her father killed or revealed anything else about the shooting.

Jordan said he was best friends with Scott Windhurst, Eric's older brother, and that they still spoke weekly. Jordan said he suspected Scott's ex-wife started the rumor that Eric killed Danny Paquette.

"And I don't take stock in rumors," he reportedly told the cops.

* * *

SERGEANT Mudgett interviewed the fourth member of the "Gang of Five" in the office of his attorney. Like his old friend Eric, Matthew Quinn hadn't worked too hard in high school, but in his late twenties he'd rededicated himself to his education. He was now a practicing veterinarian.

At this point, the investigators expected more of the same kind of denial of knowledge they'd received from the other members of Eric's old clique.

"Can you tell us," Mudgett began, "do you possess truthful information in regard to this death?"

"I do," Quinn said.

Quinn then told the whole story of how Melanie had approached him and Eric in the gym and told them about Danny's sexual abuse. He told them how he'd warned Eric in the boy's room not to go through with it and how Eric had lied to him about killing Danny the night before he actually committed the shooting.

"I wish now I had reacted differently," Quinn said of the way he'd supported Eric when his friend had tested him with the lie. "Because maybe he wouldn't have gone through with it. That's something I've had to live with," he said ruefully.

* * *

"I'VE been deathly afraid," Eric Prescott told Trooper Gilbert in the interview room at the Hooksett Police Department. The last member of the "Gang of Five," he surprised the investigator by admitting, "I've been afraid for a lot of years." He added, "[And I'm] even more afraid now."

"Why are you more afraid now?" Gilbert asked.

"Retaliation." Prescott said.

"From him?" Gilbert asked.

"Not just him, but somebody."

Prescott described himself as angry and scared. He was unwilling to meet with authorities at the state police headquarters, in Concord, for fear that someone from adjacent Hopkinton would see his truck there. He also wanted police to start a disinformation campaign that "many" people were coming forward to talk, so as to divert attention from him. Prescott said that for the past two decades he'd been afraid to go deer hunting for fear of an "accident" befalling him.

"I've been dying to tell somebody about this for twenty years," Prescott said. "I've always known it was the right thing to do. But there's been more than one victim in this crime. It's all of us that have lived in fear for twenty years."

Prescott told the investigators he had an image of Eric Windhurst burned into his mind, pulling him into the bathroom at Hopkinton High and asking him if a kid named Andrew Cheney had been spreading rumors about him.

* * *

ANDREW Cheney, Melanie's boyfriend at the time of the shooting, met with a NHSP investigator in a hotel room near his home in Albany, Ohio. Cheney said that Melanie had broken up with him immediately after the 1985 field hockey championship. He remembered that he'd waited for her at the game, but she never showed up.

Shortly afterward, he read in the paper about a man in Hooksett being killed in a suspicious hunting accident. Cheney wondered if the victim, Danny Paquette, could be related to his ex-girlfriend Melanie Paquette, and whether that would account for her sudden decision to end their relationship. Cheney knew that Melanie had hated her father for some reason, and he was aware Melanie and Eric Windhurst had been spending more and more time together. He found the whole thing too coincidental.

Cheney went to Eric's house to confront him, to ask him if he had anything to do with Danny's death. Although two decades later he couldn't recall the exact words, Cheney said Eric answered in a peculiar way. He gave his answer as a hypothetical. He said something like, "*If* that happened, maybe it would have happened like this."

Cheney had walked away with no answers but with the definite feeling that Eric was indeed involved.

* * *

MARTHA Windhurst had been living alone in Warner, New Hampshire, since her husband, Trapper John, had died of liver cancer in 2000. The death had hit his younger half-brother Eric very hard. He told friends it wasn't fair that Trapper had spent years fighting for his benefits from the Veteran's Administration only to receive them shortly before he died.

On November 3, 2004, Martha told Sergeant Mudgett and

Trooper Gilbert how Eric came to her and Trapper around New Year's Eve 1985 and confessed to shooting Danny. Records showed that Eric had been questioned on December 31, 1985. Trying to gauge whether his confession to Trapper and Martha had occurred before or after the interview, the detectives pushed her for a more definitive date. Martha admitted that at the time she'd been struggling with alcoholism and that there was very little she could be 100 percent sure of.

The investigators were about to leave when Martha's attorney suggested she had other information of interest.

"Tell them about the letter you wrote," he urged his client.

Mudgett was stunned. "You're the author of the letter?"

"Do you know about that?" she asked.

"I had the letter in my hand before we left," Gilbert said.

Martha admitted to typing up the shorter of the two anonymous letters authorities received in 1992. She wrote the one signed "a former neighbor"—which technically she had been. She remembered having typed the letter in the vault at Vital Records, where she worked. She'd done it at the end of the workday when no one was around and she knew she'd be sober. Martha even remembered that the typeface had left some the letters red, because she was working with a red-and-black ribbon.

"I told you a female wrote it," Mudgett said to Gilbert. He had done statement analysis on the letter and deduced by word selection and syntax that a woman had crafted it. From lines such as "it is a bad example to the many young people who know the facts about the murder," there was reason to believe the letter was not written by a contemporary of Eric's, but the level of detail it included suggested it was from someone who knew his version of events.

"I wanted him to pay," she said. "I wanted it known. People in town knew this. This was not uncommon knowledge."

"Who else knew?" they asked her. Martha wrote down a list, giving them several names they already had and several more that they didn't. She then became agitated with the investigators. She said she didn't sign the letter but had thought it was obvious where it had come from.

"Why wasn't anything ever done? Why wasn't I contacted then? Why wasn't the family contacted?"

* * *

WITH his lawyer beside him, Craig Metzger finally made the trek from Colorado to the conference room at the State Police Major Crime Unit in Concord on December 15, 2004, just days before the grand jury would convene. At first, Trooper Scott Gilbert ran the interview. After getting some biographical information from Metzger, Gilbert asked what he knew about the Paquette homicide.

"There was a lot of talk around high school that Eric killed somebody. That was the constant rumor that did flow through."

"What do you know more than a rumor about what happened to Danny Paquette?"

"I don't," he said.

Sergeant Mark Mudgett, who had been listening patiently, pounced. "Have you had any conversation with Eric about this?"

"No."

"You telling the truth?"

"Yes."

"Eric didn't tell you to say that if you were contacted by the police?"

"No."

"You and he to this day have not discussed his involvement in Danny Paquette's death?" Gilbert asked.

"No."

"Why do you think he would have told all these people about it and not told you, one of his best friends?"

Metzger denied that he and Eric had been good friends. He claimed he hung with a different crowd in high school and that afterward he and Eric got into a huge fight—which Metzger lost—and the two hadn't been close since. Metzger didn't explain, if that were the case, why he and Eric came to be roommates while they were ski bums in Colorado.

"I have a hard time with your answer," Mudgett said. "I don't believe it at all."

"OK," Metzger said, unconcerned.

"Are you prepared to take a polygraph?"

"If I have to."

"That's not what I'm saying," Mudgett shot back. "Are you prepared to do so?"

Metzger's attorney, Jim Moher, tried to break it up. He said he wouldn't advise his client to take a polygraph, that the tests were not reliable. Mudgett turned his frustration on the lawyer, saying he was head of the polygraph unit and disagreed.

"I'm asking you, not your attorney," Mudgett said, pointing a finger at Metzger. "I'm asking you if you want to take a polygraph test."

"He's hired me, and he's going to be deferring to my decision on these things," Moher said.

"Understood," the sergeant said. "Let him defer to you, but he can answer that question."

"If it would clear everything up," Metzger said, "I'd probably definitely look into it."

"Definitely look into it or be willing to take one?"

Attorney Moher asked for a moment alone to confer with his client. When Gilbert and Mudgett returned to the room, the questioning resumed.

"So I'm going to ask you again," Mudgett said. "Did you have any conversation with Eric about this?"

"No, I didn't."

"And you're prepared to stay with that."

"Absolutely," Metzger said. Then he qualified the statement by saying, "Yes, I've had conversations with other people. The whole friggin' school."

"Well, we all know that," the sergeant said. "It's pretty damn common knowledge in the town of Hopkinton what happened."

Metzger would not change his statement. Mudgett and Gilbert ended the interview, reminding Metzger that he was under subpoena and should expect to give a sworn statement before the grand jury that Friday.

* * *

WITH or without the help of the complete "Gang of Five," investigators now had more than enough. They were going to indict Eric Windhurst for the first-degree murder of Danny Paquette.

— 25 —

The Prosecutor

JEFFERY Strelzin had a problem with the Windhurst case.
Senior Assistant Attorney General Strelzin was head of the Criminal Bureau and in charge of the Homicide Unit. It was the position that Kathleen McGuire had held before being nominated to a seat on the superior court. It had occurred to him that there could be the appearance of a conflict at some point. Strelzin and his team did come before Judge McGuire often to argue motions, seek warrants, and try murder cases. She would have to be handled diplomatically, but thoroughly. But Judge McGuire was not the problem Strelzin had with the case.

The prosecutor had reviewed the I-85-147 case file—now numbering more than twenty-five hundred documents—and was aware of the Paquette family's justifiable suspicion and mistrust of authorities. He knew they had a historical beef with the New Hampshire Office of the Attorney General dating back to Rena Paquette's mysterious death, forty years earlier. Victor Paquette seemed like a wild card; his method of seeking justice was at times abrasive, at times self-defeating. How the tall, tough-looking biker would react to developments in the case was anyone's guess. But the Paquette family was also not the problem Strelzin had with the case.

There were still several members of Eric's old high school clique, the so-called Gang of Five, who would not break their so-called code of silence. Some were still loyal; some were afraid they would be charged with hindrance or, worse, conspiracy. Some were simply afraid. Several potential witnesses had obtained lawyers and were seeking immunity from the prosecution. But the silence of high school friends and potentially valuable witnesses was not the problem Strelzin had with the case.

Melanie Paquette Cooper had agreed to cooperate fully with their investigation. Several times she had flown from Idaho—and then from Wyoming after her family moved there, and her husband opened a Yamaha dealership—to meet with New Hampshire police or prosecutors about the case. She was to be their star witness, but the defense would likely attack her credibility because just like the accused, she had spent decades hiding the truth. There were other concerns with Melanie's testimony, as well, but they were not the problem that Strelzin had with the case either.

Eric Kimball Windhurst was a handsome, clean-cut guy. He would look good to a jury. He had one of the state's best defense attorneys, Mark Sisti. Strelzin anticipated Sisti would argue third-party self-defense: that Eric was acting to protect Melanie from imminent harm by killing Danny Paquette. All the jury would see, he feared, was that this nice young man in a well-fitting suit had killed a child molester when he was a minor. Though Sisti could not argue jury nullification, there was a distinct possibility that twelve men and women could say, "Good riddance, Mr. Paquette. Here's your medal, Mr. Windhurst."

The problem that Strelzin had with the case was not the defense attorney or the jury or the evidence or the victim or the suspect, Eric Windhurst. The problem Strelzin had was with the motive for the crime.

He simply didn't believe it.

* * *

JEFFERY Strelzin had the tall, well-built frame of an athlete, with features that were not classically handsome but striking in their intensity. He had dark hair and deep-set eyes in a face that looked easily a decade younger than his forty-three years. When Strelzin spoke, it was always with animated passion, whether he was discussing a legal case or the motorcycle ride he'd taken to work that day. His idol was Abraham Lincoln, and a framed portrait of the president hung proudly behind his desk.

Strelzin was a native son, raised in Concord, New Hampshire. As head of the Criminal Bureau, he had a corner office just blocks from his childhood home. Strelzin had been a self-described "screwup" as a young man. He was kicked out of college after his freshman year, and wondered what he would do with his life. His mother, an office worker for the New Hampshire State Police, thought he should get a job as a police dispatcher for a small town. That turned into a stint as a part-time cop. Strelzin found the work to be thankless and sometimes tedious. He realized the road to doing anything interesting in police work was so many years down the career path that it would be faster for him to finish college and go to law school. Strelzin graduated in the top 10 percent of his class at Concord's Franklin Pierce Law Center in 1991. He joined the attorney general's office in 2001 after spending several years clerking for a judge and serving as a prosecutor in Merrimack County.

At the time the grand jury heard testimony on the Paquette case, there was a new state attorney general. A young prosecutor named Kelly Ayotte took over the post in July of 2004, becoming New Hampshire's first female attorney general. Peter Heed, the attorney general who'd approved Chief Agrafiotis's plan to reopen the Paquette case, abruptly stepped down from the office after an allegation surfaced that he'd displayed inappropriate behavior in—of all places—a hotel barroom Conga line during a sexual-assault-awareness workshop. Heed was later exonerated.

Having come from the criminal division, Ayotte had an affinity for the complex work of a homicide prosecution. She had never lost a homicide case herself. Senior Assistant Attorney General Jeff Strelzin shared his concerns about the Windhurst case with Attorney General Ayotte, his boss, as well as the other prosecutors on his team and the police investigating the crime.

"What are the things we evaluate when someone convicted of a murder is up for parole: what danger do they pose to society? What is their likelihood of reoffending? We try to project ten or twenty years into the future and see what their behavior is going to be like."

Strelzin would lay all this out in front of his colleagues.

"Here's what we know about Eric Windhurst." He'd continue, "He allegedly commits this crime at age seventeen, then for twenty years never reoffends. Except for some minor stuff, he never gets into any more trouble. Some would say he lived like a model citizen."

"So what?" some would counter.

"So why does this kid, with no other history of violence, with his entire life in front of him, walk through the woods to kill a man he doesn't even know for a girl he's not in love with? Look at the guy through the scope of a rifle and wait for the flavor to go out of his chewing gum before blowing him away? Something doesn't add up."

* * *

IN preparing for the grand jury, Strelzin dug into the transcripts of past interviews, looking for something to answer the question of why Eric had volunteered to kill Danny Paquette. There was no indication that the two had ever met, so it was unlikely that Eric had a personal grudge against the victim. Melanie received only about twenty thousand dollars from Danny's estate, and the money stayed in her savings account, so it didn't seem she'd paid him. Nor did the unaccounted cash Pauline Gates had embezzled turn up in Eric's bankbook. Lastly, although Melanie had stated her belief that Eric wanted to be a "Rambo" and just go out and shoot someone for the thrill of it, that didn't jibe with Eric's adult behavior.

Then Strelzin was struck by something Christine Windhurst had said in her interview, something later repeated by other people. He believed this information had meaning, that perhaps he had deduced the real reason Eric Windhurst had shot Danny Paquette.

* * *

DURING her July 2004 interview with state police, Christine Windhurst revealed a surprising secret about her ex-husband's family. Sergeant Mark Mudgett was asking her to recall what

Eric had told her about what had happened in November 1985.

"They had become good friends," Christine said of Eric and Melanie. "And her stepfather was sexually abusing her. And she was afraid of him and confessed this to Eric. And for personal reasons of Eric's, it hit home that this was happening to her."

"Did he tell you why he chose to do it?" Mudgett asked.

"He told me that his father had abused his stepsisters."

"That Eric's father had abused his sisters?" The detective wanted to be sure he heard her correctly. "Was this well known among the family that Eric and Scott's father had abused the sisters?"

Christine said that her ex-husband, Scott, never mentioned it to her, and Eric only told her when he was confessing his crime to her. But she did say that she had heard it herself from one of the sisters who had been molested.

* * *

THE theory was bolstered during the grand jury testimony in December 2004. Strelzin questioned Eric's girlfriend, Heather Bouchard, before the secret panel. Of all the people whom the homicide prosecutor had run across in this case, the one he liked the most was Heather. He really felt for her, felt that she had found herself in an impossible situation. Although she continuously denied that Eric had exuded any pressure on her to alter her testimony, Strelzin didn't believe it. It wasn't that he thought she was perjuring herself; he just found the line too hard to swallow. He imagined how Eric would have pulled on Heather's heartstrings.

Strelzin also appreciated the demands the justice system was making on Heather. There was no question that she loved Eric, and here Strelzin was, demanding that she clandestinely testify against him. Her heart clearly belonged to Eric.

"Did Eric Windhurst ever tell you that he killed Danny Paquette?" Strelzin asked her in front of the panel.

"Yes, he did."

"Did he tell you why he did it?"

Strelzin recalled Heather telling the grand jury that back in high school, Eric had discovered that his father had molested his stepsisters.

"Eric said he couldn't bring himself to confront his own father, so he was able to turn his anger on Paquette," Heather claimed.

To Strelzin, it was the first thing about the case that made sense. Eric couldn't reconcile the horrible thing his father had done. He couldn't focus that rage on John Windhurst, someone he loved so much. So instead, he displaced that pain and used it to fuel his deadly potshot at an unsuspecting Danny Paquette.

* * *

THE new wrinkle in case I-85-147 was that they seemed to have turned up evidence of another crime: sexual assault. But had John Windhurst in fact molested the Windhurst girls? This family secret suddenly became key to proving the murder case.

Both of Eric's half sisters had moved out of New England after getting out of school. Lisa, the older of the two, found her way to Virginia, and Kimberly relocated to California but had since passed away, the victim of a tragic accident.

In January 2006, Sergeant Mark Armaganian flew to Norfolk, Virginia, to interview Lisa Windhurst Terry in person.

"I was ten, eleven years old when it started," Lisa told him of the crimes, which began in the early 1970s. "I woke up in the middle of the night, and the bottom of the covers from the end of my bed was being lifted up. My stepfather was there, and he had a flashlight. He was touching me, and I didn't know what he was doing." Kimberly, who was two years younger, had also been in the room. Lisa said that when she got older, John Windhurst would come in at night and go to her sister's bed instead.

"If you tell anyone, this will ruin your mother," John allegedly told them in order to buy their silence.

The molestation continued for years. Scott and Eric were babies at the time, and Lisa said her mother, Barbara, never suspected a thing. As a teen, Lisa would stay out all night with friends just so she wouldn't have to go home. At one point, she ran away to New York to be with her grandfather, Harold Kimball, only to have police sent after her to bring her home.

In 1990, Kimberly Windhurst Pollard had been killed in a bicycle accident along Highway 118 in Moorpark, California. Investigators think she lost control of the bike when her wheel got snagged in a groove at a railroad crossing. She was thrown from the bicycle and fell into the path of an oncoming car.

To help process her grief, Lisa called Kimberly's mother-in-law in California. She asked if Kimberly ever told her that their stepfather had molested them, and Mrs. Pollard confirmed that she had. The conversation fueled Lisa's rage against her parents, a rage that lasted for years.

In October of 2005, Lisa decided to travel to New Hampshire to confront her parents. Lisa told Armaganian that her mother picked her up from the Manchester airport, and they stopped at a restaurant in Bedford. It was there that Lisa told Barbara the whole story, believing that her mother would be horrified to find out what her husband had done to her daughters. Lisa began to cry and her mother soothed her.

"It's not your fault. I love you," she said. "I know it must be very hard to tell your mother something like that."

Barbara asked many questions, asking for specific details about what John had done, as if she were a detective herself. Lisa soldiered on, telling her mother how her husband had performed oral sex on her. It was humiliating, but when it was over, Lisa felt unburdened for the first time in her life.

After the tears subsided, they left the restaurant and sat in the car while rain poured down, washing away the emotional stain Lisa felt. Barbara then reached in the backseat and pulled out a pad with several questions on it about the abuse. Lisa was stunned. Barbara had clearly been preparing for their reunion and had written the questions before her daughter had landed.

There is no evidence that Barbara had known of the molestation at the time it occurred, in the 1970s. According to Lisa, Eric was the one who told their mother about the abuse a year earlier—the spring of 2004—and Barbara had confronted John about it prior to Lisa's return trip to New Hampshire. But how Barbara said John had defended himself was the thing that Lisa couldn't get over.

"He supposedly told her things like I had started it. That I approached *him*," Lisa told Armaganian. "It was disgusting."

"But there was no denial on his behalf? It was just 'she came on to me?'"

"His thought was he should be the one to show me instead of someone else. Some boy down the street or something."

Lisa said she had called law enforcement in New Hampshire five years earlier to inquire whether anything could be done. The person on the other end of the phone said that for a crime that had taken place thirty years earlier, there was little action they could take. He suggested she could sue in civil court. Lisa knew her stepfather, who was then approaching eighty, had had knee replacements, hip replacements, arthritis, and all sorts of physical pain from years of doing carpentry.

"I'm not a very churchgoing person," she said, "but my feeling is that it's his payback. God is paying him back for all the pain he has caused."

* * *

THERE was no doubt in the mind of police investigators that they had enough evidence to charge John Windhurst Sr. with Aggravated Felonious Sexual Assault, a class-A felony in New Hampshire. When Armaganian returned to New Hampshire, he drew up the paperwork himself and passed it on to his superiors.

No one at the New Hampshire State Police or the attorney general's office had any delusions about how far they were going to get on this. Investigators passed their findings on to the Merrimack County Attorney's Office. Although they were confident that they could meet their burden of proof for an indictment and eventual conviction of the old man, the statue of limitations for these crimes, which occurred in the 1970s, had long passed. The case file against John Windhurst, MC-060-1290, was closed.

For prosecutor Jeff Strelzin, the details of Lisa Terry's claims were horrifying, and the injustice of the Windhurst patriarch's escape from punishment felt like a slap on the face. However, the point of the exercise was never to indict and convict John Windhurst. The goal was to establish their alternative theory of the case: that Eric Windhurst acted not in defense of another person but out of a displaced anger for his own father's misdeeds. Strelzin believed he got what he had been looking for from the start, an answer to his problem with case I-85-147. He had finally found the motive for Eric Windhurst's crime. With that problem solved, Strelzin was ready to go to trial.

— 26 —

A Model Life

Iₙ the pre-dawn morning of December 14, 2005, Heather Bouchard found herself struggling to keep warm as she drove home from working the night shift at Concord Hospital, where she worked in the maternity ward. She turned her car down the frozen path off of Main Street in Hopkinton. She wanted nothing more than to drag herself upstairs and climb into bed.

Heather raced inside to escape the wind chill that threatened to harm her nose and ears, and she took off her coat and gloves. Eric Kimball Windhurst was standing at the door, waiting for the woman he loved. The tiny home they shared was among the old Kimball Cabins on Kimball Lake, the same cabins he'd partied in as a high school student. They had only been living here full-time for a few months, during which time Eric had worked day and night to completely renovate the place, adding a second story and a screened porch, new plumbing and electrical, a new kitchen. The old stone cabin had been transformed into a one-bedroom fairy-tale cottage, the perfect home for two.

Earlier on that cold morning, Eric had dressed for work while waiting for Heather to come home. He'd put on a long bib-style pair of insulated coveralls and a turtleneck, which he planned to top with the new Carhartt jacket he'd purchased to replace the ancient one he'd worn for a decade. He'd made some coffee and cranked up the propane fireplace to chase the morning chill from the room. Eric wanted to custom fit the gas burner in the old stone fireplace. It had taken him forever to cut the stone to his liking. Like all the other modern conveniences he'd added to the cabin, he wanted to make it look like they had been there all along.

"They said on the radio it was eleven below zero in Concord. It won't get above freezing all week," she warned him. She knew Eric wasn't looking forward to another day spent on scaffolding, hanging siding on the new house he was helping to build. But he didn't mind the work, as this was his first job for a builder whom he'd long hoped would recognize his talent and hire him.

A view into the window that morning would've revealed a couple standing in amber firelight, discussing work and the weather. It would seem they had their whole lives ahead of them, but both knew time was getting short.

* * *

IT had been nearly a year and a half since Melanie Paquette Cooper had called him out of the blue, shaking him to the core. The state's determination—sending investigators all the way to Idaho to question Danny Paquette's stepdaughter—scared Eric. Although he'd never called her back, he assumed that Melanie had hired a lawyer and circumnavigated the interrogation. But even if she had, he knew it would not stop the state's investigation.

Eric told friends that he felt like the end was coming. He was able to express his anxieties openly with people in Hopkinton, because Eric had, over two decades, systematically confessed his teenage deed to an ever-growing group of confidants. People he'd known since high school, friends he'd made through work or social obligations. Eric's assassination of Danny Paquette was something of an open secret to a select social circle in town.

The code of omertà was honored for several reasons. There were those who knew that Danny Paquette had been accused of molesting Melanie, and they felt Eric had been justified in his crime. There were those who thought that the thirty-seven-year-old man had indeed lived a "model life," just as he had described to Melanie during their July 2004 phone call. But there were also those who were afraid of Eric Windhurst, and didn't want to be accused of turning him in.

* * *

HEATHER Bouchard was an attractive nurse who worked in the maternity ward at Concord Hospital, a unit widely known for providing delivering mothers with an environment not unlike that of a high-end hotel. Her best friend was Christine Windhurst, Eric's sister-in-law. Christine also worked in the maternity ward, sharing the crazy hours and intangible joys of helping to deliver babies. It was Christine who'd brought Heather into the Windhurst fold around 2002 or 2003 to meet her husband Scott's divorced brother. Later, Christine and Scott would divorce as well, but even after that, the two women would remain good friends. At least for a time.

By then in his midthirties, Eric Windhurst still had a boyish charm about him. He was ruggedly handsome, his former soccer player's frame broadened to the expansive shoulders and strong back of a carpenter. He still had the dark hair and striking blue eyes of his youth, and the mischievous smile to match them. Heather fell for Eric hard and fast.

At first their relationship was tempestuous, full of drama. They were passionate but sometimes fought, once splitting up after a fight about how to do the laundry. Over time, however, their relationship stabilized, growing into a deep and steady bond. Eric told friends that making it work with Heather was like "love college," that he'd never really had a healthy relationship before and had to learn how to pass the tests. He often said she made him want to be a better person. Heather told people she thought Eric was a truly decent man, the most inwardly thoughtful person she had ever known. The couple eventually laughed over their early problems, created something real, and moved forward into a deeper phase of connection.

According to almost everyone who knew them as a couple, they were "it" for each other.

* * *

"ARE you going up to bed?" Eric asked. Heather, who could barely keep her eyes open after a grueling twelve-hour shift, nodded. "I'll go with you."

Heather threw herself across the mattress. Eric, dressed in his rugged work clothes, sat on the bed next to her. He rubbed her back; Heather's back always hurt after work. Eric's hands were small, but they were strong.

They shared bon mots. Eric told her he loved her over and over again. It was the kind of exchange they'd shared often in recent weeks, as though reminding themselves every day that what they had was good . . . too good to lose.

Eric hated leaving Heather in the warm bed tucked under the shingled eaves of their cabin. He dreaded his day's work in the cold but was never late for a job if he could help it. He kissed Heather good-bye and left her where she lay.

He wouldn't see her again for eighteen months.

* * *

ALMOST a year and a half earlier, in July 2004, a week after state police investigators had visited Melanie Cooper in Idaho, those same officers paid a visit to Christine Windhurst at Concord Hospital. The authorities thought Christine might be candid because she and Scott Windhurst had been divorced for a year and were in the middle of a prolonged custody battle.

In a taped interview, Christine told investigators that even before she and Scott were married, in 1992, she had heard that Eric had killed a man. Over the years, she had suspicions that Scott might have been involved, might have done the shooting himself and that Eric was covering for *him*. Christine had at one point told Heather Bouchard and all of her coworkers that she had an "ace up her sleeve" to play against Scott if their divorce got too nasty.

But Christine also told investigators an odd story about how when she and Scott were dating, he'd told her that *he* killed Danny Paquette. For years, she thought Scott was the triggerman. When the *Unsolved Mysteries* episode aired in 1990, Martha Windhurst, Trapper John's wife, told Christine that in fact it was Eric who shot Danny. Christine confronted her husband about the lie, and he came clean, but she never understood why he told it.

Christine had by this time moved from the apartment she'd shared with Scott in one of the many Windhurst properties to a house in neighboring Warner. She told investigators that sometime during 2003 Eric had surprised her with a visit.

"What did Eric say to you?" asked Sergeant Mark Mudgett, the New Hampshire State Police trooper who'd gotten Melanie to confess to him a week earlier. Sergeant Mark Armaganian was also present in the nursing director's office for questioning.

"That he killed Danny Paquette."

"That's what he told you?"

"He told me that he thought he was having a bad time in his current relationship. He was basically telling me that this was his punishment for what he had done. He said, 'This is my punishment. I'll never be happy in a relationship.'"

"Was this common knowledge with the family?" Mudgett asked, referring to Eric's involvement in the shooting.

"Yes."

"Why didn't you go to the police before now?"

"I kind of feared the whole thing." Christine said Scott Windhurst had told her to never talk about it. She claimed he thought all their telephones were tapped and that no one was allowed to speak about the crime in the house, even if they whispered. "It kind of scared me so I didn't talk to anybody about it."

"Eric had, for the past couple of years," Christine said, "been dating my best friend."

"Who's your best friend?"

"Heather Bouchard."

* * *

AFTER being interviewed in July 2004, Christine told Heather that the police had grilled her. Even though she hadn't grown up in Hopkinton, Heather, too, had heard scuttlebutt about Eric's involvement in a killing, even before they'd begun dating. She ignored it as rumor, until Christine told her the story was true. Eric understood that Heather knew about the murder, but the couple rarely discussed it. He would later compare his crime to the beginning of a termite infestation in a tall, ancient tree. They knew it could someday harm them, but they did their best to ignore it.

Now, Christine was telling Heather the police were poking

around. She also said the investigators' visit was a secret that should be shared with no one, especially not with Eric, and made Heather promise to keep the secret.

Heather made good on her promise for about a week, when she could no longer put aside the questions in her head. She confronted her boyfriend with these developments. At first Eric was dubious of his ex-sister-in-law's claims.

"She's in the middle of this nasty custody battle," he said. "Maybe she's just pulling your chain."

Neither of them felt they knew for sure what Christine's angle was. Instead, the couple came up with a plan. If anything came of it, Heather was to say that she had only been dating Eric for a year and a half and didn't know much about him.

* * *

A couple of months later, in the autumn of 2004, Heather Bouchard got pulled into investigation I-85-147 with a subpoena to appear before a Merrimack County grand jury. Not only did she get served, but Eric's brother and parents got subpoenaed as well. Heather was sure there were many other witnesses she didn't know about.

Heather asked Eric to meet her in the parking lot of the Border's bookstore in Concord. When he got there, she told him what had happened.

"Whatever you do," Heather remembered Eric saying, "please don't say that I ever told you that I did it."

"Come on, you know now I'm sucked in. Give me a break."

Eric told her he needed to talk to his lawyer, Mark Sisti, because despite his knowledge of these investigative rumblings, he had not yet discussed any of it with his attorney.

"Just don't say I told you I did it." His plea was designed to protect both of them.

"I don't know what I should be doing right now," Heather said, tears streaming down her face. "Now I could be in trouble. I don't want to be involved in this."

When Heather said she wasn't going to jeopardize her own safety, Eric said, "Just do what you have to do. Do what you have to do."

* * *

HEATHER claimed that after their meeting in the parking lot, Eric never again pressured her into talking about the case. The only exception was one night in November of 2004, before the grand jury would question her. Heather had been antsy, having mentally prepared for her appearance only to find out at the last minute that the date was pushed back to December.

Eric asked, "Did you tell your attorney everything?" The question came out of nowhere.

"Yes, I have."

"You don't have to tell him *everything*, you know."

"It's too late," she said. "I already have."

"I'm so sorry, Heather. I'm so, so sorry."

"Sorry for what?"

"For getting you involved in this. For telling you anything."

Eric spent the evening apologizing profusely.

Shortly thereafter, Heather and Eric broke up.

* * *

HEATHER Bouchard appeared before the grand jury in mid-December 2004. When she'd put that day behind her, she gathered some Christmas presents for Eric's parents and drove to Hopkinton to drop them off. Barbara and John Windhurst invited her to stay a while; they now lived in a comfortable home they'd built on land Eric had showed off to Melanie on his tour of the town nearly twenty years before. The Windhursts knew Heather and Eric had stopped seeing each other a month before, and Heather assumed they knew the reason why.

During her visit, Eric came to the house to see his parents. Seeing him there, the man she loved, Heather knew she could no longer stay away from him. They were so in love, they said, that they didn't care how it looked. Heather had already testified and had truthfully said she was no longer with Eric. They decided to pick up where they had left off.

* * *

IN 2005, the couple renewed their plans for a life together, mindful that the world was slowly closing in around them. There was no open talk of marriage, for that seemed like too cruel of a gesture for either of them. But they had something special, and Heather adopted Eric's long-held view of making the most of today because of an uncertain tomorrow.

Prosecutors would later say the couple also agreed that if Eric were ever to be arrested, Heather would again claim they were broken up.

Instead of Heather and Eric jointly purchasing the Kimball Lake cabin from Eric's parents, Heather bought it alone. This was Eric's idea, one she had to be talked into. He planned to fix up the old property to make it livable but to also make it sellable. After some convincing and terse negotiation, she finally agreed with his plan.

Eric began working like a dog on the project. He added a second story to the stone cottage for a cozy master bedroom. He built the kitchen cabinets from scratch, giving them a rustic look that did not disguise their meticulous craftsmanship. He made solid wood countertops and installed a floor made of Douglas fir. He updated all the systems and built a screened porch that stretched the length of the bungalow, affording full views of placid Kimball Lake.

Eric would spend all day on a job site, then come home to work on the cabin until he collapsed from exhaustion. In the end, the tiny house was beautiful. It had taken most of the spring and summer of 2005, but Eric had created more than just a storybook love nest for Heather; he had built a gem in one of the most sought-after neighborhoods in Hopkinton.

During this time, Heather's relationship with Christine, Scott Windhurst's ex-wife, had become strained. Christine seemed surprised and upset that Heather was going forward with plans to move in with Eric on a Windhurst property. Scott Windhurst's ex could not understand why her best friend would throw herself into that abyss of family dysfunction and paranoia. One day, in the maternity ward nurses' lounge, the two friends got into an ugly argument about the investigation. After that, Heather Bouchard stopped talking to Christine Windhurst.

* * *

ERIC continued to tell close friends the truth about his involvement in the death of Danny Paquette twenty years earlier. There was no strategic need for him to do so. He didn't need further alibis. The rumors, such as they were, were not so loud and pervasive that they needed to be addressed. His reputation as a hard worker, good friend, and model citizen was likely to suffer as more people found out about his darkest secret. But somehow Eric *needed* to tell people. It might have been that he was testing people's reactions, measuring the strength of their friendships—much as he had with sixteen-year-old Matt Quinn before the shooting. It might have been his need to unburden himself of the guilt and the sin—something he hadn't been able to muster the courage to do at that church in Colorado. It also might have been a desire to enlist the protection and moral support of as many people as possible that he admired—as he did by first confessing the crime to his older half brother and hero, Trapper John.

Any one of these people could have called the police. Any one of these people could have come forward to accuse, to testify. Any of them could have said, "I don't want you telling me this. How dare you put the welfare of me and my family in jeopardy by making me complicit in your crime." But it seemed that none of them did. All of them kept it secret from authorities (which is not the same as keeping it secret—many passed their firsthand knowledge on to wives, friends, and other intimates). There is something to be said about having a friend you know would literally kill for you.

Hopkinton, it seemed, was a lot like *Peyton Place*, the novel of small-town life by New Hampshire author Grace Metalious. Much like a rumor of infidelity that is told to everyone except the transgressed spouse, the knowledge that Eric Windhurst had long-ago killed a child molester circulated among nearly everyone, except for the law-enforcement officers who might have been compelled to do something about it. Danny Paquette's murder had become, in effect, everyone's little secret.

When he was finally arrested, those "in the know" simply said, "They picked up Eric today." No further explanation was necessary.

* * *

RICKY Patenaude left his large new house in Henniker, New Hampshire—a town that shares a border with Hopkinton—on that frigid morning of December 14, 2005, and jumped into a preheated car to drive to work. As he drove out of the neighborhood, perched on a hillside with panoramic views of Pat's Peak, he passed a construction site where another luxury home was being built by well-known local contractor George Sharpe. As he had done the day before—and for the weeks previous to that—Patenaude looked for Eric Windhurst among the laborers on the job site.

Ricky and Eric's relationship had never recovered from the Rolex watch incident. Ricky had no idea that any of the Windhursts suspected him of writing one or both of the anonymous letters. He just figured that they had naturally grown apart.

Sometimes, the two men would run into each other at the market or at a local restaurant. Eric would always say hello and ask how he was doing, but Ricky felt tension between them.

It was an entire year earlier, in December of 2004, that Ricky Patenaude had appeared before a grand jury and been quizzed on what he knew of Eric's involvement in the 1985 murder. "I don't know anything about it," he recalled telling the panel. The prosecutor asked tougher questions. "Eric never told me anything. There were things I heard around town, but it's all hearsay."

Suddenly, one of the grand jurors stood up and said, "I don't believe you." Soon, all the grand jurors were yelling at him, throwing questions at him.

"What do you want me to say?" he begged. "You want me to lie and make shit up?"

The cacophony continued with accusations that he was covering for Eric, was part of a code of silence. Patenaude just threw his hands up. Finally, one grand juror shouted out, "Enough!" and quieted the mob.

Ricky Patenaude had never understood why Eric hadn't told him about the shooting, why he'd had to trick the information out of Matt Quinn. He chalked it up to not being one of Eric's "A-list" friends when they were in high school, something he'd resented for years. But after the grand jury proceeding, Patenaude was finally glad he had been on the "B-list" and not heard it from Eric firsthand. The truth, or at least Ricky Patenaude's version of the truth, had finally set him free.

* * *

ERIC Windhurst watched Ricky Patenaude's car leave the neighborhood as he continued hanging siding on the front of the house. Despite the temperature, he was comfortable in his new Carhartt coat. Eric was working for the high-end builder George Sharpe, and he considered the job a feather in his cap, as Sharpe hired only the best. Sharpe was highly regarded for his craftsmanship, a trait that Eric deeply valued. Ironically, it was a value he had in common with Danny Paquette.

From his place on the scaffolding, Eric noticed a dark-colored domestic sedan pull up in front of the job site. Two men in suits and overcoats got out and began asking for Eric Windhurst. They hadn't identified themselves, but he could tell that the men, Sergeants Mark Armaganian and Mark Mudgett, were cops.

Eric took off his tool belt and put it down on the scaffolding. He turned to the man next to him and, nodding to the troopers before beginning the descent to the ground, said, "They're here for me."

— 27 —

The State Versus . . .

For all intents and purposes, the investigation into case I-85-147 was over. Only the trial was left. In the end, there were more than three thousand pages of investigative notes, police reports, legal filings, and interview transcripts, plus dozens of hours of audio- and videotape. It was now a legal docket at the Merrimack County Superior Court clerk's office, number 05-S-1749, *The State of New Hampshire v. Eric Kimball Windhurst*.

Eric was detained at the Merrimack County House of Corrections. The facility was not as hard-core as the state prison, but was a clear preview of what his life might become. On December 22, 2005, Eric was shuttled into the Merrimack County Superior Court for his formal arraignment on the felony charges. Unlike his brief appearance in Hooksett District Court on December 14 after his arrest—where he looked like a ruggedly handsome carpenter in his Carhartt coat, bib coveralls, and tousled hair—Eric entered this court wearing the standard orange jumpsuit given to every prisoner.

Accompanied by one of the associates at the Sisti law firm, Jonathan Cohen, Eric entered a not-guilty plea to the single charge of first-degree murder. The penalty for this charge was life in prison without the possibility of parole.

The hearing drew a crowd of curious media. New Hampshire had no cold-case unit, so the announcement of an arrest in a twenty-year-old homicide was a local cause célèbre. Newspapers were speculating as to whether Eric could have the case transferred to juvenile court, just as the lawyers for Kennedy cousin Michael Skakel attempted to do in his belated trial for murdering Martha Moxley in 1975.

The affidavit Sergeant Mark Armaganian filed for the arrest warrant detailed that Melanie Paquette Cooper's confession was what broke the case open and that members of the Windhurst family and his circle of friends all had knowledge of the crime. This initial paperwork failed to mention why the killer committed the crime, prompting the headline in the *Concord Monitor*: "Question of motive remains unanswered." When asked by a reporter where Melanie was at the time of the shooting, Senior Assistant Attorney General Jeff Strelzin said "in the vicinity" and "out of the car."

* * *

VICTOR Paquette went to the hearing to see the man who was being accused of killing his brother. It was not the first time Victor had seen Eric Windhurst with his own eyes. He would later admit to "taking field trips" to Hopkinton, presumably to spy on the man implicated in those letters.

Even with the circumstantial evidence that had existed for years, not even Victor had been convinced at first that Eric Windhurst was the killer. Victor and Richard Baron, his boyhood friend who'd helped to get the story on *Unsolved Mysteries*, continued to investigate Danny's death on their own. The cops didn't like Victor and Baron calling people who were potential suspects or witnesses in a crime, so the men got private-investigator licenses. This allowed them to continue their operation and give a big "fuck you" to the police, who they felt were dragging their feet.

Victor said they had created a timeline of index cards that they posted on a wall. There were actually two timelines: one for Eric Windhurst and one for another suspect, whom Victor declined to identify. Over the years, he and Baron would trace out the probabilities for both suspects. Victor said the timeline for the other suspect would only get so far before petering out, which left only Eric.

After Victor walked out of the courtroom following the

arraignment, reporters asked him how he felt about the developments. He gave a surprising answer, considering that his pursuit of the truth had been so fervent for so long.

"In all of this, I have had to walk away from it to keep it from making me crazy."

* * *

ERIC Windhurst told friends that his attorney had said to him this was the most winnable homicide case he'd ever taken on. Everyone knew what he meant. Who would vote to convict him? Eric was accused of killing a child molester. Plus, the crime had occurred when Eric was a minor, and he'd grown to be a well-liked man in a town populated with plenty of high-profile residents. Some defense attorneys hope to hypnotize just one juror, get a mistrial, and then work out some kind of favorable deal with a prosecutor leery of trying the case a second time. But that was not the plan with this trial. For Eric's lawyers, acquittal was the goal.

On February 28, 2006, defense attorney Mark Sisti filed notice with the court that they might offer a self-defense claim at trial. It's a standard filing in any proceeding, but it was like more blood in the water for the media sharks following the case. Reporters polled legal scholars about whether Eric Windhurst would be successful with that strategy. Most thought it was a stretch. They commented that the premeditated planning of the shooting didn't fit with the duty to retreat. They worried about a precedent that would set a rule that Good Samaritans could become vigilantes. Yet others thought if Sisti could prove that Melanie Paquette lived in perpetual fear of Danny, then he could evoke a type of "battered woman's syndrome" case, with Eric as a third-party defender.

Senior Assistant Attorney General Strelzin objected to the motion to argue a defense-of-others claim. A hearing on a series of motions was scheduled for June 2006. The murder trial was slated for August 28, 2006.

* * *

ROBERT Lynn was the presiding judge. He was the chief justice of the superior court—in essence the boss of all the judges, including the Honorable Kathleen McGuire. Lynn had been on the bench since 1992, and he had a colorful past that included a stint in the DEA before law school, working undercover buying and selling drugs. Lynn was known for having a very interactive style in the courtroom, unafraid to ask questions of attorneys and witnesses alike. He was smart and very well respected by jurists and politicians; he had an obvious love of the law. Lynn was also in charge of the court's softball team, a duty that he administered with much gusto during warmer months.

Lynn drew the Windhurst case, and because of the single-docket policy he enacted as administrative judge, he alone would follow the case from beginning to end. This meant Lynn would also hear the Cooper case, which seemed rather perfunctory because it was assumed that Melanie already had made a deal with the prosecution.

Defense Attorney Sisti came out swinging. Among the first requests he made at a closed-door meeting was a suggestion that Chief Justice Lynn recuse himself from the case. He argued that as the supervisor of Judge Kathleen McGuire, a figure who might play an important role in the case and would surely be a witness at trial, that Lynn could not be objective. Lynn denied the request.

Sisti also filed a motion asking that the tape-recorded phone calls between Melanie Paquette Cooper and Eric Windhurst be excluded from trial. The authority to conduct the "one-party intercepts" was granted by members of the New Hampshire attorney general's office. Sisti contended the prosecutors had no proper authority to bless such an operation when the agents of the state were actually conducting the calls from Idaho. Lynn eventually denied the motion, allowing the recordings to be slated as evidence at trial.

The defense also wanted to introduce evidence of Danny's abuse of Melanie to prove the other Paquettes lived in fear of the man. They sought counseling records from Peggy Upton, the therapist who tried to help teenage Melanie and had been compelled to report the molestation to authorities. They hoped the counselor would be able to testify to the level of Melanie's panic, that she truly believed her life would be in danger once Danny learned she was in New Hampshire. But the effort was fruitless. Upton had moved to Florida and was, according to a relative, now too aged to be of any assistance. The counselor's notes from the 1980s were not retained.

* * *

AT the June 23 hearing, Sisti presented arguments that the defense needed access to Upton's files as well as the two hundred pages of evaluations of Danny Paquette during his time at the state mental hospital. Appearing for the state, Strelzin said they didn't have copies of those medical records and didn't see what evidence could be obtained from them.

Judge Lynn seemed suspicious of why the defense needed that information, and Sisti explained they might argue at trial that Melanie was in fear for her safety at the time of the shooting. This opened a whole can of worms that didn't bode well for the defense.

"Self-defense requires imminence. You do not get to kill somebody—to use deadly force—to go after them," the judge said, clearly not buying the claim. Unless convinced otherwise, Lynn could bar Eric's attorneys from bringing up the claim at trial, effectively undercutting their entire strategy.

"We will assert that Melanie Cooper thought at any second she would be harmed," said Sisti. He said everyone—the police, her mother, her aunt and uncle—had all failed to safeguard Melanie. "We have her living under the roof of a law enforcement officer who had a duty to protect her and didn't."

Sisti made it clear that Kathleen McGuire, who at the time of the murder was an assistant attorney general, was going to be a factor in the trial.

"The victim was shot from afar," the judge said. "Do you have any evidence that the victim knew that Melanie Cooper or the shooter was anywhere in the area?"

"I'm not going to say yes to that," Sisti answered. "First of all, we don't perceive Mr. Paquette as a victim."

Sitting in the gallery with his sister and nephew, Victor Paquette ground his teeth. "This is plain, coldblooded murder," he softly growled.

"I have a hard time accepting that this could be a third-party self-defense claim," Lynn said.

"We will assert that Melanie Cooper thought that any second, she was going to be raped or killed. We will make that showing. I have no question that we will make that showing.

"Your honor, you have to look at this from the point of view of these two teenagers," Sisti continued. "You have a young girl, terrified, clinging to this guy right here." The lawyer pointed dramatically to Eric, seated next to him at the defense table. "Danny Paquette had terrorized that family. He had violated a restraining order. He had brutalized and repeatedly raped Melanie. The family fled to Alaska. Melanie was living in hiding in New Hampshire, and now the legal system is going to notify Danny Paquette where his stepdaughter is. And Melanie says to Eric, 'Nobody will protect me from a guy who is going to kill me or rape me.'"

Judge Lynn, still dubious of the self-defense position, said he'd give Sisti another chance to plead that argument before trial. As Eric was escorted out, he waved to his brother Scott, who had come to the hearing, the only member of the Windhurst family who did. Eric looked for Heather Bouchard but did not see her in the courtroom. She had yet to visit him behind bars, and he hadn't seen her face since he left for work that December 2005 morning. Sisti briefly talked to reporters before blowing out of the courtroom.

"We're not going to plea-bargain," he said.

* * *

STRELZIN found that the more press the case got, the more public opposition he found for the state's decision to prosecute Eric Windhurst. While at the gym or grabbing a drink after work, people would corner him about the case.

"Why are you going after this guy?" some would say. Some would seem rather angry about the case, about punishing a man for an act that seemed courageous, even chivalrous. What bothered Strelzin wasn't so much that he had to defend his prosecution, but to whom he had to defend it. The people who felt bold enough to confront him were prominent citizens; some even worked in the legal system.

"Because you can't have people taking the law into their own hands," Strelzin would tell them. "Imagine if someone had a grudge against you, or someone knew somebody with a grudge against you. Would you want it to be OK for that person to kill you? There's a fine line between degrees of grudges; who's to say where that line should be drawn?"

In *Murder in the Cathedral*, T. S. Eliot wrote, "The last temptation is the greatest treason: / To do the right deed for the wrong reason." Strelzin could see the case in this quote. Though the prosecutor believed the boy's anger with his own father motivated him, Eric Windhurst did not have the right to kill another person. It didn't matter whether the person was a rapist or a murderer or a molester. Or a monster. Maybe T. S. Eliot had it wrong. Perhaps the greatest treason was to do the wrong deed for the right reason.

Strelzin found himself making the case against "frontier justice" over and over again during the weeks preceding the trial.

"Think about this," Strelzin would say. "What if Eric was wrong about Danny? What if he wasn't a child molester at all? What then?"

At the heart of it, Strelzin was also deeply troubled by the enormous hypocrisy he saw in the legions who supported Eric Windhurst after his arrest. The moral question Strelzin always wanted to ask Eric's defenders was, *If it was OK to shoot Danny Paquette for what he did to Melanie, why didn't Eric shoot his own father, who did the same thing to his half sisters?*

* * *

ABOUT a month before the trial, Strelzin filed a motion to prevent Eric from offering a defense-of-others claim at trial. It was among a series of rabbit punches he delivered to the Windhurst defense. Strelzin also moved that no evidence of Danny Paquette's crimes or bad behavior be allowed.

Then the upper cut: a motion to allow testimony to be presented to the jury about John Windhurst's sexual assaults. Strelzin was ready to play his trump card. This strategy was meant to counteract any self-defense claim with an alternative motive that the defense might not be able to disprove.

It also added an additional layer of psychological pressure to the defendant. His dear friends were already going to be dragged into court and grilled about their roles in covering up the murder—placing them in some legal peril. Now his family would be called to testify—not against him—but against his elderly father. Lisa Windhurst Terry would be compelled to detail the perverted acts that she'd been subjected to for years. Elderly John Windhurst would be forced to take the stand and would get humiliated by the prosecution and devoured by the press. The knockout punch would come during Strelzin's closing. He'd ask the jury to consider John Windhurst's crimes and his character. Then he'd point to the defendant and ask, If John Windhurst didn't deserve to die, why would Danny Paquette?

* * *

TWO weeks before trial, Judge Lynn had yet to rule on whether Sisti and his team could present a defense-of-others claim. The judge wanted to know what evidence the defense had that Danny Paquette, welding unaware in his field, posed an imminent threat to Melanie Paquette. Sisti was reluctant to do so before trial and within earshot of the prosecution, so Lynn agreed to let Sisti present his evidence for private review. The state objected; Strelzin was fighting at every turn to keep Sisti from arguing a third-party self-defense. Lynn overruled the state's objection, but he said the defense had done little to convince him up until that point that Windhurst's actions could be viewed as anything but premeditated. It was a clear indication to both attorneys that Judge Lynn was likely to bar Windhurst's lawyers from making any kind of defense-of-others claim at trial. Eric's case was effectively eviscerated.

As soon as Lynn left the bench and the defendant was taken away by the sheriff's deputies, Strelzin closed his briefcase and began to collect his voluminous files on the case. Sisti motioned to one of the other prosecutors if he might have a private word.

"We're ready to make a deal," he said.

* * *

THE idea of a plea bargain for Eric was not greeted with enthusiasm by the members of Danny Paquette's family. Before the hearing, Strelzin met privately with Victor and several other relatives. They had been expressing their anger and disappointment on television and in the papers.

"What happened?" Victor complained. "You said we were all set to go to trial. 'Bring it on.' Now you cut this deal!"

One of Danny's nephews said that anything less than first-degree murder would be a miscarriage of justice. Strelzin sympathetically explained this was the best way to ensure Eric went to jail and that Danny got justice.

Victor wasn't buying it. He never gave up his belief that Kathleen McGuire had something to do with the glacial pace of the investigation. He accused the prosecutors of deliberately keeping the case from going to trial so the truth about McGuire's involvement wouldn't come out. Victor said they were afraid of what would happen if she got on the stand.

Strelzin explained, as he had many times before to Victor, that there was no evidence that Judge McGuire had at any time withheld information or obstructed the investigation.

Victor was so viscerally angry that he screamed at the prosecutors. Again, he felt the attorney general's office stabbed him the back, just like it had in 1964, just like it had in 1985.

"We're going to stand up in court and tell the judge we object to this deal and demand that he reject it."

After the meeting, Victor drew up war plans in his mind. He wanted Danny to have his day in court. He received a call from his sister, Nadine. She had been growing weak with age and illness.

"Victor, why don't we let this go? Let's support the plea bargain." Her brother was not ready to end the fight. "Do it for me," she begged him.

In the end, he relented.

* * *

ON August 21, 2006, Eric Kimball Windhurst, wearing a French blue dress shirt and tie, walked into a Nashua courtroom to plead guilty to a charge of second-degree murder. The structured sentence was fifteen to thirty-six years in the New Hampshire State Prison for Men and offered the possibility of parole. Given the relative weaknesses in both of their cases, it was considered a good deal by both the prosecution and the defense.

When asked if there was anything he wanted to say before sentencing, Eric turned to the members of the Paquette family.

"I'm sorry," he said, his voice quivering.

"Yeah, bullshit." It was Doug Paquette, Victor's son.

"I have . . . I have . . ." Eric was overcome with emotion.

"Spit it out!" Doug Paquette yelled across the court at him.

"I have no words to express how sorry I am for what I've done." His fingers absently touched his face, an instinctive reaction to fighting off tears. "I just hope someday that you can forgive me." He swallowed hard, visibly, and sat down.

The Paquette family said they weren't happy with the plea deal, but they accepted it. Victor couldn't bring himself to speak in court, so he asked his son, Doug, to read his written statement for him.

"Eric Windhurst pronounced himself judge, jury, and executioner of Danny Paquette. Eric, I now promise you that my family will take every opportunity to remind the court of what a coldblooded killer you really are."

Nadine's son read a statement on her behalf. "Were it in my power, I would have everyone that was part of this twenty-one-year secret—some would say cover-up—be standing beside Mr. Eric Windhurst to share in his guilt and sentencing."

Chief Justice Robert Lynn signed off on the negotiated plea. "To shoot someone you never met at a distance, it doesn't get more deliberate than that," he said.

With that, the bailiffs put Eric Windhurst in handcuffs. He acknowledged his family and friends on the left side of the courtroom, and then was taken out a side door for transfer from the county lockup to state prison.

— 28 —

Surprise Ending

MELANIE Paquette Cooper, along with her husband, David, and their five children, boarded a plane to Manchester, New Hampshire, to be formally sentenced for her role in the murder of her stepfather. The charge she faced on December 1, 2006, was felony hindering apprehension, for lying to police in 1992 on her written questionnaire. She did not face any charges for events that occurred in 1985. They were hopeful about getting back to Wyoming in time to enjoy Christmas, with this finally behind them.

* * *

VICTOR Paquette's animus toward Melanie was a different color than that he held for Eric. Eric was a killer; Melanie was a traitor. To Victor, both were capital offenses. At one point leading up to the trial, prosecutor Jeff Strelzin had met with Victor and the rest of the Paquette family to brief them about the status of the case. He explained how Melanie had been traveling to New Hampshire and assisting in their investigation and prosecution. At the table was Paul McDonough, a Manchester-based attorney who was representing Melanie in the case.

"Perhaps," McDonough suggested to no one in particular, "the Paquettes would like to meet with Melanie privately."

Victor Paquette reportedly responded that he would love

to have that meeting with his niece alone behind closed doors. "I wouldn't kill her, but it would be a near-death experience for her."

Shortly after the meeting a postcard arrived for Melanie at the dealership in Wyoming. It said, cryptically, "Sorry I missed you. Wanted you to know your Uncle Victor is really looking forward to seeing you!"

The card was signed "D."

* * *

AT the hearing, Senior Assistant Attorney General Jeff Strelzin represented the state. He presented the deal to Judge Robert Lynn. Melanie would plead guilty to the felony hindering apprehension charge and ask that all of it be suspended. Strelzin said it was a fair deal. He said that no one should have to go through the emotional and physical abuse that Melanie Paquette had suffered.

Mark Mudgett, by then a lieutenant with New Hampshire State Police, did something he had never done in his twenty-six years in law enforcement: he testified on behalf of a defendant. Mudgett said Melanie had cooperated fully with authorities for more than a year without a deal in place. It wasn't until this past autumn, after the sentencing of Eric Windhurst, that an agreement had been struck.

Civilian investigator Bill Shackford also testified for Melanie. He said that without her cooperation, there would have been no way to arrest and convict Eric Windhurst, the target of their probe.

The Paquette family then read their witness-impact statements. The tone of the statements was angrier at this sentencing than at Eric's. They wore buttons with Danny's picture and the words "Never Forgotten."

"We're here because you convinced a human being to murder another human being," one of Danny's nieces said. "You used twenty-one years of our suffering to build a life. I ask the court to consider that twenty-one years doesn't make you any less guilty. You were and you are the architect of this murder. You killed him. You orchestrated this murder. Without you, there wouldn't have been a murder."

A man who Melanie had never seen before approached the podium. His name was Keith Bastek. He was the son that teenage Denise and Danny had put up for adoption all those years ago, the boy whom Danny had pledged to find if only Denise would leave her boyfriend and start a family with him.

Bastek now lived in Florida. He grew up to be—of all things—a welder. A few years previously, he had begun looking through probate records in an attempt to track down his biological parents. When he finally learned their identity and of this father's death in 1985, he reached out to his mother's family, the Messiers. But after the news of Eric's arrest and Melanie's complicity, he felt that the Messiers had lied to him about his father.

Bastek sat with the Paquettes at the hearing. When he walked to the stand, he brought with him Danny's army shirt and cap, and he held them up while he spoke. "You have robbed me of any chance of meeting my biological father," he cried, and then he asked the judge to reject the plea and to send Melanie to prison.

* * *

MELANIE Paquette wore an angelic white blouse to the sentencing hearing. Her husband and children were in the courtroom, and she looked over at them several times during the proceeding, giving the gathered press ample photo opportunities. During the course of the previous months, New Hampshire residents who followed the case noted that Melanie still looked much like she did as a teenager, except that now she had slightly longer hair and a more rounded face. Melanie was a slight woman and undeniably beautiful, even though she was unadorned by much makeup, and wore a simple hairstyle, and modest clothing.

When it was Melanie's turn to speak, she told Judge Lynn the story about how she and Eric had met in the gymnasium, how he called her at home telling her he would do it, and how she'd practically begged him to take her. She said she never thought Eric would actually go through with it, would actually pull the trigger and shoot Danny.

"I did not ask for Danny to be killed. I did not ask for Eric to do what he did," she said, apologizing to the Paquettes. "I was really scared and I didn't do the right thing. And I'm sorry for that."

Judge Lynn pondered Melanie's words for a moment. Both attorneys expected that he would deliver a reprimanding statement, and then accept the deal as they'd brokered it.

"I have very serious questions about the accuracy of what you've told me." Lynn said. There was a stir the courtroom, then a hush. No one was sure where the judge was going with this. "An objective person just would find it very, very difficult to accept the idea that you really didn't understand that he was going to do this."

Lynn turned to the investigators. "Was there ever any evidence that she played a larger role in this crime?" They said there was not.

* * *

BUT in fact, there *was* a mixed bag of evidence pointing to the possibility that Melanie Paquette did much more than sit on a stone wall and chew gum while Eric Windhurst murdered her stepfather. There was enough evidence to at one point cause heated discussion within the attorney general's office as to whether they should charge Melanie Paquette Cooper with a crime instead of making her a deal in exchange for her cooperation. Some in the office felt they should absolutely do so, that she should be charged with accessory or conspiracy to commit murder.

* * *

WHEN Bill Shackford, Mark Mudgett, and Mark Armaganian arrived in Idaho and convinced Melanie Paquette Cooper to tell the truth about 1985, the young mother was very complete on the details. She remembered what clothes she wore, the conversation they had, she even remembered that the brand of gum that Eric produced had been Trident.

On July 14, 2004, investigators noticed Melanie gave very straight answers to all but one of the questions they asked. On the most important question in regard to her own culpability, Melanie would not give a direct answer.

Mudgett: Did you have to tell Eric who Danny was or point him out?

Cooper: I just, I don't think, because I don't remember seeing him. I mean maybe he was out there. I don't know if I could remember seeing him. I have, there was a tractor, maybe he was working on the tractor? I think he asked. I'm not sure if he did, I really don't remember now.

(Later)

Mudgett: Did you have to point Danny out to him? Is it possible that you had to point Danny out to him?

Cooper: I don't remember that.

Mudgett: Is it possible you did?

Cooper: Possibly but I don't remember seeing a person. And I don't remember doing that. And I don't, I mean I don't remember seeing Danny on there or near that.

Mudgett: Could you see Danny by the tractor?

Cooper: No. I didn't see. I mean I couldn't see that, I don't know. I don't. I remember seeing a person. Maybe someone, maybe a figure, maybe, I mean vaguely.

After that day's session, Melanie was free to go home to her family and to speak with her husband about what happened in those many hours spent with the men from New Hampshire. The next day, on the fifteenth, when Melanie returned to the Ada County Sheriff's Office, she told the investigators that she remembered another detail about the case. It was one that would portray her in a better light.

Mudgett: . . . You said you have some other information that you forgot to talk to me about.

Cooper: . . . I don't know exactly when it was he told me that he was planning on doing it himself. But I do remember that when he told me that I was very against it. That I said no, I mean you're not going to do this and that [I] was very adamant that I did not want him to do it. . . . I don't know what he was trying to live out. . . . But I think he also had his own ulterior motives. I think that, I think that he thought about killing people before I ever came along. I think that it was something that was in his mind and I think he saw this as an opportunity. . . . And I think part of me was searching for was he serious? Is this for real? . . . So then it never became a reality in my mind that it was really going to happen . . .

Mudgett: What, you're vacillating between reality and fantasy based on what you're telling me and at some point in time this had to sink into reality. When was that?

Cooper: When my aunt and uncle sat me down when I came back from the field trip . . .

Months after her confession, at the start of another round of interviews with New Hampshire authorities, Melanie said she recalled an incident that occurred several days before the shooting. She said that Eric had come to her and asked what Danny looked like, but he never said why he was asking. This memory, which materialized months after the interviews began, offered an answer to the elusive question of how Eric Windhurst might have been able to identify Danny Paquette from three hundred yards away. However, not all of the investigators bought it.

* * *

MATT Quinn, Eric's friend who said he'd tried to talk him out of the shooting, was unique among all other witnesses in that he was the first to hear the true story, and had heard it almost immediately. Quinn already knew the details of the Saturday morning shooting by the time he got on the bus to Quebec Sunday morning—before most of the Messiers had even read about the death in the paper. By all accounts, it was Eric who had told Matt himself. And it was at least a month before Eric told anyone else.

Matt Quinn told police that Eric had said that both he and Melanie stepped out of the woods and hid together behind an abandoned car on the edge of Danny's field. Melanie then pointed out who Danny was, and Eric shot him through the heart.

* * *

OF the two anonymous letters received by Richard Baron, Martha Windhurst claimed authorship of one. Sabrina Patenaude had seemed to admit—then retract—that she wrote the other. But Sabrina claimed all she learned about the case came from her brother Ricky, who had heard rumors about the murder within Eric's circle of friends.

Details in the second letter suggest it was written by one of Melanie's confidants, not one of Eric's. In fact, the author states, "Melanie Paquette, Danny's daughter told me Eric Windhearst [sic] (who was going to Hopkington [sic] High School with her) shot and killed her father." Taken at face value, the letter writer didn't even know how to spell Eric's last name. Nor did the writer know how to spell Hopkinton, so perhaps it wasn't a local resident.

Unlike Eric, who couldn't seem to help himself from telling more and more people, Melanie told very few about her role in the shooting. She admitted to telling her mother and her husband, and to purposely not telling her aunt Kathy McGuire for fear she'd lose her job in the attorney general's office. There was only one other person to whom Melanie said she confessed. She said she'd told the Messiers's nanny, Wendy Smith, who hailed from the neighboring town of Dunbarton.

Bill Shackford tried to track down Wendy Smith in 2004, only to learn that Wendy had died two years earlier in Mesa, Arizona, at age forty-five. Shackford got in touch with her parents, who said Wendy had led a troubled life and had struggled with substance abuse. They said in 1986, Wendy's car had been forced off the road on the back way from Hopkinton to her parents' home in Dunbarton one night; Wendy was then kidnapped at knifepoint and driven to a secluded location and raped. Her parents say she was never the same after the incident, and that for her, it was the beginning of a lifelong downward spiral.

Shackford asked the Smiths if Wendy had ever discussed Melanie or Danny Paquette. They could not recall whether she had.

The significance of Wendy Smith to investigators was that she, like Matt Quinn, was likely to have gotten the freshest recollection from Melanie, a first draft before time and conscience could blur the details. In this second anonymous letter, the author states:

> She said Eric took his father's 270 rifle. They drove to her fathers [sic] house in Hooksett, parked on a road near the house and walked through the woods where they could see the house. She pointed out her father working in the yard. Then Eric told her to go back to the car. He shot him and ran back to the car.

* * *

MELANIE told investigators that she had also told her mother over the telephone about her involvement in the murder. She also explained that she had written to her mother regularly and that Denise Paquette had likely saved the letters. The detectives contacted Denise at her home in Portland, Oregon, and inquired about these letters. She gave them a packet of neatly tied envelopes but explained that she had destroyed at least one of the letters that arrived after November 9, 1985. Its contents are a mystery.

* * *

THE most compelling of the circumstantial evidence indicating that Melanie had pointed out Danny came from Melanie herself. In relating the story of Eric's phone call on the morning of November 9, the day of the murder, Melanie wasn't able to convince him to bring her along until she said, "You don't even know who to shoot." It seemed to be the only reason he brought her along.

It's possible that Eric would have known Danny was a welder. But just before the shooting, there were two men working on the bulldozer: Danny Paquette and Court Burton. The apprentice, Burton, was holding a piece of metal while Danny welded it in place. As soon as Burton left to go mix paint and disappeared into the garage, Richard Duarte heard the crack of the rifle and saw Danny's helmet roll on the ground.

* * *

ALTHOUGH he never revealed what side of the argument he came down on, prosecutor Jeff Strelzin admits there was debate among the prosecutors in the attorney general's office about whether to bring charges against Melanie. In the end, they determined the evidence against her was too thin, too circumstantial to get an indictment.

It would have come down to a "he-said, she-said" argument between Eric and Melanie. In the past Melanie admitted she had lied about being raped, lied about being mugged, and had lied to fellow students at UNH about dying from a terminal disease. But both Eric and Melanie had lied about their involvement in the shooting, and neither one would make a credible witness against the other on this point.

* * *

ON that December 2006 morning in Chief Justice Robert Lynn's courtroom, Melanie Paquette Cooper continued to contend that she really did not believe that Eric Windhurst would actually go through with the act and shoot her stepfather in 1985.

"I didn't question him because I didn't think it was going to happen," she said to the judge. "I don't even know if Eric knew he was going to do that that day." She went on to say that when Eric called her and said he was going to "do it," she thought he was saying it for effect: "I thought he was putting on an act like a person from a movie. I didn't think he was serious."

Even when they were at the Paquette property, Melanie claimed, she still didn't believe what was about to happen was real.

"I just followed him. I don't know why I couldn't see what he was going to do. It didn't register."

To the more than a dozen assembled members of the Paquette family, Melanie spoke nervously, her voice trembling.

"I'm very sorry that you suffered all these years.... I know it's hard for you to understand, but I didn't ask for Danny to be killed," she said. "Danny has done a lot of things to me, but he didn't deserve to die that way."

* * *

JUDGE Lynn listened carefully to Melanie's version of events, and then spoke thoughtfully, deliberately.

"For me to accept the view that you ask me to accept is just too much," the judge said. Referring to the teenager's thirty-minute drive to Danny Paquette's home before the shooting, and then the conversation Melanie said she had with Eric on the stone wall before he walked away to complete the act, he said, "I guess I have real difficulty accepting the idea that at some point the lights didn't go on."

To the shock of all assembled in the courtroom, Judge Lynn rejected the idea of a suspended sentence. Instead, he sentenced Melanie Paquette Cooper to three to six years in the New Hampshire State Prison for Women, in Goffstown, for felony hindering apprehension. Having already pleaded guilty to the crime, Melanie had effectively waived her right to appeal.

Hearing the judge speak, Melanie just shook her head and mouthed the word *no*. She turned and gave helpless looks to her husband, David, and her five children. Her body began to tremble. The children were all whisked from the room before they could see their mother shackled.

It seemed so unfair. Melanie had grown up the victim of intense physical and sexual abuse. As a young adult, she carried the emotional scars. She'd struggled to find herself, to be comfortable in her own skin. Despite all this, she had settled down and become a devoted wife and mother. The family had opened their Yamaha dealership in Wyoming. Some would say they were living the American dream. Now she was trapped in a nightmare from which she could not awake.

"My heart goes out to your family," Judge Lynn said. "It is clear to me that you have done some tremendous things with your life since this tragedy."

The bailiff placed handcuffs on Melanie as she wept. She would not be going home for Christmas as they had hoped.

"Bye-bye, Melanie," one of the Paquettes said in a voice filled with satisfaction.

"It's a beautiful thing," another said.

* * *

AFTER the courtroom cleared out, one person remained behind sitting in the back row. It was Denise Paquette, Melanie's mother. The whole time she was there, she had not spoken in open court in support of her daughter. In fact, she spoke to no one. She did not even acknowledge Keith Bastek, her first-born child. She simply sat in the courtroom, staring ahead.

When she finally pulled herself up and walked into the hallway, she did not stand with Melanie's other supporters, not even with her grandchildren.

"She was crying out for help and I couldn't help her," Denise told a reporter. In that moment, she acknowledged the reality that struck Eric Windhurst in that school gymnasium back in 1985, a realization that spurred him on to deadly action.

"I failed my daughter miserably," she said.

— 29 —

Many Rivers to Cross

VICTOR Paquette, the one-time black sheep of the Paquette family, had become somewhat of a leader among his many nieces and nephews, sisters and brothers. They certainly looked up to him during those days in court, fighting for the honor of their deceased uncle. Many of them who were kids when he died fondly remembered Danny taking them for rides on his motorcycle or playing catch with them. They didn't know the Danny whom Melanie described; they didn't believe her.

Victor refuted the claim that Danny ever molested his stepdaughter. He believed it was a divorce tactic used against his brother, one that was too quickly believed and impossible to disprove. He also held tight to his belief that Kathleen McGuire and her colleagues used their influence to slow or stall the murder investigation.

"Eric Windhurst was a little rich boy who found a place to put his Joe Jock testosterone," Victor said. "So he sat there and chewed gum until the flavor ran out, and executed my brother."

Victor mellowed with age. He stopped drinking and carousing. But he still enjoyed a good game of pool in some of the area's less-desirable bars.

Victor had praise for one man in this case, the young patrolman who had worked his way up to becoming the Hooksett chief of police. "I have a lot of respect for Agrafiotis," he said.

"That little guy can't buy a pair of pants, because his balls are too fucking big."

* * *

CHIEF Agrafiotis maintained a good relationship with Victor because he showed the man respect. Agrafiotis recognized that, as a biker, Victor lived by a code. Although his code was a different one from the police's, Victor expected the cops to live by their code, too.

Although some said the little town's police department didn't get its proper share of the spotlight for cracking the case, Agrafiotis felt that solving the 1985 homicide sent a message that those who commit crimes in Hooksett would be punished. He expressed authentic sadness for all the families' pain.

Bill Shackford stayed on at the Hooksett Police Department as a civilian investigator one day a week, working on other unsolved crimes. In May 2008, the Hooksett Lions Club held an awards ceremony to honor Shackford's investigative work.

Both Agrafiotis and Shackford wondered how things might have been different for both Eric and Melanie had the case gone to trial. They believed that if more details about Danny Paquette had been made public, more sympathy would have been generated, particularly for Melanie.

* * *

KELLY Ayotte, attorney general for the state of New Hampshire, was recognized as one of the nation's leading young prosecutors. Ayotte argued a brief before the U.S. Supreme Court in October 2005 in defense of New Hampshire's parental-notification law. Though she lost the case that bore her name, *Ayotte v. Planned Parenthood* was recognized as an important precedent in modern abortion law.

* * *

SENIOR Assistant Attorney General Michael Delaney left the Attorney General's Office in 2004 to become legal counsel to Governor John Lynch. When Kelly Ayotte resigned her post as attorney general in July 2009 to explore a run for the U.S. Senate, Delaney took her place as AG.

* * *

ATTORNEY General Peter Heed, the one who authorized the Hooksett police operation, had regrets about resigning in 2004 over the flimsy allegations of inappropriate behavior. An independent investigator later cleared Heed of any wrongdoing. In 2004, Heed ran for his old job of Cheshire County Attorney. He was nominated by both the local Republican and Democratic parties and won back the position.

* * *

JOHN Barthelmes, the New Hampshire State Police (NHSP) corporal who first caught the Paquette shooting case before Roland Lamy took over, rose through the ranks to become colonel, the highest ranking officer in the state police. After he retired, he took a job with the White House Office of Drug Policy. In 2007, his friend and neighbor, Governor John Lynch, asked him if he would accept an appointment to be commissioner of the Department of Safety. Among the divisions Commissioner Barthelmes would oversee was the New Hampshire State Police.

* * *

RETIRED NHSP sergeant Roland Lamy continued to be a regular at the Concord restaurant that unofficially had a booth perpetually reserved for him, and where he escorted his mother out to dinner every week.

In his other big case, the disappearance of Denise Bolser, the woman who vanished from Raymond in 1985—she turned up alive and well in 2002, living a new life in Panama City, Florida. She had faked her own kidnapping.

When discussing the Paquette case after the fact, Lamy spoke only in riddles. He never quite explained why the murder probe was abruptly declared a hunting accident, why he was compelled to send Melanie typewritten questions, or why for one year the NHSP did almost nothing with the answers. He referred to "certain people" who wanted it done that way and said nothing more.

Lamy contended they would have solved the case ten years sooner if they had only had one critical piece of information:

Lamy claims that he did not know at the time that Melanie had gone to a counselor, or that a child abuse investigation by the state into Danny Paquette was about to get underway.

"I nearly spit my coffee out when I read that in the paper," he exclaimed.

Whether that knowledge might have expedited a confession from one of the participants back then can never be known; nor was it clear whether or not this information had been withheld, available, or simply overlooked. In the numbered case file of I-85-147, there was a single document dating back to 1985 from a caseworker at the New Hampshire Department of Health and Human Services assigned to investigate the counselor's complaint. The document was numbered 139 in a case file of three thousand pages. This document was removed from the case file—along with various other nonpublic or redacted files—when it was made available to the public during a "Right To Know" request.

"I'll tell one thing. After all these years, that Victor Paquette was right." Lamy conceded that he'd been wrong about his nemesis. "No one would stick up for his brother, but he did. If everyone had a brother like Victor Paquette, there would be fewer unsolved murders."

* * *

REPORTER Lisa Brown bounced around to a few more jobs in journalism before starting a corporate video production house. Brown covered Melanie's 2006 sentencing as a freelancer for the Associated Press, and said she felt a great deal of sympathy for Melanie, and thought the sentence Melanie received was unfair. The AP photograph of Melanie looking lovingly at her family broke her heart, Brown said. She also refused to believe that prosecutors truly suspected Melanie of pointing out Danny working in the field.

* * *

SENIOR Assistant Attorney General Jeff Strelzin said that although he did not agree with Judge Robert Lynn's jail sentence for Melanie, he understood why the judge imposed it. He also felt that the sentence was fair, considering that Melanie did play a role in taking another person's life.

"This is definitely a case I will never forget," he stated. "I have no sympathy for Danny Paquette," he said of the accused child molester, "but I do have sympathy for his family." Nevertheless, he noted that in the last two and a half years of his life, Danny Paquette appeared to have started to turn things around: he was becoming more artistic with his welding and trying to live a decent life.

Strelzin continued his winning record for the attorney general's office. In 2008, both he and Attorney General Kelly Ayotte successfully argued New Hampshire's first death-penalty case in more than seventy years. The accused was a man who shot a Manchester bike patrol officer in the head. The judge for that case was the Honorable Kathleen McGuire.

* * *

DESPITE the insinuations of Victor Paquette and the like, there was never any evidence that Kathleen McGuire knew of her niece's involvement in the killing of Danny Paquette. Nor was there any evidence that McGuire or agents acting on her behalf interfered with the investigation or withheld information. Prosecutor Jeff Strelzin was quick to point out that the records show McGuire was not only cooperative in 1985, but every time since then.

In 2005, Kathy McGuire received the Lawyer of the Year Award from the Merrimack County Bar Association. One of the initiatives sponsored by the judge was a program that brought master furniture makers into the state prison to lecture to promising inmates and teach them advanced techniques in woodworking. Ironically, inmate Eric Windhurst has been attempting to land a coveted spot in the program, but as of this writing has been unable.

Kathy McGuire has declined numerous requests to discuss this case.

* * *

FOR embezzling $23,782.74 from her employer, Pauline Gates eventually received a deferred two- to four-year prison sentence and two years of probation. Gates was ordered to pay $5,000 in restitution to the victim.

* * *

MARK Sisti continues to practice law out of his office in Chichester, New Hampshire. Sisti declined to contribute to this book, and his advice for his client, Eric Windhurst, was to do the same.

* * *

WHAT Craig Metzger, one of Shackford's so-called Gang of Five, said to the grand jury in December 2004 was not known. Neither was whether investigators ever took him up on his offer to "probably definitely" take a polygraph. But when the prosecution released the names of sixty-five potential witnesses they had planned to use against Eric Windhurst, Craig Metzger's name was not on it.

Matt Quinn's name was on the list. Eric Prescott, the man who said he'd lived in constant fear of Eric Windhurst since 1985, was also slated to testify, but the plea deal meant he never had to face his deepest fear: everyone knowing that he'd cooperated with the police. It isn't clear whether he understood that his interviews would eventually become a part of the public record.

Although he claimed to have no firsthand knowledge at the grand jury, the state had also been prepared to call Ricky Patenaude to take the stand.

Ricky Patenaude continued to work for his father, operating the family's artesian-well company. His memories about events from the 1980s and 1990s remained cautiously sketchy.

"When I think about Eric today, all I can say is, 'What a waste,'" Patenaude said, preferring not to dwell on the difficult post–high school years with Eric, but on the pleasant memories of the two of them riding dirt bikes in his backyard when they were kids.

* * *

DECEMBER 2007 was the last time Heather Bouchard spoke about Eric Windhurst with anyone other than her immediate family and close friends. At that point, she hadn't yet moved on, at least not in her heart.

"He is a constant specter in our lives," she said at that time of the man who was taken from her at the peak of their relationship. "I really think sometimes it would have been better if he'd died, because then, we'd be able to fully grieve, to know that someday we could get past it."

Heather Bouchard may have succeeded in moving on with her life, just the way Eric told her he hoped she would. In 2008, she sold the cabin he'd renovated for her and moved to a neighboring town. The reason for the sale was that she needed more space; she was expecting a child with the new man in her life.

* * *

THE identity of Rena Paquette's killer was never officially determined.

An attorney for Edward Coolidge said he was being grilled by Manchester police about the murder of Pamela Mason until 2:30 a.m. on Sunday, February 2, 1964, and had to appear in court on an unrelated larceny charge on Monday morning, February 3, 1964. The implication was Coolidge was either in custody or in court when Rena was murdered.

Attorney General William Maynard lost a bid to run for governor of New Hampshire. Despite his other accomplishments as a lawyer, Maynard was always remembered for the Coolidge case and for how the killer's sentence had been overturned by the U.S. Supreme Court because Maynard had signed the search warrant. Maynard died in a nursing home in 1996.

Victor Paquette said he also had another suspect, a high school friend who would often visit the Paquette farm but who then left town immediately after Rena's body was discovered burning in the pigsty.

* * *

RICHARD Baron remained good friends with Victor Paquette. Next to Chief Agrafiotis, Victor credits Baron with seeing this case to completion and keeping him going.

Baron moved to Florida, where he worked in printing and graphic design. In 2001, he self-published a fictionalized version of the events surrounding Danny's death in a book titled *Deadly Visions*.

* * *

MICHAEL Manzo, Melanie's college boyfriend, left the *Union Leader* and the newspaper business in the mid-1990s. Mike began a new career in public relations specializing in high-tech firms.

* * *

THE two female bodies discovered in Bear Brook State Park the day after Danny's death continued to haunt police. Incredibly enough, ten years after the incident, an investigator revisiting the scene discovered a barrel not far from the original site with the bodies of two more children stuffed inside of it. Testing showed that these children were blood relatives of the woman and girl discovered there in 1985, likely killed at the same time but not discovered in the park for another decade.

The four family members were never identified, and their killer has never been apprehended.

* * *

IN spring 2009, several investigators—including the then NHSP Sergeant Scott Gilbert and Bill Shackford—testified before a legislative panel in support of establishing a cold-case unit for the state of New Hampshire. Supporters said there were more than one hundred unsolved homicides in the state going back decades. They said the apprehension of Eric Windhurst and the closure to the Danny Paquette case was the first cold case they'd cracked in fifty years.

On January 1, 2010, a law went into effect in New Hampshire that removed the statute of limitations for prosecuting crimes related to murders. They include such infractions as falsifying evidence, threatening witnesses, or lying. Legislators said the intent was to keep the pressure on those who back up false alibis or otherwise hinder a murder investigation.

Strelzin said they have no interest in prosecuting anyone else who might have helped Eric Windhurst and Melanie Paquette Cooper keep their secret.

* * *

THE house that Danny Paquette owned at 898 Whitehall Road, and all the surrounding property, was sold to a construction company. The house and outbuildings remained, but the yellow field that Eric Windhurst's .270 bullet had sailed across was occupied by a large industrial building, blocking the view of the old house from the woods that lay behind it.

* * *

JOHN and Barbara Windhurst remained in their house in a quiet part of Hopkinton. Friends said that the parents' relationship with Scott Windhurst and Lisa Windhurst Terry was strained. Issues included money, property, and the lingering sexual assault allegations against John by Lisa.

According to Eric Windhurst, neither of his parents ever came to visit him in prison; however, they did stay in touch by telephone.

* * *

AT the twenty-year reunion of the Hopkinton High School Class of 1987, classmates set a place at a table for Eric Windhurst. Attendees left Windhurst photos and other memorabilia. The reunion was held at Pat's Peak, the ski resort owned by Ricky Patenaude's parents.

* * *

THE pale, thin Melanie Paquette Cooper who was seen leaving the courtroom to start her prison sentence did not exist for long. While serving her time in Goffstown, Melanie became noticeably tan because of her many hours in the rec yard. She also was heavier—a product of the starchy prison food her fit body was unaccustomed to.

While incarcerated, Melanie studied English at Brigham Young University through the mail. She read and worked on arts and crafts. She tried to burn off the mess-hall mashed potatoes by running six miles a day in the yard. She worked thirty hours per week in the prison's career and technology department, tutoring inmates and giving computer instruction. For the first time since her aunt's ill-fated attempt to get her help, Melanie began to receive counseling to deal with the post-traumatic stress of her childhood abuse.

On Monday nights, Melanie would call home to Wyoming and have family night on the phone. The children would play hide-and-seek among the household furniture, while Melanie called each child by name and guessed under which table or chair he or she was hiding. She tried to choke back the tears of saying good-bye every time she had to hang up.

By all measures, Melanie was considered to be a model inmate.

Attorney Paul McDonough filed a sentence review. Although unable to appeal Melanie's guilty plea, the lawyer asked a three-judge panel to consider whether Chief Justice Lynn's three- to six-year sentence was appropriate. The move had some risk, as sentence reductions only occurred in 11 percent of reviews. The percentage of sentences that were actually *increased* upon review was higher.

In June of 2007, a judicial review panel denied the request to throw out Judge Lynn's sentence, but the panel did agree to reduce the time of her incarceration. They ruled that Lynn had relied too much on circumstantial evidence during sentencing. The panel cited Melanie's "teenage cluelessness" for her passivity during the crime. Her sentence was changed to fifteen to thirty months.

In January 2008, after serving thirteen months, Melanie appealed to the state parole board for release at the fifteen-month mark. For the last time, Victor Paquette faced off with Melanie. The prisoner appeared at the hearing via closed-circuit television.

Victor, the one-time renegade biker, still tall and shorn and imposing, approached the podium to address the parole board. His tattoo peeked out from his sleeve. The card had one large spade with a bullet piercing it. But on closer look, it wasn't the ace; it was the king. To Victor, Danny had been the King of Spades.

"Forty years ago, I took an oath to that flag to defend my country and its Constitution along with a little pledge that says, 'There will be liberty and justice for all.' I'm here today to fight for justice." Victor's voice quivered, the only time he'd ever shown emotion in public. "There is a debt to be paid, and I ask you, gentlemen, that it be paid in full."

Senior Assistant Attorney General Jeff Strelzin testified on Melanie's behalf. He said that the amount of childhood trauma she'd suffered had factored into their decision to offer her a suspended sentence. At that, Victor Paquette shouted out, "Those allegations have never been proven! They're a smear campaign against my brother!"

The parole board was impressed by Melanie's exemplary record. She was granted parole and allowed to leave prison after fifteen months, the bare minimum of her sentence.

Melanie Paquette Cooper walked out of prison on March 1, 2008. After visiting several people to thank them, including Jeff Strelzin, Melanie boarded a plane and returned to her family in Wyoming.

* * *

VICTOR Paquette was disappointed when Melanie's sentence was cut short. The fight for justice for Danny didn't seem to get any better, even when the truth was known.

"Don't worry, kid. This will all work out for you."

Ever since some disingenuous guy in a trench coat had said that to Victor on a chilly 1964 day, he'd been waiting for everything to "work out." But instead of dwelling on the "what could have been," Victor turned his focus to "what is": the love of his family, the satisfaction of work well done, and the dream that someday, this *would* still all work out.

Epilogue

THE vending machines are at either end of the enormous room. There is a sign near them that reads, "Use of the vending machines by inmates will result in a terminated visit." It wouldn't occur to most people on the outside that simply pushing a button to choose a soda or snack could be considered a privilege of freedom, but here, it is.

When he sees visitors, Eric Windhurst prefers the hot breakfast sandwiches and cheeseburgers that can be purchased from the Automat-style machine and then heated in one of the room's many industrial microwaves. He eats fervently, like he's skipped a meal, but he doesn't complain much about the food he is served in the prison mess hall.

Eric takes out a sheet of paper and pencil and starts sketching. In his four years behind bars, he's had a lot of time to design the house he wants to build someday when he finally gets out. Every time he draws it, he improves the design in some small way that he's eager to share.

It's easy to imagine Eric sitting at a customer's kitchen table going over plans for a renovation. He converses easily while his hand draws straight lines, even squares. His renderings are impeccable.

Eric's dream house has evolved over the four years he's been here. His latest iteration is a cozy open-concept saltbox with arts and crafts elements. He's been reading *The Not So*

Big House and explains his use of space, the rules that apply when designing rooflines, installing dormers, placing toilets. But there's something else to his design that a casual glance might miss. Eric's house has a one-car garage. One bedroom. One closet.

Eric believes that when he gets out of jail after serving as much time as the state decides he must, he will likely be alone for the rest of his life. When asked why, he says at first that he's "damaged goods." Then he says that being alone is what he deserves. Then he says that it's what he wants. Designing this little house has been Eric's only creative outlet since his arrest. Now, it seems as if he's drawing another prison for himself to occupy when he finally leaves this one.

* * *

TO say Eric Windhurst doesn't belong in prison wouldn't be quite right. The man who murdered Danny Paquette seemingly without thought and then concealed it for twenty years believes he deserves the sentence he got, and perhaps even more. There are men in the New Hampshire State Prison for Men who don't "have a body"—the jailhouse term for *murder*—but who received longer sentences than the one he did. But Eric certainly doesn't *fit* in prison. The man that he is today is thoughtful, kind, evolved. He spends his days in jail working in the woodshop, hitting the gym, or watching trashy cable TV shows like *The Hills*.

Eric spent twenty years after murdering Danny Paquette living like a man with a terminal disease. He initially pretended to be fine, then went through a period of extreme volatility, then slowly grew into deep awareness of the impact of what he'd done. As a young adult, he sentenced himself to a life without meaningful relationships or children. At the end, just before his arrest, he finally vowed to strive to be a good person, to live each day to the fullest, to at last allow himself to feel and give the kind of love he'd refused to feel for his entire life.

To call Eric remorseful is an understatement. The man Heather Bouchard described as "inwardly thoughtful and remarkably sensitive" is sitting at this bolted-down table, eating vending machine hamburgers, and wearing dull green from head to toe. That man talks about what he did with so much pain for the lives he destroyed that it is hard to listen to him describe it. But here also is the boy he was at seventeen, at least in brief flashes when the conversation gets heated or particularly funny. His eyes dance; his face hardens. And then, as fast as it came, the storm passes, and there is Heather's Eric again, kind and quiet.

Eric doesn't deny that he used to be a wild kid, a "total fuckup," and that he's fought a constant battle since his twenties to grow beyond that. But even when he talks about his wild streak, he tends to stop short of acknowledging the darkest stories in his history; his youthful violence and brushes with the law, his volatility with girlfriends, his constant manipulations of his friends. It's hard to tell if it's because he doesn't want anyone to know what he was really like or because he himself doesn't fully realize who others knew back then.

Eric freely admits that concealing his crime for twenty years was the morally wrong choice to make. He says he hid the murder because he was afraid to go to jail, and now that he's here, he admits that fear was justified. But Eric doesn't regret his incarceration, aside from the toll it takes on the people he loves. He takes responsibility for it, claims he believes justice is being served at last.

What Eric does regret is being stupid enough at seventeen to think that he could solve Melanie Paquette's problems. Being foolish enough to make a promise that would wreck his life, all in the name of keeping her safe. And with that, he says something once again that hasn't wavered in the time since he's agreed to discuss his story.

To seventeen-year-old Eric Windhurst, killing Danny Paquette felt like a selfless act.

"Every adult, every person in that girl's life failed her from the moment she was born until the day I met her," he says. "She came to me, and her fear was more palpable than anything else I can remember. She believed her life was in danger. She made me believe it. Did I do the right thing? Of course not. For me, I was rescuing a friend, stepping up to the plate when no one else would. And I can't tell you enough—it was the biggest mistake of my life."

The one thing Eric refuses to discuss is the murder itself, sticking to his assertion that "no good" could come from his version of the truth at this point. He says only two people really know what happened that day, and he is not completely sure that Melanie's recollection hasn't been tainted by her own confession to the police. He feels that Melanie is not a malicious liar but has a tendency toward vivid fantasy, and he now wonders if her public version of events has taken the place of her real memory of the murder.

Eric admits at times to feeling bitter about the deal Melanie was able to make after stating she did not accompany him to the edge of the woods the day he shot Danny Paquette, but he doesn't want to say anything that contradicts the version of events that allowed her that deal.

"She has five children at home," he says, ever the protector. "For her, it's over. I don't see any reason to fuck that up."

Though Eric won't talk about the murder itself, he will discuss the investigation and his case. He had read a lot about himself in the papers, and he refutes much of what has been written about him.

"The chewing-gum story is bullshit," he laughs, referring to Melanie's confession to police, in which she stated that Eric said he'd "do it" when the flavor ran out of his gum. "What kind of idiot would say something like that?"

Instead, he claims that on that morning, he didn't plan to wait around for as long as it took to get a clear shot. He goes so far as to assert that he secretly hoped that there wouldn't be an opportunity at all. He told Melanie they'd only stay in those woods for a finite period of time. "How long?" he says she asked him, clearly hoping he'd have an opportunity to finish the task. He said he was frustrated by her impatience and just said the first thing that came to his mind: "We'll stay until the flavor goes out of my gum."

About the "shotgun incident," the night he allegedly threatened a classmate for bringing an outsider to his party, he says that the version told to police was a "gross exaggeration."

"I don't care how drunk I was, or how stupid," Eric says. "What looked like a shotgun to those people was actually just the stock, the wooden part of my hunting rifle. Yeah, I wanted the guy out of there; I didn't know if he'd brought drugs or what. But I'd never threaten someone with a shotgun. I never even had my rifle assembled unless I was going hunting."

Eric also believes that the story of how the investigation that led to his arrest unfolded is a "total fabrication." Like most of the Windhurst clan and their allies, he doesn't buy that Hooksett police chief Steve Agrafiotis was motivated by unresolved angst and found the funding that brought Bill Shackford into the case. Instead, he maintains that his ex-sister-in-law, Christine Windhurst, had been a secret informant to police for years as part of her vendetta against his brother Scott. He sticks with this theory even when told that the timeline outlined in the nearly three thousand pages in the case file doesn't jibe with his belief, given police notes written about him long before Christine ever had reason for revenge.

"You just don't understand how some people really are," he says, shaking his head when confronted with evidence that contradicts his theory.

One thing that has come strongly to light during the course of researching this story is that many people who still live in the small towns where they were raised have one thing in common—their beliefs don't waiver, no matter what evidence they see to the contrary. There is no gray, no room for self-doubt or reflection about alternative possibilities. There is only black, and there is only white.

Another thing Eric vehemently denies is the alternative-motive theory the prosecution planned to introduce at his trial. Jeff Strelzin, the senior assistant attorney general, says the alternative-motive theory is the only one that makes sense to him. "It just didn't make sense to me that a boy like Eric could have shot Danny Paquette for a girl he'd only known for a few weeks unless there was something else eating at him. Otherwise that would have made him a psychopath."

Eric denies being a psychopath at seventeen and instead says the factors at hand—his raging hormones, his overdramatized sense of protectiveness, his desire to fix the problem, but mostly his sincere belief in Melanie's expression of fear—combined to make him a killer. He absolutely refutes learning about his father's abuse while in high school, insisting repeatedly that the first time he ever heard about it was when he visited his half-sister Lisa in Williamsburg, Virginia, on his 1991 trip down south with Ricky Patenaude, the trip that culminated in the Rolex watch incident.

Though Ricky Patenaude doesn't recall the visit to Eric's half sister on that trip, Lisa does. She says she has perfect recall of the night she stayed up until 2:00 a.m., talking with her half-brother Eric on her back porch. She says she remembers telling him about the abuse, and then later going upstairs and telling her husband, who had also never been aware of her molestation. Lisa says she is absolutely certain that this night in 1991 was the first Eric had ever heard of it, because his reaction was so emotional. Of the claim Eric shot Danny to avenge Lisa's and Kimberly's molestation by his father, Lisa tearfully asserts, "What he did, he did not do for me."

As for Eric's father, John Windhurst, Eric acknowledges an ingrained respect for the man, and he skirts the issue of the sexual abuse of his two half sisters. Senior Assistant Attorney General Strelzin finds this to be one of the most enigmatic things about Eric. Strelzin recounts the recorded telephone conversations he listened to between Eric and his father after Eric's arrest. While homicide suspects are incarcerated and still awaiting trial, it is common procedure to listen in on the phone calls they would make from prison. Eric would speak with John Windhurst matter-of-factly, even after it became known that the prosecution intended to introduce the incest evidence at trial. At the end of these conversations, Eric would tell his dad how much he loved him. For Strelzin, the idea of someone who'd once murdered a man for the very crime he seemed to be able to ignore in his own father is one of the great puzzles of Eric's character.

When Eric is asked about his present-day relationship with John, and all that he knows about what his father did, he shapes his words carefully. "What would be the benefit," he says, "of punishing a very elderly man for something he did so long ago?"

* * *

THERE is no doubt what Eric would wish for above all else if he could. He says over and over that the power to go back to that day in the gym is one he'd trade his life for. He should have told Melanie to talk to a school counselor, or he should have told her that he'd fix it and then gone himself to find someone who could help her. Though Eric doesn't believe what he did was right on any level, he also feels deeply that something had to be done on her behalf.

"Unfortunately, she told the right guy about this," he says mournfully. "I had the temperament and the ability to do what I did. God, I wish I could just go back and punch myself, do whatever it took to keep myself from making that choice."

* * *

WHEN visiting hours are over, the lights flash in the room, signaling that three and a half hours have passed. The feeling that comes with leaving that table and walking out into the fresh air should be gratitude for the escape from the realities of incarceration and for the return to the outside, where privileges like choosing one's own dinner are often taken for granted.

There should also be some relief at leaving this tale of human tragedy behind, at momentarily forgetting about Melanie Paquette's young life, a life no one should have had to bear; the brutal murder of Danny Paquette's mother; Victor Paquette's deep and terrible bitterness, which tainted the purity of his tireless quest for justice; and Eric Windhurst himself, a man born with limitless promise, stunted by the stifling culture of silence in which he was raised.

But leaving here isn't easy. There are so many unanswered questions still, and dangling threads, too . . . the constant wondering about how or why a family would bury a poisonous truth about one of their own, and then an entire community would conspire to bury yet another secret—perhaps one even more toxic than the first—all in the name of loyalty or love or fear.

Eric Windhurst could answer many of these questions if he would only acknowledge so many truths, but there is only one truth he is well aware of.

"When I finally walk out those doors in however many years it might be," he says, "it will be the first time since I was seventeen years old that I will actually be free."

Penguin Group (USA) Online

What will you be reading tomorrow?

Patricia Cornwell, Nora Roberts, Catherine Coulter,
Ken Follett, John Sandford, Clive Cussler,
Tom Clancy, Laurell K. Hamilton, Charlaine Harris,
J. R. Ward, W.E.B. Griffin, William Gibson,
Robin Cook, Brian Jacques, Stephen King,
Dean Koontz, Eric Jerome Dickey, Terry McMillan,
Sue Monk Kidd, Amy Tan, Jayne Ann Krentz,
Daniel Silva, Kate Jacobs…

You'll find them all at
penguin.com

*Read excerpts and newsletters,
find tour schedules and reading group guides,
and enter contests.*

Subscribe to Penguin Group (USA) newsletters
and get an exclusive inside look
at exciting new titles and the authors you love
long before everyone else does.

PENGUIN GROUP (USA)
penguin.com